SIGNIFICANT
DECISIONS
OF THE
SUPREME COURT

DATE DUE			
Mar 7 7 9			
Dec 8 7 9			

SIGNIFICANT DECISIONS OF THE SUPREME COURT, 1975-1976 TERM

Bruce E. Fein

American Enterprise Institute for Public Policy Research
Washington, D.C.

Bruce E. Fein is an attorney with the U.S. Department of Justice.

The views of the author do not necessarily
represent those of the Department of Justice.

348.7346
F325
103647
Jan. 1978

Library of Congress Cataloging in Publication Data

Fein, Bruce E
 Significant decisions of the Supreme Court,
1975-1976 term.

 (AEI studies ; 183)
 Includes indexes.
 1.   United States—Constitutional law—Digests.
I. United States. Supreme Court. II. Title.
III. Series: American Enterprise Institute for
Public Policy Research. AEI studies ; 183.
KF4547.8.F422 1977   348'.73'413   77-26165
ISBN 0-8447-3283-4

AEI studies 183

Printed in the United States of America

CONTENTS

INDEX OF CASES   189

SUBJECT INDEX   193

1
OVERVIEW

The 1975–1976 term of the Supreme Court marked a significant change both in the membership of the Court and in the speed and confidence with which it has charted a diminished role for the federal judiciary and an increased role for the states in the process of governing.[1] On December 19, 1975, Justice John Paul Stevens filled the vacancy caused by the retirement of Justice William O. Douglas because of ill health. Douglas's departure left the liberal bloc of the Court with only the votes of Brennan and Marshall. It seemed to encourage the remaining seven justices in their general belief that an unelected federal judiciary should avoid imposing constitutional and, thus, nationwide shackles on other levels or branches of government in their attempts to treat intractable and complex political, economic, and social problems.

After avoiding controversial decisions during the preceding term, the Court rendered a series of opinions with wide political and public reverberations. It upheld the constitutionality of the death penalty for murderers if imposed pursuant to specified procedural safeguards. In seeming to depart from its general approach to consti-

---

[1] See, for example, Stone v. Powell, 428 U.S. 465 (1976) (reducing the scope of federal habeas corpus review in suits raising Fourth Amendment claims); Paul v. Davis, 424 U.S. 693 (1976) (holding an individual's interest in reputation is not a liberty interest protected by the Fourteenth Amendment); Simon v. Eastern Kentucky Welfare Rights Organization, 426 U.S. 26 (1976) (holding that indigents lack standing to challenge an Internal Revenue Service ruling concerning the charitable obligations of tax-exempt hospitals); Rizzo v. Goode, 423 U.S. 362 (1976) (overturning an injunction requiring a police department to adopt a program for effectively dealing with complaints by civilians); Bishop v. Wood, 426 U.S. 341 (1976) (upholding the discharge of a policeman without a hearing); National League of Cities v. Usery, 426 U.S. 833 (1976) (holding federal regulation of the wages and hours of state and municipal employees an unconstitutional infringement of state sovereignty).

tutional questions in other areas, the Court expanded a woman's right to an abortion by striking down restrictions requiring spousal and parental consent. The planning of several presidential candidates was shaken when the Court invalidated several provisions of the Watergate-inspired amendments to the Federal Election Campaign Act and thereby impaired the financing of their campaigns. Both broadcasters and the press won a controversial battle to stop the growing use of judicial gag orders imposed to prevent the pretrial publication of news that could be prejudicial to the accused.[2] The Court erected such high constitutional standards of necessity as virtually to prohibit the issuance of gag orders against the press in any circumstances. Finally, for the first time in several decades, the Court established a restraint on the authority of Congress to encroach upon state sovereignty in legislating pursuant to the commerce clause.

With regard to questions of criminal law, the Court restricted and virtually overruled liberal decisions of the Warren Court that greatly expanded the constitutional rights of suspects and prisoners.[3] In weighing and balancing the interests of individuals in privacy and the interests of society in effective law enforcement in an era of increased crime, high rates of recidivism, and public clamor for better law inforcement, the Court generally leaned in favor of law enforcement needs.[4]

Death Penalty Decisions

Justice Holmes once observed:

> Great cases, like hard cases, make bad law. For great cases are called great, not by reason of their real importance in shaping the law of the future, but because of some accident of immediate overwhelming interest which appeals to the

---

[2] See Reporters Committee for Freedom of the Press, *Press Censorship Newsletter* no. 9 (April-May 1976), pp. 2-34.

[3] Compare Mapp v. Ohio, 367 U.S. 643 (1961), with United States v. Janis, 428 U.S. 433 (1976), and Stone v. Powell, 428 U.S. 465 (1976); compare Miranda v. Arizona, 384 U.S. 436 (1966), with Michigan v. Mosley, 423 U.S. 96 (1976), United States v. Mandujano, 425 U.S. 564 (1976), and Beckwith v. United States, 425 U.S. 341 (1976); compare Fay v. Noia, 372 U.S. 391 (1963), with Estelle v. Williams, 425 U.S. 501 (1976); compare Kaufman v. United States, 394 U.S. 217 (1969), with Stone v. Powell, 428 U.S. 465 (1976).

[4] See, for example, United States v. Watson, 423 U.S. 411 (1976); United States v. Martinez-Fuerte, 428 U.S. 543 (1976); South Dakota v. Opperman, 428 U.S. 364 (1976); United States v. Miller, 425 U.S. 435 (1976); Fisher v. United States, 425 U.S. 391 (1976); Andresen v. Maryland, 427 U.S. 463 (1976); Imbler v. Pachtman, 424 U.S. 409 (1976).

feelings and distorts the judgment. These immediate interests exercise a kind of hydraulic pressure which makes what previously was clear seem doubtful, and before which even well settled principles of law will bend. [*Northern Securities Co. v. United States*, 193 U.S. 197, 400–401 (1904), Holmes, J., dissenting.]

The five written opinions of the Supreme Court regarding the death penalty this term involved, in the words of Justice Holmes, "great cases" and made "bad" or at least poorly reasoned law. At stake were the lives of more than 450 prisoners. The enormous increase in crime over the past fifteen years and a growing belief that deterrence, as opposed to rehabilitation, should be the primary purpose of criminal punishment heightened public interest in the issue. These circumstances seem to have distorted the judgment of the Court in its decisions that virtually prohibited mandatory death penalty statutes, but upheld the death penalty if imposed pursuant to specified procedural safeguards.[5] An examination of the plurality opinions by Justices Stewart, Powell, and Stevens in the leading cases of *Gregg* v. *Georgia*, 428 U.S. 153 (1976), and *Woodson* v. *North Carolina*, 428 U.S. 289 (1976), reveals the use of inconsistent and unpersuasive reasoning in striking down mandatory death penalty statutes.

In *Gregg*, a convicted murderer sentenced to death challenged the constitutionality of the Georgia death-sentencing provisions. They provide for a bifurcated trial procedure; sentence is imposed at a separate hearing only after a guilty verdict in the initial trial stage. At the sentencing hearing, any evidence relevant to the sentencing decision, including any mitigating or aggravating circumstance, is admissible. In order to impose a death sentence, the sentencing authority must find, beyond a reasonable doubt, the existence of at least one of ten statutorily defined aggravating circumstances.[6] Judicial review of all death sentences by the Georgia Supreme Court is required to ensure that the sentence is not arbitrarily imposed. The defendant argued that Georgia's death-sentencing provisions violated the prohibition of the Eighth and Fourteenth amendments against

---

[5] The Court left open the question of whether mandatory death penalty statutes applicable to murder committed by prisoners serving life sentences violated the Eighth and Fourteenth amendments. See Woodson v. North Carolina, 428 U.S. 280, 292 n. 25 (1976).

[6] One aggravating circumstance was commission of a murder for the purpose of avoiding lawful arrest. Another was commission of murder by a person with a substantial history of criminal convictions for serious assault. See Gregg v. Georgia, 428 U.S. 153, 165 n. 9 (1976).

"cruel and unusual" punishments on two alternative grounds.[7] First, he claimed that the death penalty was unconstitutional per se. In the alternative, he contended that the discretion permitted the sentencing authority resulted in the arbitrary and capricious imposition of the death penalty in violation of the mandate of *Furman* v. *Georgia*, 408 U.S. 238 (1972).[8]

The plurality opinion rejected the claim that the punishment of death for the crime of murder is, under all circumstances, unconstitutionally "cruel and unusual." It asserted that the Eighth Amendment prohibited a particular punishment only if it violated contemporary community standards of decency or was "excessive." A punishment was excessive, the plurality stated, if it involved "the unnecessary or wanton infliction of pain" or was grossly disproportionate to the severity of the crime.

In concluding that the death penalty was consistent with contemporary standards of decency, the plurality relied principally on two facts. First, thirty-five states and the federal government had enacted new death penalty statutes since the 1972 *Furman* decision of the Court. Second, juries imposed the death sentence in a substantial number of cases under these statutes.

The death penalty is not an excessive punishment, the plurality stated, because it serves the legitimate penal function of retribution. In addition, although numerous and exhaustive studies on the deterrent effect of the death penalty have been inconclusive, the plurality concluded that legislatures could constitutionally assume that capital punishment does deter crime. Finally, the plurality failed to find any disproportionality in imposing capital punishment for murder.

The *Woodson* decision involved a North Carolina statute which required the death penalty for all persons convicted of first-degree murder. The Court invalidated the statute on the ground, *inter alia*, that mandatory sentencing provisions for capital crimes violate contemporary standards of decency. In reaching this conclusion, the Court relied predominantly on the fact that virtually all mandatory sentencing laws had previously been repealed by Congress and state legislatures, thus manifesting, in the reasoning of the Court, an indication that "contemporary standards of decency" inexorably move forward and inevitably reject an ever greater number of punishments.

---

[7] In Robinson v. California, 370 U.S. 660 (1962), the Court held that the due process clause of the Fourteenth Amendment incorporated the prohibition against cruel and unusual punishments embodied in the Eighth Amendment.

[8] In *Furman*, the Court held that the standardless discretion provided juries in imposing the death sentence resulted in its infliction in an arbitrary and capricious manner in violation of the Eighth and Fourteenth amendments.

What the Court failed to consider, however, is the fact that ten states had chosen to enact mandatory death penalty laws since the *Furman* decision and that juries had convicted hundreds of persons under those laws. These developments appear to contradict the notion that American society has grown progressively more reluctant to inflict death as the punishment for serious offenses.

The decision to enact mandatory statutes cannot be satisfactorily explained, as the Court attempted, by attributing to the motives of state legislators a mistaken belief that *Furman* precluded the existence of sentencing discretion for capital crimes. In any event, the validity of such an observation would depend upon an examination of the legislative history of the laws passed by all ten states, but in the *Woodson* decision the Court was content to explore the genesis of the North Carolina statute alone. It is at least as likely that a return to mandatory sentencing can be ascribed to heightened fears about rising crime rates as to a mistaken interpretation of *Furman*. The state of Hawaii, for example, where capital punishment was abolished in 1957, may well enact a new death law in 1977 because of public anger over recent murders.[9] The 33 percent increase in murder rates in the United States from 1969 to 1974 could have precipitated a shift in public attitude toward the death penalty as a means of dealing with violent crime.[10] A 1966 Gallup poll found a plurality of 42 percent against the death penalty, but by the spring of 1976 a Gallup poll found a majority favoring the death penalty by 65 to 28 percent.

The plurality opinion in *Woodson* also found mandatory death laws constitutionally defective for two other reasons. First, it was reasoned in the opinion that since many juries in the past have refused to convict persons charged with murder when death was the obligatory punishment, they would continue to do so under modern statutes. Inasmuch as juries lack standards to determine whether acquittal is the appropriate remedy for avoiding the imposition of death, the Court concluded that mandatory sentencing laws encourage the very application of capricious justice which *Furman* condemned. It is possible to argue, however, that acquittal under these circumstances is heavily dependent upon the importance which society places upon the curbing of serious crime. Juries may be less disposed to render verdicts of innocence when crime rates are high than when they are low. Indeed, this proposition seems to be validated by the fact that sixty-three persons were sentenced to death under North Carolina's

---

[9] See *Washington Post*, August 15, 1976.
[10] See Federal Bureau of Investigation, *Crime in the United States*, 1974 Uniform Crime Reports, p. 11.

mandatory statute [11] while only seventy-five persons were found guilty of capital crimes throughout the United States in 1972.[12]

The *Woodson* decision also created a unique rule for death penalty cases by stipulating that, when death is at stake, the sentencing authority is constitutionally required to take into consideration the character of the offender and the circumstances of the crime before imposing sentence. This requirement seems to be an odd throwback to the time when persons could be convicted on the basis of their status or life style, rather than for the commission of specific acts. Criminal laws, after all, inflict punishment for certain deeds, not for the habits, character, or reputation of the accused. The Supreme Court has itself accepted this reasoning by deciding that states may not punish a person simply on the basis of his status as a narcotics addict (*Robinson* v. *California*, 370 U.S. 660 [1962]). By refocusing the attention of the sentencing authority to the character of the convicted person and away from the nature of the criminal act in death penalty cases where retribution and deterrence, not rehabilitation, are the purposes of punishment, the Supreme Court may have injected a degree of constitutionally-based distortion into the system of criminal justice. In recent years, in fact, the wide disparity of sentences received by different offenders convicted of the same crime has been severely criticized and has generated proposals and laws to reduce discretion in the sentencing process.[13]

Abortion

The Court's major decisions concerning abortion this term manifested a seeming departure from other decisions reflecting a presumptive deference toward legislative choices and a rejection of the view that requirements for obtaining standing—a limitation of the jurisdiction of the Court imposed under Article III of the Constitution—be applied loosely in federal courts. The Court also may have foreshadowed the eventual evisceration of its central holding in *Roe* v. *Wade*, 410 U.S. 113 (1973); it specifically held that a state may prohibit abortions, except when an abortion is necessary to preserve the mental or physical health of the mother, at any stage of fetal development where existing medical technology could sustain the life of the unborn child indefinitely outside the womb.

---

[11] See Brief for Petitioner, Woodson v. North Carolina, No. 75-5491, Appendix A.
[12] See Gregg v. Georgia, 428 U.S. 153, 182 n. 26 (1976).
[13] See for example, Maurice Oppenheim, "Computing a Determinate Sentence. . . New Math Hits the Courts," *California State Bar Journal*, vol. 51, no. 7 (November-December 1976), p. 604.

In *Planned Parenthood of Central Missouri* v. *Danforth*, 428 U.S. 52 (1976), the constitutionality of several provisions of a Missouri abortion statute was attacked. One provision made an abortion unlawful during the first twelve weeks of pregnancy unless the written consent of the spouse was obtained.[14] Writing for the Court, Justice Blackmun asserted that the husband's interest in preventing an abortion was virtually indistinguishable from that of the state. Thus, he reasoned, since the state was constitutionally barred under *Roe* from preventing abortions during the first trimester of pregnancy, so was the father. To bolster that conclusion, Blackmun stated that since the mother physically bears the child and is more directly and immediately affected by the pregnancy, her wishes should prevail over those of the father.

Blackmun's equating of the interest of the husband in preventing an abortion with that of the state is hard to justify. A husband, unlike the state, has a strong and legitimate interest in the birth of a child he has helped to conceive. In addition, the husband's interest in giving and receiving the love, affection, and friendship of his child throughout his life is enormous. The Court has recognized a constitutionally protected interest of unmarried fathers to raise their children in preference to state custody.[15] Blackmun's conclusive assertion that the interests of the husband and the state are identical for purposes of preventing an abortion is inconsistent with the spirit of *Stanley* v. *Illinois*. It seems to rest on a type of male stereotyping that Blackmun and the Court found constitutionally impermissible as applied to women only last term.[16]

Roe v. *Wade* acknowledged that a state may properly prescribe certain health and safety procedures in abortions necessary for the well-being of the mother after the first trimester of pregnancy. Missouri attempted to exercise its discretion in this regard by prohibiting abortions performed by the saline amniocentesis method after the first twelve weeks of pregnancy. The Supreme Court, however,

---

14 However, an abortion was permitted after the first trimester of pregnancy over the spouse's objection if necessary to preserve the mother's life.

15 Stanley v. Illinois, 405 U.S. 645 (1972).

16 See Stanton v. Stanton, 421 U.S. 7 (1975). There the Court struck down a state statute specifying a greater age of majority for males than for females for purposes of receiving support payments. In rejecting the claim that the age differential could be justified by the greater interest of a male in obtaining an education while assured of parental support, Justice Blackmun wrote: "To distinguish between the two on educational grounds is to be self-serving: if the female is not to be supported so long as the male, she hardly can be expected to attend school as long as he does, and bringing her education to an end earlier coincides with the role-typing society has long imposed."

refused to accede to the judgment of the Missouri legislature and ruled that such a prohibition was an unconstitutional infringement of a mother's right to abort an unwanted fetus. In doing so, the Court emphasized the fact that saline amniocentesis is a widely accepted medical procedure throughout the country and is considered to be safer than some alternative methods of abortion. That a legislature has acted unwisely or even improvidently is not, however, ordinarily enough to justify the nullification of a statute relating to health or welfare on constitutional grounds. It is possible to argue that Missouri was entitled to seek higher standards of safety than those prevailing in other states and that its action was within the discretionary ambit of the regulatory scope permitted by *Roe*.

The inclination of the Court to expand the constitutional rights of women to obtain abortions was consistent with its decision in *Singleton* v. *Wulff*, 428 U.S. 106 (1976). At issue there was whether physicians participating in Missouri's Medicaid program could assert the constitutional rights of their female patients in challenging a statute precluding Medicaid reimbursement for abortions that are not "medically necessary." Both in this and recent terms, the Court has strictly construed the requirement of standing in dismissing the claims of several plaintiffs.[17] The decisions in part reflect a belief that the federal judiciary is not constitutionally designed to be the primary arbiter of all societal disputes.[18]

In *Wulff*, however, the Court departed from the underlying philosophy of its rigorous standing rules. It ruled that the physicians could advance the constitutional rights of their female patients to obtain an abortion in challenging the restriction on Medicaid reimbursement. The Court reasoned that if the relationship between a litigant and a third party is sufficiently close, the litigant should be permitted to advance the constitutional rights of that party if "genuine obstacles" prevent the assertion of his own rights. The Court found two obstacles to the assertion by indigent females of their rights to an abortion. The first was a desire to protect the privacy of an abortion decision from the publicity of a court suit. But this privacy interest can be readily protected by the use of pseudonyms in bringing suit.[19] The second obstacle was the virtual impossibility of deter-

---

[17] See Simon v. Eastern Kentucky Welfare Rights Organization, 426 U.S. 26 (1976); Warth v. Seldin, 422 U.S. 490 (1975); United States v. Richardson, 418 U.S. 166 (1974).

[18] See Schlesinger v. Reservists Committee to Stop the War, 418 U.S. 208 (1974).

[19] Justice Powell dissenting in *Wulff* noted: "Our docket regularly contains cases in which women, using pseudonyms, challenge statutes that allegedly infringe their right to exercise the abortion decision" (428 U.S. 106).

mining the abortion rights of an indigent woman before such rights would be irrevocably lost because of fetal development. The Court asserted that physicians would not provide abortions to impecunious women unless eligibility for reimbursement under Medicaid was established. Indigent women, however, are not faced with genuine obstacles in seeking to assert their alleged constitutional rights to abortions covered by Medicaid. Indeed, a case on the 1976–1977 docket of the Supreme Court raising virtually the same Medicaid question at issue in *Wulff* was brought under a pseudonym by an indigent female plaintiff, who obtained an abortion from her physician during the pendency of the litigation (*Westby* v. *Doe*, No. 75–813). The decision of the Court in *Wulff* seems understandable only by inferring a strong desire to have claims concerning abortion speedily adjudicated in federal courts.

The constitutional rights of women to obtain abortions, however, may be sharply curtailed by the development of medical technology. In the *Planned Parenthood* case, the Court emphasized that a state may prohibit abortions unnecessary for the preservation of the mother's health or life whenever the fetus is potentially able to live indefinitely outside the womb. Although that point is reached at present after approximately twenty-eight weeks of pregnancy, future developments in medical knowledge and technology will undoubtedly reduce that period. Whether such reduction would in fact curtail opportunities for abortions is uncertain. In *Doe* v. *Bolton*, 410 U.S. 179 (1973), the Court held that, even after viability, a state could not forbid an abortion necessary to preserve the life or health of the mother. *Doe* seemingly held that a physician must be permitted to consider all factors relevant to a woman's well-being—physical, emotional, psychological, familial, and age—in determining whether an abortion is necessary to preserve health. If *Doe* is interpreted to permit an abortion after viability if the mother states that childbirth would be psychologically or emotionally upsetting, then reducing the number of weeks to viability would have little effect on a mother's constitutional right to an abortion.

Campaign Financing

On January 30, 1976, shortly after the selection of delegates to the national Democratic and Republican conventions had begun, the Supreme Court issued a landmark decision upholding the constitutionality of some, but not all, of the major provisions of the Federal Election Campaign Act (*Buckley* v. *Valeo*, 424 U.S. 1 [1976]). The

9

provisions upheld in *Buckley* included the limitation on contributions from individuals and political committees to candidates for federal office to $1,000 and $5,000, respectively, and the general program to provide public financial support for presidential primary and general election campaigns.

The most important aspects of the statute which were invalidated by *Buckley* imposed limitations on the expenditures of candidates for federal office and established the Federal Election Commission (FEC) dominated by congressional appointees to enforce the provisions of the Federal Election Campaign Act.[20] Because the FEC was the only body authorized to certify eligibility for public funds under the act, its demise deprived several candidates, including Ronald Reagan, Morris Udall, and Henry Jackson, of matching funds badly needed in their primary campaigns.[21] The Court stayed the effective date of its judgment invalidating the FEC for thirty days to give Congress an opportunity to rectify the constitutional deficiencies in the manner of selecting the members of the commission. The Federal Election Campaign Act was not finally amended until May 11,[22] however, and the reconstituted commission first resumed the dispersal of matching funds on May 21, leaving primary candidates without federal support for a full sixty days.

The *Buckley* decision in effect invalidated numerous state and local laws which imposed limitations on expenditures in campaigns for state and local elections.[23] In California, for example, an expenditure ceiling of approximately $1.1 million applicable to the controversial Nuclear Power Initiative proposition[24] was nullified, thus allowing the opponents of the proposition to spend almost $3.5 million in working for its eventual defeat.[25] The prohibition of ceilings on expenditures for federal elections, however, promises to be of little practical consequence. *Buckley* approved restrictions on expenditures when they are linked with a candidate's acceptance of

---

[20] The six-member commission had two members appointed by the President, two members appointed by the speaker of the House of Representatives, and two members appointed by the president pro tempore of the Senate, all subject to the concurrence of both houses of Congress (2 U.S. Code 437 [c]).

[21] See *Congressional Quarterly*, vol. 34, no. 17 (April 24, 1976), pp. 998-99.

[22] P.L. 94-283. That law provides for presidential appointment and Senate confirmation of all commission members.

[23] See *The Book of the States, 1976-77* (Lexington, Kentucky: Council of State Governments, 1976), Table 10, p. 223. That table indicates that thirty-one states had limitations on expenditures applicable to elections at the time of the *Buckley* decision.

[24] See "Government," *California Annotated Code*, section 85303.

[25] See *National Journal*, vol. 8 (June 12, 1976), p. 827.

public subsidies. Although that exception is now applicable only to presidential campaigns, legislation may be enacted to provide public funding for congressional elections,[26] and President Carter has expressed support for the concept.

Despite the fact that both Senator McGovern and President Nixon spent far more from private sources in their 1972 presidential campaigns than is authorized under the existing Federal Election Campaign Act for presidential candidates receiving public funds,[27] no substantial candidate in the 1976 race declined an available subsidy to avoid the ceiling on expenditures. This is probably in part because the Watergate scandal has caused the electorate to view with suspicion any candidate who spends large sums from private sources. Congressional candidates would probably also be politically constrained to accept both public funds and a ceiling on spending if they were provided for by law.

Fair Trial—Free Press

In recent years, the news media and the judiciary have clashed increasingly over the publication of information relating to judicial proceedings.[28] Several courts have enjoined the news media from reporting on particular cases in the belief that such action was necessary to ensure a fair trial for the accused. There is evidence to support the belief that these so-called gag orders are necessary to ensure fair trials.[29] Nevertheless, despite massive pretrial publicity concerning their cases, defendants such as John Mitchell, Maurice Stans, Kenneth Parkinson, Angela Davis, and John Connally have been acquitted.

The Supreme Court addressed the constitutionality of judicial gag orders in criminal cases for the first time in *Nebraska Press Association v. Stuart*, 427 U.S. 539 (1976). It characterized judicial in-

---

[26] See S. 926, H.R. 2979, 95th Congress, 1st session (1977).

[27] President Nixon spent approximately $60 million and Senator McGovern $30 million in the general presidential election campaign.

[28] See Reporters Committee for Freedom of the Press, *Press Censorship Newsletter*, no. 9 (April-May 1976).

[29] Allen H. Barton and Alice M. Podawer-Singer, "The Impact of Pre-Trial Publicity on Jury Verdicts," in *The Jury System in America: A Critical Overview*, volume 4, chapter 5, of the Sage Criminal Justice Series, Rita James Simon, ed. (Beverly Hills, California: Sage Publishers, 1975). The study found that mock juries exposed to pretrial publicity prejudicial to the defendant convicted 80 percent of the time, while they convicted only 39 percent of the time when exposed to "neutral" coverage of the case. The validity of the study has been questioned because of the controlled manner in which jurors were exposed to the publicity. See Reporters Committee for Freedom of the Press, *Press Censorship Newsletter*, no. 8 (October-November 1975), p. 60.

junctions against publication as a prior restraint on free speech and press and, thus, presumptively unconstitutional. Such injunctions would satisfy First Amendment guarantees, the Court concluded, only if it is proven that no alternative measures could ensure a fair trial and that the injunction would be effective in protecting that right. Alternative measures include a change of trial venue, postponement of the trial, extensive questioning of prospective jurors to screen out those with clear bias, sequestration of jurors, and injunctions proscribing extrajudicial statements by any lawyer, party, witness, or court official that divulge prejudicial information. It is difficult to imagine any case in which a substantial threat to a fair trial created by prejudicial publicity could not be avoided by the use of such alternative measures. Moreover, to prove that an injunction will be effective in keeping prejudicial information from prospective jurors is extremely difficult. It requires a court to know what information will in fact undermine the impartiality of jurors. In addition, constitutional due process may preclude a court from enjoining publication by national news media operating outside its territorial jurisdiction. As a practical matter, therefore, the *Nebraska Press Association* decision probably bars the issuance of judicial gag orders against the news media in criminal cases for the purpose of ensuring a fair trial.

Nebraska Press Association represents one in a series of decisions strengthening the constitutional protection of the news media to report on political and governmental matters.[30] These decisions reflect in part the increasing importance of the news media and the declining importance of Congress in uncovering corruption in government and informing the public about important political issues.

With reference to Congress, Woodrow Wilson observed:

> Quite as important as legislation is vigilant oversight of administration, and even more important than legislation is the instruction and guidance in political affairs which the people might receive from a body which kept all national concerns suffused in a broad daylight of discussion. The informing function of Congress should be preferred even to its legislative function.[31]

---

[30] See New York Times v. Sullivan, 376 U.S. 254 (1964); New York Times v. United States, 403 U.S. 713 (1971); Columbia Broadcasting System, Inc. v. Democratic National Committee, 412 U.S. 94 (1973); Miami Herald Publishing Co. v. Tornillo, 418 U.S. 241 (1974); Cox Broadcasting Company v. Cohn, 420 U.S. 469 (1975); but see Branzburg v. Hayes, 408 U.S. 665 (1972).

[31] Woodrow Wilson, *Congressional Government* (New York: World Publishing Company, 1956), pp. 195-98.

Vice President Mondale, while still in the Senate, wrote that congressional power has declined over the past decades largely because of the failure of Congress to exercise its oversight and informing functions diligently.[32] The national news media have filled this power vacuum to a large extent.

In the view of Justice Stewart, the primary purpose of the constitutional guarantee of a free press was to create a private institution that would act as a watchdog on governmental abuse. He has stated that a free press was meant to provide "organized expert scrutiny of government," and that this constitutional understanding provides a unifying principle underlying recent decisions of the Supreme Court concerning the organized press.[33]

Federalism

The Great Depression of the 1930s and the Second World War triggered an enormous increase in the power of the national government and a reduction in the importance of state powers. The national budget grew from approximately $4.6 billion in 1932 to approximately $365.6 billion in fiscal 1976. The aggregate budgets of all state and local governments in 1976 totaled only $185 billion. A present member of the Rhode Island legislature has stated: "In state government you become very aware that many of the opportunities to have a real impact, to make a difference, have long ago been removed to the federal government."[34]

In recent years, however, significant public dissatisfaction with the slowness and inefficiency with which many national programs are operated has resulted in national legislation returning important decision-making authority and revenue to the states. The several revenue-sharing statutes are leading examples of this trend.

An increase in the power of the states and municipalities and a corresponding reduction in national powers might be healthy for several reasons. It would increase the probability of discovering the most appropriate role for government in dealing with seemingly intractable social and economic problems. The Supreme Court has observed that the science of government is the science of experiment.[35]

---

32 Walter Mondale, *The Accountability of Power* (New York: David McKay Company, 1975), chapter 5.

33 See address of Potter Stewart, "Or of the Press," Yale Law School Sesquicentennial Convocation, New Haven, Connecticut, November 2, 1974.

34 *Harvard Law Record*, vol. 64, no. 4 (February 18, 1977), pp. 5 and 9.

35 Anderson v. Dunn, 19 U.S. 226 (1821).

As with progress in the physical sciences, more effective ways of treating social science problems are most readily discovered through the trial-and-error method.[36] If fifty states and numerous municipalities have both the responsibility and authority to seek improved ways of treating social problems, it is far more likely that improvements will be discovered than if experimentation is stifled by a uniform approach of the national government. In addition, if a state or local approach fails, only its constituency will suffer the adverse effects.[37] This fact has the salutary consequence, however, of generating political pressure in the affected state or local electorate to seek a different approach. In contrast, a national program may be unworkable in several parts of the country without generating sufficient political pressure to remedy its defects, because in a majority of congressional districts or states it is operating satisfactorily. In addition, the Congress considers such a large volume of proposed legislation each year that it lacks the time needed to determine whether national programs are operating well.[38] Effective experimention and appropriate adjustment of government programs may thus be more likely to occur at the state and local levels than at the national level.

Returning important powers to state and municipal governments will also promote an invigorated democracy and political freedom by multiplying the centers of significant government authority. A dispersal of power reduces the likelihood that one part of society will be able to take action inimical to another part. As Madison observed in *The Federalist* Number 51: "It is of great importance in a republic not only to guard the society against the oppression of its rulers, but to guard one part of the society against the injustice of the other part."

In addition, an increase in state and municipal authority would promote the diffusion of political knowledge and perhaps expand public participation in the political process.[39] Greater knowledge of political issues and increased participation by the public in govern-

---

[36] See New State Ice Co. v. Liebman, 285 U.S. 262 (1932) (Brandeis, J., dissenting).

[37] As Justice Brandeis observed in New State Ice Co. v. Liebman, "It is one of the happy incidents of the federal system that a single courageous State may, if its citizens choose, serve as a laboratory; and try novel social and economic experiments without risk to the rest of the country."

[38] In 1975, 11,351 bills were introduced in the House of Representatives and 2,840 bills were introduced in the Senate. See *Congressional Record*, December 19, 1975, p. D1571.

[39] In Montana during 1976, popularly elected study commissions in the 181 counties of the state proposed alternative forms of local government subject to local ratification. The educational value of the effort promises to be enormous. See Neal R. Peirce, "A Model of Self-Government at Last Chance Gulch," *Washington Post*, July 24, 1976.

ment affairs are necessary to the maintenance of a vigilant and healthy democracy in the United States.

Finally, local and state legislators can be held accountable more easily than can congressmen. The cumbersome system of congressional committees, the myriad of procedural rules, and the size of the Congress make it difficult for the constituency of a congressman to hold him accountable for the fate of particular legislation, such as the recent congressional pay raise.[40] Because state and local legislatures generally are significantly smaller and more simply organized than Congress, it is easier for constituents to hold their members, as opposed to congressmen, accountable for their actions. Political accountability, of course, is the hallmark of an effective democracy.

Three of the decisions of the Court this term promoted the interests of federalism by reducing the power of the national government and increasing those of the states. In *National League of Cities v. Usery*, 426 U.S. 833 (1976), the Court held that Congress lacked authority under the commerce clause to apply the minimum wage and overtime provisions of the Fair Labor Standards Act to state and municipal employees. It concluded that state sovereignty would be unconstitutionally impaired if Congress could regulate the wages and hours of state and municipal workers. The practical significance of the *National League of Cities* decision is unclear. The AFL-CIO Executive Council has voted to lobby Congress to make receipt of federal grant monies by state and local governments conditional upon observance of the Fair Labor Standards Act.[41] States and municipalities now receive approximately $60 billion in federal grant monies annually. *Steward Machine Co. v. Davis*, 301 U.S. 548 (1937), however, provides support for the view that Congress may not exercise its spending authority in a manner that would impair the essence of statehood.[42] If that is true, Congress lacks authority to frustrate the

---

[40] On February 20, 1977, a proposed $12,900 pay raise for members of Congress submitted by President Ford took effect without either house of Congress having voted on the question. The proposal by law was to become effective unless vetoed by either house within thirty days after submission. See *Congressional Quarterly*, vol. 35, no. 7 (February 12, 1977), p. 268.

[41] See *Washington Post*, August 2, 1976.

[42] In *Steward Machine*, the Court upheld the constitutionality of a federal employment tax with a maximum 90 percent credit against the tax for contributions made to an unemployment fund that was under state law and met certain federally prescribed conditions. By negative implication, however, the Court indicated that states may not contract with Congress in a fashion that impairs their statehood (301 U.S. 548, 597). *Steward Machine* also suggested that Congress may not condition the receipt of federal benefits upon state adoption of a statute or policy "unrelated in subject matter to activities fairly within the scope of national policy and power" (301 U.S. 548, 590).

holding of *National League of Cities* through use of conditional grant-in-aid programs to state and local governments.

In *Hughes* v. *Alexandria Scrap Corp.*, 426 U.S. 794 (1976), the Court upheld the authority of a state to discriminate in favor of its own citizens in the purchase or subsidization of goods or services.[43] It was claimed that the commerce clause constitutionally forbade such preferences to ensure free and open national economic markets.

In *Stone* v. *Powell*, 428 U.S. 465 (1976), the Court reduced the supervisory powers of the federal judiciary over state courts. It held that federal courts lack jurisdiction to entertain a habeas corpus petition raising a Fourth Amendment claim if the state prisoner has obtained a "full and fair" hearing on the issue in a state court. This decision followed a long series of cases greatly expanding the habeas corpus jurisdiction of federal courts.[44]

General Analysis

Justice Potter Stewart recently stated that in the 1950s and 1960s, the Supreme Court for the first time in history was leading the nation in many areas.[45] Whether the Supreme Court ought to play a role of leadership in the governing of the nation is much disputed. What is clear, however, is that the Supreme Court in the 1970s, during the tenure of Chief Justice Warren Burger, has increasingly aligned itself with the existing political mood of the nation. During the 1975–1976 term, the Court generally refused to extend and in some instances reduced the rights of suspects, criminals, and prisoners. These decisions reflect in part the public concern with high crime rates. The decisions of the Court expanding the constitutional powers of the states and reducing those of Congress are consistent with a pervasive anti-Washington mood throughout the country. Many have criticized decisions of lower federal courts that resulted in close judicial supervision of the operation of public agencies such as schools,[46] prisons,[47] mental

---

[43] The Court did not reach the question of whether Congress could prohibit such discrimination.

[44] See "Developments in the Law, Federal Habeas Corpus," *Harvard Law Review*, vol. 83 (1970), p. 1038. See also Braden v. 30th Judicial Circuit Court of Kentucky, 410 U.S. 484 (1973); Hensley v. Municipal Court, 411 U.S. 345 (1973).

[45] See *Newsweek*, July 4, 1976, p. 36.

[46] Morgan v. Kerrigan, 401 F. Supp. 216 (D. Mass. 1975), *affirmed*, 530 F.2d 401, 530 F.2d 431 (1st Cir. 1976), *cert. denied sub nom.* White v. Morgan, 426 U.S. 935 (1976).

[47] Pugh v. Locke, 406 F. Supp. 318 (M.D. Ala. 1976), *affirmed in part, remanded in part sub nom.* Newman v. Alabama, 46 U.S.L.W. 2192 (5th Cir. 1977).

health institutions,[48] and fire departments.[49] These critics charge that such decisions are creating an "imperial federal judiciary."[50] In accord with these views, the requirement of standing was raised as a barrier to prospective federal plaintiffs.[51] And the Court declined to recognize claimed constitutional rights that would place the federal judiciary in the position of overseeing school systems,[52] police departments,[53] and prisons.[54] The Court generally followed the spirit of Chief Justice Stone's remark that "courts are not the only agency of government that must be assumed to have the capacity to govern." (*United States v. Butler*, 297 U.S. 1, 87 [1936], Stone, J., dissenting.)

Voting Alignments

The voting patterns of the justices in the cases concerning the system of criminal justice, federalism and federal courts, and civil rights and civil liberties is revealing.

With regard to issues of criminal justice, all the justices except Brennan and Marshall generally voted against suspects, defendants, or prisoners in nonunanimous decisions. Rehnquist failed to cast a single vote in support of their claims in twenty-eight such cases. Burger and Blackmun twice voted in their favor. Powell supported them in three and White in six of the twenty-eight cases. Stewart and Stevens followed more complex voting patterns. Stewart cast nine votes in favor of suspects, defendants, or prisoners, while Stevens supported them six times in the fourteen nonunanimous decisions in which he participated. In contrast, Marshall and Brennan voted only

---

[48] See Wyatt v. Stickney, 344 F. Supp. 373, and 344 F. Supp. 387 (M.D. Ala. 1972), *aff'd in part, remanded in part sub nom.* Wyatt v. Aderholt, 503 F.2d 1305 (5th Cir. 1974).

[49] See Carter v. Gallagher, 452 F.2d 315 (8th Cir. 1972) (*en banc*), *cert. denied* 406 U.S. 950 (1972).

[50] See Nathan Glazer, "Towards an Imperial Judiciary?" *The Public Interest*, vol. 41 (Fall 1975), pp. 104-23. Justice Holmes cautioned the judiciary against an unrestrained willingness to constitutionalize rules of governing. He observed: "Great constitutional provisions must be administered with caution. Some play must be allowed for the joints of the machine, and it must be remembered that legislatures are ultimate guardians of the liberties and welfare of the people in quite as great a degree as the courts." (Missouri, Kansas & Texas Ry. Co. v. May, 194 U.S. 267, 270 [1904]).

[51] Aldinger v. Howard, 427 U.S. 1 (1976).

[52] Pasadena City Board of Education v. Spangler, 427 U.S. 424 (1976).

[53] Rizzo v. Goode, 423 U.S. 362 (1976); Kelley v. Johnson, 425 U.S. 238 (1976); Bishop v. Wood, 426 U.S. 341 (1976).

[54] Baxter v. Palmigiano, 425 U.S. 308 (1976); Meachum v. Fano, 427 U.S. 215 (1976); Montanye v. Haymes, 427 U.S. 236 (1976).

once in favor of law enforcement officers and prison officials in the nonunanimous decisions.

In the cases concerning federalism and ease of access to federal courts, the voting patterns are not so marked when compared to those in the criminal justice cases. Rehnquist, Burger, and Stewart voted in favor of states' rights and limited access to federal courts in all five of the nonunanimous decisions raising these issues. Powell voted with this trio in four of the five cases. Blackmun and Stevens occupied a middle position, casting three of five and two of four votes, respectively, in favor of national authority and broad access to federal courts. White voted that way in all but one of the five decisions, while Brennan and Marshall voted against states' rights and in favor of expanded access to federal courts in every case.

In cases dealing with racial discrimination, the justices split along somewhat different lines from the way they were divided over federalism and federal courts. In the nonunanimous decisions, Rehnquist voted to reject the claim of racial discrimination in all six cases. He was joined by Burger and White four times. Stewart, Powell, Blackmun, and Stevens occupied a centrist position, casting half their votes to uphold and half to reject claims of racial discrimination. Brennan and Marshall voted to support claims of racial discrimination in every case.

The nonunanimous decisions concerning freedom of speech and press revealed voting patterns similar to those in the area of criminal justice. Rehnquist voted against claims of freedom of speech or press in all seven cases. Burger and Powell joined Rehnquist five times. Blackmun, Stewart, and Stevens had mixed voting records. The former two justices divided their votes four to three in support of claims of freedom of speech and press, while the latter cast one of his two votes that way. Brennan and Marshall cast all their votes to uphold claims of freedom of speech and press and were joined by White five times.

On the basis of these voting patterns and other decisions, the justices can be placed on a spectrum running from judicial conservatism to judicial liberalism, as those terms are popularly understood, as follows: Rehnquist, Burger, Powell, Blackmun, White, Stewart, Stevens, Marshall, and Brennan. Rehnquist and Burger vote very conservatively. Powell, Blackmun, White, Stewart, and Stevens in particular areas occupy middle positions. Marshall and Brennan vote as the liberal counterweight to Rehnquist and Burger.[55]

---

[55] For a more complete record of the voting behavior of the justices, see *Harvard Law Review*, vol. 90 (1976), p. 277.

Table 1
ACTION OF INDIVIDUAL JUSTICES

| | Opinions Written[a] | | | | Dissenting Votes[b] | | |
| | | | | | In disposition by | | |
	Opinions of court	Concur-rences	Dis-sents[c]	Total	Opinion	Memo-randum	Total
Blackmun	16	7	9	32	19	1	20
Brennan	16	10	27	53	56	8	64
Burger	17	10	5	32	16	5	21
Douglas[d]	0	1	1	2	2	1	3
Marshall	17	8	19	44	50	11	61
Powell	16	20	5	41	7	8	15
Rehnquist	16	1	15	32	30	8	38
Stevens[e]	9	9	17	35	19	6	25
Stewart	16	7	16	39	25	3	28
White	15	16	12	43	21	0	21
Per curiam	21	—	—	21	—	—	—
Total	159	89	126	374	245	51	296

Note: A complete explanation of the way in which the tables are compiled may be found in "The Supreme Court, 1967 Term," *Harvard Law Review,* vol. 82 (1968), pp. 93, 301-302, and "The Supreme Court, 1969 Term," *Harvard Law Review,* vol. 84 (1970), pp. 30, 254-55.

Table 1, with the exception of the dissenting votes portion, deals only with full-opinion decisions disposing of cases on their merits. Twenty-one per curiam decisions were long enough to be considered full opinions. The memorandum tabulations include memorandum orders disposing of cases on the merits by affirming, reserving, vacating, or remanding. They exclude orders disposing of petitions for certiorari, dismissing writs of certiorari as improvidently granted, dismissing appeals for lack of jurisdiction or for lack of a substantial federal question, and disposing of miscellaneous applications. Certified questions are not included.

[a] A concurrence or dissent is recorded as a written opinion whenever a reason, however brief, is given, except when simply noted by the reporter.

[b] A justice is considered to have dissented when he voted to dispose of the case in any manner different from that of the majority of the Court.

[c] Opinions concurring in part and dissenting in part are counted as dissents.

[d] Justice Douglas retired on November 12, 1975.

[e] Justice Stevens acceded to the bench on December 19, 1975.

Source: *Harvard Law Review,* vol. 90 (November 1976), p. 276, as corrected.

1975–1976 Statistics

The total number of cases on the docket of the Supreme Court rose slightly from 4,668 last term to 4,761 this term. The number of cases disposed of, in contrast, fell from 3,847 in the 1974 term to 3,806 in the 1975 term, leaving 955 cases remaining on dockets at the conclusion of the term. The Court heard 179 cases argued, disposed of 161 by signed opinion, and set 3 cases for reargument. The corresponding figures for the 1974–1975 term were 175 cases argued, 144 disposed of by signed opinion, and 11 cases set for reargument. Statistics reflecting the work of individual justices and the Court as a whole may be found in Tables 1 through 3.

Table 2

CASES FILED, DISPOSED OF, AND REMAINING ON DOCKETS AT CONCLUSION OF OCTOBER TERMS 1973, 1974, AND 1975

Type of Case	On Dockets	Disposed of During Terms	Remaining on Dockets
Original			
1973	14	4	10
1974	12	4	8
1975	14	7	7
Appellate			
1973	2,480	1,868	612
1974	2,308	1,877	431
1975	2,352	1,810	542
Miscellaneous			
1973	2,585	2,004	581
1974	2,348	1,966	382
1975	2,395	1,989	406
Totals			
1973	5,079	3,876	1,203
1974	4,668	3,847	821
1975	4,761	3,806	955

Source: Office of the Clerk of the Supreme Court of the United States.

Table 3
DISPOSITION OF CASES,
1973, 1974, AND 1975 OCTOBER TERMS

Number of Cases	1973 Term	1974 Term	1975 Term
Argued during term	170	175	179
Number disposed of by full opinions	161	144	160
Number disposed of by per curiam opinions	8	20	16
Number set for reargument	1	11	3
Cases granted review this term	183	172	172
Cases reviewed and decided without oral argument	188	157	186
Total cases to be available for argument at outset of following term	89	100	99

Source: Office of the Clerk of the Supreme Court of the United States.

Retirement of Justice William O. Douglas and Appointment of Justice John Paul Stevens

On November 12, 1975, Mr. Justice Douglas retired from the Supreme Court after having served for more than thirty-six years, the longest tenure of any justice in history. On December 17, 1975, John Paul Stevens, formerly a judge on the Seventh Circuit United States Court of Appeals, was confirmed by the Senate to the vacancy created by Douglas's retirement.

2
SUMMARIES OF SIGNIFICANT DECISIONS

Criminal Law: Powers of the Police and Prosecutors

The Court decided twenty-seven significant cases concerning criminal law, reflecting its continuing preoccupation with the system of criminal justice.[1]

The United States experienced an increase of 157 percent in its crime rate between 1960 and 1974, and only 20 percent of reported felonies resulted in the arrest of a suspect.[2] Many have attributed increased crime to decisions in cases of criminal law by the Warren Court that are alleged to have shackled the police in apprehending suspects and prosecutors in obtaining convictions. The decisions of the Supreme Court in the field of criminal law, however, have at best a marginal effect on the crime rate.[3] The primary defect of the criminal justice system is in sentencing. Because of the enormously high rates of recidivism, the majority of criminals are probably prosecuted successfully for at least one of their many crimes.[4] Instead of incapacitating these repeat offenders with lengthy prison sentences, however, many judges choose leniency. This is, in part, because prisons are

[1] See Bruce Fein, *Significant Decisions of the Supreme Court, 1974-75 Term* (Washington, D.C.: American Enterprise Institute, 1976), p. 13.

[2] Federal Bureau of Investigation, *Crime in the United States,* 1974 Uniform Crime Reports, pp. 11, 47.

[3] One study of six large cities found that the percentage of criminal prosecutions terminated because of due process obstacles ranged from one to fourteen. *PROMIS Newsletter,* vol. 2, no. 1 (Institute for Law and Social Research, July 1977), p. 4.

[4] In fiscal 1974, approximately 43 percent of all prisoners received by the Federal Bureau of Prisons had at least one known prior commitment. Approximately 9 percent of that group had two known prior commitments, and 17 percent had three or more known prior commitments. See Federal Bureau of Prisons, *Statistical Report, Fiscal Year 1974,* Table B-4.

overcrowded and, in part, because some judges believe that rehabilitation is the only proper purpose of punishment of criminals.[5] Many parole authorities are also too willing to grant parole for these reasons.[6] If repeat offenders received long prison sentences, the crime rate would probably fall because of their criminal incapacity and because the deterrent effect of the criminal law would be raised.[7] Decisions of the Supreme Court, however, cannot achieve this result.

In every important case concerning the police and prosecutors this term, the Court ruled in their favor. The Court held that under the Constitution:

- Evidence seized by state officers in violation of the Fourth Amendment may be used in a civil proceeding by or against the United States (*United States* v. *Janis,* 428 U.S. 433 [1970]).

- Police may make warrantless arrests of suspects in public places without any showing that exigent circumstances justified the failure to obtain an arrest warrant (*United States* v. *Watson,* 423 U.S. 411 [1976], *United States* v. *Santana,* 427 U.S. 38 [1976]).

- After refusing to be questioned about one crime, a suspect held in police custody may be questioned about another crime after the passage of a significant period of time and the receiving of a fresh set of *Miranda* warnings (*Michigan* v. *Mosley,* 423 U.S. 96 [1975]).

- Border patrol agents may operate permanent traffic checkpoints near the border to stop and to observe motor vehicles briefly for the purpose of detecting illegal aliens (*United States* v. *Martinez-Feurte,* 428 U.S. 543 [1976]).

---

[5] In several southern states the problem of crowded prisons has reached crisis proportions. Arkansas, Alabama, Florida, Louisiana, and Mississippi are under some type of court order designed to relieve overcrowding and correct other prison deficiencies. In Georgia more than 1,000 prisoners were released to relieve severe overcrowding. See *New York Times,* October 24, 1975, October 28, 1975, and January 25, 1976.

[6] Maurice Sigler, chairman of the United States Parole Commission, has stated that present policies on the parole of violent and habitual criminals give inadequate consideration to the victims of their crimes and the danger to the community created by their release. *Washington Star,* August 14, 1975.

In fiscal 1974, an average of only 50 percent of a federal prisoner's sentence was served before he received parole. The comparable figure in 1964 was 63 percent. See Federal Bureau of Prisons, *Statistical Report, Fiscal Year 1974,* p. 16.

[7] In Washington, D.C., a focus of investigative and prosecutorial resources on repeat robbery offenders and an increased willingness by the judiciary to set high monetary bonds or revoke probation or parole for these suspects contributed to a 19.3 percent reduction in armed robberies during the first seven months of 1976.

- Police may conduct routine inventory searches of impounded cars without reason to suspect evidence of crime (*South Dakota v. Opperman*, 428 U.S. 364 [1976]).

- An individual lacks any Fourth Amendment protection from government seizure of his bank records from a bank (*United States v. Miller*, 425 U.S. 435 [1976]).

- A taxpayer lacks a Fifth Amendment right to prevent the government from compelling the disclosure of documents prepared by his accountant and in the possession of the taxpayer's attorney (*Fisher v. United States*, 425 U.S. 391 [1976]) or from using income tax information to prosecute federal gambling offenses (*Garner v. United States*, 424 U.S. 648 [1976]).

- The government does not violate the Fifth Amendment in obtaining a warrant to search the business files of an individual suspect (*Andresen v. Maryland*, 427 U.S. 463 [1976]).

- *Miranda* warnings are not required before questioning a grand jury witness who is also the target of its investigation (*United States v. Mandujano*, 425 U.S. 564 [1976]) or a suspect in noncustodial circumstances (*Beckwith v. United States*, 425 U.S. 341 [1976]).

- Police officers violate no constitutional rights in falsely characterizing an individual as a criminal (*Paul v. Davis*, 424 U.S. 693 [1976]).

- A prosecutor may not be sued for damages under 42 U.S. Code 1983 for knowingly using perjured testimony in a criminal case (*Imbler v. Pachtman*, 424 U.S. 409 [1976]).

- Federal courts should generally abstain from supervising the internal disciplinary practices of police departments (*Rizzo v. Goode*, 423 U.S. 362 [1976]).

Many of these decisions seem at least inconsistent in spirit with earlier decisions protecting the constitutional rights of suspects and defendants.[8] Constitutional rights are not generally absolute, how-

---

[8] Compare Fisher v. United States, 425 U.S. 391 (1976), United States v. Miller, 425 U.S. 435 (1976), and Andresen v. Maryland, 427 U.S. 463 (1976), with Boyd v. United States, 116 U.S. 616 (1886); compare United States v. Martinez-Fuerte, 428 U.S. 543 (1976), with Terry v. Ohio, 392 U.S. 1 (1968); compare South Dakota v. Opperman, 428 U.S. 364 (1976), with Camara v. Municipal Court, 387 U.S. 523 (1967), and See v. City of Seattle, 387 U.S. 541 (1967).

ever; they are in part responsive to the circumstances of the time.[9] In the present era of high and rising crime rates, the Court may believe that the societal interest in detecting and prosecuting criminals is entitled to greater constitutional weight than in times of low crime rates.

A notable development in recent years has been the increased willingness of state courts to find in state constitutions and laws rights protective of suspects and defendants that the Supreme Court failed to find in the United States Constitution.[10] This trend tends to refute those who argue that only federal courts are attentive to claims of individual and human rights.

Future significant constitutional issues concerning the investigative powers of the police are likely to develop from the use of new electronic technology. The police in a number of communities are using twenty-four-hour closed-circuit TV systems to "patrol" whole neighborhoods. The first such system was installed in Mount Vernon, New York. Cleveland police are assisted by the use of low-light-level color TV images transmitted to police headquarters by laser beam.[11] In the past, the Supreme Court was compelled to overrule its initial rulings on the constitutionality of wiretaps under the Fourteenth Amendment as their sophistication and threat to privacy increased.[12] One may hope that initial decisions of the Court regarding the constitutional issues raised by the use of electronic sensors will reflect

---

[9] The preamble to the Constitution expresses six majestic but at times conflicting purposes behind its adoption: (1) to form a more perfect union, (2) establish justice, (3) ensure domestic tranquility, (4) provide for the common defense, (5) promote the general welfare, and (6) secure the blessings of liberty. In construing constitutional provisions all these purposes should be considered and not just one to the exclusion of others. With regard to the rights of criminal suspects and defendants, the goals of establishing justice, ensuring domestic tranquility, and protecting individual liberty must be reconciled.

[10] Compare Harris v. New York, 401 U.S. 222 (1971), with People v. Disbrow, 44 U.S.L.W. 2417 (Cal. Sup. Ct. 1976); compare Schneckloth v. Bustamonte, 412 U.S. 218 (1973), with State v. Johnson, 68 N.J. 348 (1975); compare United States v. Robinson, 414 U.S. 218 (1973), with State v. Kaluna, 520 P.2d 51 (Hawaii 1974); compare Kirby v. Illinois, 406 U.S. 682 (1972), and United States v. Ash, 413 U.S. 300 (1973), with People v. Jackson, 217 N.W. 2d 22 (Michigan 1974), and Blue v. State, 45 U.S.L.W. 2348 (Ala. 1977). See generally United States v. Miller, 425 U.S. 435, 443 n. 4 (1976) (Brennan, J., dissenting), and A. E. Dick Howard, "New Paths for State Courts," Washington Post, August 22, 1976.

[11] See Paul Dickson, "Big Brother's Sensors," Washington Post, July 25, 1976.

[12] In Olmstead v. United States, 277 U.S. 438 (1928), the Court held that conversations were not protected by the Fourth Amendment and that a telephone wiretap was not a "search" subject to the restrictions of that amendment. These holdings were overruled in Berger v. New York, 388 U.S. 41 (1967), and Katz v. United States, 389 U.S. 347 (1967).

a thoughtful consideration of future technological developments and their impact on individual rights.

United States v. Janis, 428 U.S. 433 (1976)

Facts: On the basis of certain wagering records seized by state police officers pursuant to a defective warrant and thus in violation of the Fourth Amendment, the Internal Revenue Service assessed Janis approximately $90,000 in federal wagering excise taxes. Janis brought suit in federal district court and successfully claimed that the assessement was void because it was based upon evidence seized unconstitutionally.

Question: Is evidence seized by a state criminal law enforcement officer in good faith, but nonetheless unconstitutionally, inadmissible in civil proceeding by or against the United States?

Decision: No. Opinion by Justice Blackmun. Vote: 5–3, Brennan, Marshall, and Stewart dissenting. Stevens did not participate.

Reasons: In order to enforce the prohibitions of the Fourth Amendment against unreasonable searches and seizures, the Court has created the so-called exclusionary rule. This rule prohibits federal and state governments from using evidence in a criminal prosecution that has been obtained in violation of the Fourth Amendment rights of the accused. The primary if not exclusive purpose of the exclusionary rule is to deter Fourth Amendment violations.

Application of the rule can sometimes operate to frustrate justice by excluding evidence conceded to be relevant and reliable in many proceedings. For that reason, in determining whether the exclusionary rule should be applied in noncriminal proceedings, the Court has weighed the probable increased deterrence of applying the rule against its adverse effects on the interest of society in fair and effective law enforcement.

In this case, state officials violated the Fourth Amendment. The exclusionary rule prohibits state and federal governments from using the evidence seized as a result of the violation in any criminal proceeding against Janis. Applying the rule to a federal civil tax proceeding as in this case would provide little additional deterrence to violations of the Fourth Amendment by state officials. In contrast, the cost to society would be high.

In short, we conclude that exclusion from federal civil proceedings of evidence unlawfully seized by a state criminal enforcement officer has not been shown to have a sufficient likelihood of deterring the conduct of the state police so that it outweighs the societal costs imposed by the exclusion. This Court, therefore, is not justified in so extending the exclusionary rule. . . .

In the past this Court has opted for exclusion in the anticipation that law enforcement officers would be deterred from violating Fourth Amendment rights. Then, as now, the Court acted in the absence of convincing empirical evidence and relied, instead, on its own assumptions of human nature and the interrelationship of the various components of the law enforcement system. In the situation before us, we do not find sufficient justification for the drastic measure of an exclusionary rule. There comes a point at which courts, consistent with their duty to administer the law, cannot continue to create barriers to law enforcement in the pursuit of a supervisory role that is properly the duty of the Executive and Legislative Branches. We find ourselves at that point in this case.

United States v. *Watson*, 423 U.S. 411 (1976)

Facts: Without a warrant, postal inspectors arrested Watson in a public restaurant for possession of credit cards stolen from the mail. After the arrest, Watson consented to a search of his car, which uncovered two credit cards in the names of other persons. The cards were the basis for charging Watson with possessing stolen mail. Watson made an unsuccessful pretrial motion to suppress the cards on the ground that they were obtained as a consequence of violating the Fourth Amendment prohibitions against unreasonable searches and seizures. He claimed that his arrest was illegal for want of a warrant and that his consent to the search was coerced and thus invalidly given. The court of appeals reversed Watson's conviction.

Question: Was either the arrest of Watson or the search of his car made in violation of the Fourth Amendment?

Decision: No. Opinion by Justice White. Vote: 6–2, Marshall and Brennan dissenting. Stevens did not participate.

Reasons: 18 U.S. Code 3061(a) expressly authorizes postal inspectors to make warrantless arrests if they have reasonable grounds for believing that the person arrested has committed a felony. Probable cause existed in this case, and thus the challenged arrest was in accord with a congressional statute entitled to a presumption of constitutionality. Moreover, in a long series of decisions, the Supreme Court has assumed that the Fourth Amendment permits warrantless arrests for felonies when probable cause exists. That was the rule under English common law. At least when the felony arrest is made in a public place, the failure to obtain a warrant does not violate the Fourth Amendment.

> Law enforcement officers may find it wise to seek arrest warrants where practicable to do so, and their judgments about probable cause may be more readily accepted where backed by a warrant issued by a magistrate. . . . But we decline to transform this judicial preference into a constitutional rule when the judgment of the Nation and Congress has for so long been to authorize warrantless public arrests on probable cause rather than to encumber criminal prosecutions with endless litigation with respect to the existence of exigent circumstances, whether it was practicable to get a warrant, whether the suspect was about to flee, and the like.

The Court rejected the claim that Watson's consent to the search was involuntary. In *Schneckloth* v. *Bustamonte*, 412 U.S. 218 (1973), the Court held that voluntariness was to be determined in light of all the circumstances. Here, consent was obtained without the use of promises or threats of coercion. Moreover, Watson was cautioned that the results of the search of his car could be used against him. Although consent was given while Watson was in custody and without a warning of his right to refuse consent, those factors alone do not demonstrate the lack of a free and unconstrained choice. To hold otherwise would be inconsistent with *Schneckloth*.

United States v. *Santana*, 427 U.S. 38 (1976)

Facts: With probable cause to believe that Santana had participated in an illegal sale of heroin, police officers drove to her house and observed her standing in the doorway with a brown paper bag. As the officers approached to make an arrest, Santana retreated into the vestibule of her house where she was apprehended. The police discovered heroin and marked money, used in the illegal heroin sale, in Santana's possession. At her trial for illegal possession of heroin with intent to distribute, Santana successfully moved to suppress the heroin and money on the ground that her arrest violated the Fourth Amendment. The district court concluded that the police were constitutionally required to obtain a warrant before arresting or searching Santana inside her home.

Question: Did the warrantless arrest and search of Santana violate the Fourth Amendment?

Decision: No. Opinion by Justice Rehnquist. Vote 7–2, Marshall and Brennan dissenting.

Reasons: In *United States* v. *Watson*, 423 U.S. 411 (1976), the Court held that the warrantless arrest of an individual in a public place upon probable cause did not violate the Fourth Amendment. For purposes of this rule, a "public place" should be construed to include those locations where an individual lacks any reasonable expectation of privacy. Accordingly, when Santana stood in the doorway as the police approached, she was in a public place. "She was not merely visible to the public but as exposed to public view, speech, hearing and touch as if she had been standing completely outside her house." She thus lacked any expectation of privacy in the doorway. Under *Watson*, a warrantless arrest there would have been proper.

Santana's retreat into the vestibule did not create any additional Fourth Amendment protection. *Warden* v. *Hayden*, 387 U.S. 294 (1967), established the rule that the police may enter a house to make a warrantless arrest if in "hot pursuit" of a suspect. When the police approached Santana standing in the doorway, hot pursuit within the meaning of *Warden* had commenced, especially because "there was . . . a realistic expectation that any delay would result in the destruction of evidence."

Michigan v. Mosley, 423 U.S. 96 (1975)

Facts: Suspected of robberies, Mosley was arrested and brought to a police station for questioning. There he was advised of certain constitutional rights as prescribed by *Miranda* v. *Arizona*, 384 U.S. 436 (1966). When Mosley objected to answering any questions about the robberies, the police interrogation ceased. Approximately two hours later, different police officers read Mosley his *Miranda* rights and commenced interrogation concerning an unrelated homicide. In responding to the questions, Mosley implicated himself in the crime. At his trial for murder, he moved to suppress the implicating statement on the ground that *Miranda* prohibited police interrogation concerning the homicide once he had objected to questions regarding the robberies.

Question: Was the police interrogation concerning the homicide prohibited by *Miranda*?

Decision: No. Opinion by Justice Stewart. Vote: 6–2, Brennan and Marshall dissenting.

Reasons: The *Miranda* opinion states that if a suspect in custody indicates, "at any time prior to or during questioning, that he wishes to remain silent, the interrogation must cease." That statement, however, fails to state under what circumstances, if any, questioning may be resumed. The answer lies in analyzing the purposes of the *Miranda* rules.

> To permit the continuation of custodial interrogation after a momentary cessation would clearly frustrate the purposes of *Miranda* by allowing repeated rounds of questioning to undermine the will of the person being questioned. At the other extreme, a blanket prohibition against the taking of voluntary statements or a permanent immunity from further interrogation, regardless of the circumstances, would transform the *Miranda* safeguards into wholly irrational obstacles to legitimate investigative activity, and deprive suspects of an opportunity to make informed and intelligent assessments of their interests.

Miranda was intended to safeguard the right of a suspect to remain silent by demanding that the exercise of his "right to cut off questioning" be "scrupulously honored." That rule counteracts the coercive features of custodial interrogation that prompted the *Miranda* decision.

Mosley's right to terminate questioning was fully respected in this case. After objection, the police immediately ceased interrogation about the robberies. Questioning was resumed only "after the passage of a significant period of time and the provision of a fresh set of [*Miranda*] warnings" and was restricted to a crime unrelated to the earlier interrogation.

United States v. *Martinez-Fuerte,* **428 U.S. 543 (1976)**

Facts: Border patrol agents of the Immigration and Naturalization Service operate several permanent traffic checkpoints inland from the Mexican border to detect illegal immigration. The checkpoints are maintained at or near intersections of important roads that smugglers and others who transport illegal aliens are likely to use. Vehicles approaching the checkpoint are informed of the necessity to stop for United States officers. At the checkpoint, an agent briefly observes each vehicle and permits most to continue without further examination.

Some vehicles, however, are referred to a secondary inspection area where the occupants are asked about their citizenship and immigration status. These referrals may occur whether or not the agent suspects that the vehicle contains illegal aliens. At checkpoints located near San Clemente, California, and Sarita, Texas, the border patrol discovered persons transporting illegal aliens. At their trials, the defendants moved to suppress all evidence obtained at the checkpoint stops on the ground that the operation of the checkpoints violated the Fourth Amendment. The fifth and ninth circuit courts of appeals rendered conflicting judgments on the constitutionality of these searches.

Question: Does the operation by the border patrol of permanent traffic checkpoints inland from the Mexican border violate the Fourth Amendment?

Decision: No. Opinion by Justice Powell. Vote: 7–2, Brennan and Marshall dissenting.

Reasons: The contours of the Fourth Amendment are determined by weighing the public interest in effective law enforcement against the interest of the individual in privacy and personal security.

There are millions of illegal aliens in the country. It is impracticable for the border patrol to control the flow of illegal aliens along the Mexican border because of its length and rugged terrain in many places. Traffic checkpoints at major highways are essential to any effective program to detect illegal aliens. Without these checkpoints

> such highways would offer illegal aliens a quick and safe route into the interior. Routine checkpoint inquiries apprehend many smugglers and illegal aliens who succumb to the lure of such highways. And the prospect of such inquiries forces others onto less efficient roads that are less heavily travelled, slowing their movement and making them more vulnerable to detection by roving patrols. . . .
> A requirement that stops on major routes inland always be based on reasonable suspicion would be impractical because the flow of traffic tends to be too heavy to allow the particularized study of a given car that would allow it to be identified as a possible carrier of illegal aliens. In particular, such a requirement would largely eliminate any deterrent to the conduct of well-disguised smuggling operations, even though smugglers are known to use these highways regularly.

Accordingly, the border patrol has a great need to make routine traffic checkpoint stops.

In contrast, the stops infringe only minimal privacy interests of the occupants of the vehicle. Inspection is limited to what can be seen in the vehicle without a search. Traffic is not stopped arbitrarily or without notice. Selective referrals of vehicles for secondary inspection

> may involve some annoyance, but it remains true that the stops should not be frightening or offensive because of their public and relatively routine nature. Moreover, selective referrals—rather than questioning the occupants of every car—tend to advance some Fourth Amendment interests by minimizing the intrusion on the general motoring public. . . . Accordingly, we hold that the stops and questioning at issue may be made in the absence of any individualized suspicion at reasonably located checkpoints.
>
> We further believe that it is constitutional to refer motorists selectively to the secondary inspection area at the San Clemente checkpoint on the basis of criteria that would not sustain a roving-patrol stop [described in *United States* v. *Brignoni-Ponce*, 422 U.S. 873 (1975)]. Thus, even if it be assumed that such referrals are made largely on the basis of apparent Mexican ancestry, we perceive no constitutional violation. . . . As the intrusion here is sufficiently minimal that no particularized reason need exist to justify it, we think it follows that the Border Patrol officers must have wide discretion in selecting the motorists to be diverted for the brief questioning involved.

The Court also concluded that a judicial warrant to conduct the checkpoints was not constitutionally required. One purpose of a warrant is to prevent the success of a search or seizure from distorting an evaluation of its constitutional reasonableness. That danger, the Court noted, does not exist in a judicial determination of the reasonableness of checkpoint stops because that decision depends on objective facts such as the location and method of operation of the checkpoint. Another purpose of a warrant is to require the judgment of a neutral third party before permitting an intrusion into individual privacy. But this need is reduced, the Court asserted, when the discretion to stop a vehicle is small and the location of checkpoints is determined by high-ranking executive officials.

South Dakota v. *Opperman*, 428 U.S. 364 (1976)

Facts: Local police in a South Dakota town impounded a car for violations of municipal parking ordinances. After observing items of personal property in the car, the police conducted a routine inventory search and secured the contents of the car. Although not searching for evidence of crime, the police discovered marijuana in the unlocked glove compartment that resulted in prosecution of the owner of the car for its unlawful possession. A motion to suppress the evidence discovered in the inventory search was denied by the trial judge and the owner was convicted. The South Dakota Supreme Court reversed the conviction on the ground that the marijuana was obtained in violation of the owner's Fourth Amendment right against unreasonable searches.

Question: Did the police inventory search of the car violate the Fourth Amendment?

Decision: No. Opinion by Chief Justice Burger. Vote: 5–4, Marshall, Brennan, Stewart, and White dissenting.

Reasons: The Fourth Amendment affords protection against "unreasonable" searches. The Court has held that a search of an automobile might satisfy the standards of reasonableness in circumstances insufficient to justify a search of a home or office. This is so for two reasons. First, persons have a lower expectation of privacy regarding automobiles than they do with respect to dwellings. Second, the inherent mobility of motor vehicles may create exigent circumstances which justify warrantless searches.

The general practice of local police departments in conducting inventory searches of impounded automobiles and securing their contents developed in response to three distinct needs: "the protection of the owner's property while it remains in police custody . . . ; the protection of the police against claims or disputes over lost or stolen property . . . ; and the protection of police from potential danger. . . . The practice has been viewed as essential to respond to incidents of theft or vandalism."

In light of these purposes, the inventory search challenged in this case satisfied the Fourth Amendment requirement of reasonableness.

The inventory was conducted only after the car had been impounded for multiple parking violations. The owner, having left his car illegally parked for an extended period, and thus subject to impoundment, was not present to make other arrangements for the safekeeping of his belongings. The inventory itself was prompted by the presence in plain view of a number of valuables inside the car. . . . [T]here is no suggestion whatever that this standard procedure, essentially like that followed throughout the country, was a pretext concealing an investigatory police motive. [Footnote omitted.]

United States v. Miller, 425 U.S. 435 (1976)

Facts: By means of a subpoena, the government obtained from two banks copies of checks and other bank records concerning a criminal defendant. The defendant unsuccessfully moved to suppress these items of evidence on the ground that they were seized in violation of the Fourth Amendment because the subpoena was defective. A federal court of appeals reversed the district court and upheld the defendant's claim.

Question: Does the Fourth Amendment protect an individual against government seizures of bank records that concern him?

Decision: No. Opinion by Justice Powell. Vote: 7–2, Brennan and Marshall dissenting.

Reasons: In *Hoffa* v. *United States*, 385 U.S. 293 (1966), the Court concluded that government investigative activities infringe Fourth Amendment interests only if they intrude into an individual's privacy. The contours of that zone are determined by an individual's legitimate expectations. In this case the defendant lacked any legitimate expectation that he could prevent the disclosure of his bank records to a third party. His records were required to be maintained under the Bank Secrecy Act; the defendant had no ownership interest in them; and even the original checks

> are not confidential communications but negotiable instruments to be used in commercial transactions. All of the documents obtained [by the government], including financial statements and deposit slips, contain only information voluntarily conveyed to the banks and exposed to their employees in the ordinary course of business. The lack of any legitimate expectation of privacy concerning the information kept in bank records was assumed by Congress in enacting the Bank Secrecy Act, the expressed purpose of which is to require records to be maintained because they "have a high degree of usefulness in criminal, tax, and regulatory investigations and proceedings."

Fisher v. United States, 425 U.S. 391 (1976)

Facts: Under investigation by the Internal Revenue Service (IRS) for possible violations of federal income tax laws, two taxpayers obtained from their accountants certain documents relating to the preparation of their tax returns and transferred them to their respective attorneys. The attorneys declined to comply with an IRS summons demanding production of the documents on the ground that they were protected by the taxpayers' Fifth Amendment privilege against compulsory self-incrimination. In separate suits brought to enforce the IRS summonses, one federal court of appeals upheld the Fifth Amendment claim and another rejected it.

Question: Does a taxpayer have a Fifth Amendment right to protect from compulsory disclosure documents relating to the preparation of his tax returns and in the possession of his attorney?

Decision: No. Opinion by Justice White. Vote: 8–0. Stevens did not participate.

Reasons: The Fifth Amendment provides in relevant part that "no person . . . shall be compelled in any criminal case to be a witness against himself." In a long series of cases ending with *Couch* v. *United States,* 409 U.S. 322 (1973), the Court has repeatedly held that this constitutional privilege prohibits only the use of compulsory process to obtain incriminating information from the accused himself, not from others. So long as the compulsion is directed at a person other than the accused, including his agent or attorney, the Fifth Amendment privilege is unavailable. In such circumstances, the ingredient of personal compulsion against the accused is lacking; he is not being coerced to provide information. Accordingly, the Fifth Amendment did not protect the taxpayers against enforcement of the IRS summonses against their attorneys.

The attorney-client privilege, however, may be asserted to protect the disclosure of information provided to the attorney by his client if that information would have been protected in the hands of the client by the Fifth Amendment privilege. The purpose of the attorney-client privilege is to encourage clients to make full disclosure to their attorneys so that fully informed legal advice may be provided. That purpose would be undermined if documents protected by the Fifth Amendment when possessed by the client lost that protection after their transfer to an attorney for the purpose of obtaining legal advice. Thus, "since each taxpayer transferred possession of the documents in question from himself to his attorney, in order to obtain legal assistance in the tax investigations in question, the papers, if unobtainable by summons from the client, are unobtainable by summons directed to the attorney by reason of the attorney-client privilege."

The claim that the Fifth Amendment prevents the compelled production of documents as opposed to testimony stems from *Boyd* v. *United States,* 116 U.S. 616 (1886). There the government sought a partnership invoice concerning a shipment of glass for use in a civil forfeiture proceeding involving customs fraud. The *Boyd* Court upheld the claim of the partnership that the compulsory production of their private books and papers in the proceeding would violate the Fifth Amendment. The rationale of *Boyd*, however, has been substantially undermined by many subsequent decisions holding that the Fifth Amendment protects only the "compelled testimonial communications" of the person asserting the privilege. The documents in this case were the work product of the accountants, not the taxpayers. Their preparation was voluntary, not compelled. The taxpayer cannot avoid the production of such documents simply because they are incriminating.

It is true, nevertheless, that the production of documents in response to a subpoena contains communicative aspects. Production tacitly concedes the existence of the documents, their possession by the taxpayer, and his belief in their authenticity. Whether these concessions are both testimonial and incriminating for purposes of the Fifth Amendment must be determined in light of all the circumstances.

In this case, the documents at issue were owned and prepared by the accountants in the ordinary course of business. Their existence and location are a foregone conclusion and the taxpayer adds little or nothing of testimonial significance by admitting that he has the documents. Moreover, seeking the accountant's work papers creates an insubstantial risk of incrimination to the taxpayer because the great majority of taxpayers lawfully obtain assistance from accountants in filing tax returns. Finally, the belief of the taxpayers in the authenticity of the accountants' documents would not be competent to authenticate them. They did not prepare the papers and could not vouch for their accuracy. Accordingly, "compliance with a summons directing the taxpayer to produce the accountant's documents involved in this case would involve no incriminating testimony within the protection of the Fifth Amendment." The Court reserved decision on the issue of whether the Fifth Amendment would shield a taxpayer from producing his own tax records while they were in his possession.

Garner v. *United States*, 424 U.S. 648 (1976)

Facts: Garner was indicted for conspiring to commit certain federal gambling offenses. The government introduced Garner's income tax returns for three years as part of its case. The returns showed that Garner reported his occupation as "professional gambler" and received substantial income from gambling or wagering. This information was used to rebut the claim that Garner's relationships with other conspirators were innocent. After a verdict of guilty, Garner appealed, claiming that the use of his tax returns violated his Fifth Amendment privilege against compulsory self-incrimination.

Question: Did the government's use of Garner's tax returns violate the Fifth Amendment?

Decision: No. Opinion by Justice Powell. Vote: 8–0. Stevens did not participate.

Reasons: In *United States* v. *Sullivan*, 274 U.S. 259 (1927), the Court held that the privilege against compulsory self-incrimination is not a defense to prosecution for failure to file a tax return. The *Sullivan* Court indicated, however, that the taxpayer could, in the return, raise objections to providing specific tax information on Fifth Amendment grounds. *Sullivan* thus compels a taxpayer to file returns but grants him a constitutional right to refuse to make incriminating disclosures.

The Court has also held that an individual who voluntarily reveals information instead of claiming the Fifth Amendment privilege loses the protections of that privilege. Since Garner failed to assert any privilege in filing his tax returns, this general rule would defeat his subsequent attempt to raise it during his conspiracy trial.

It was argued, however, that Garner's case should be excepted from the general rule because his failure to claim the Fifth Amendment privilege was necessitated by certain provisions of the income tax code. In *Marchetti* v. *United States*, 390 U.S. 39 (1968), and *Grosso* v. *United States*, 390 U.S. 62 (1968), the Court carved an exception to the general rule of Fifth Amendment waiver by ruling that gamblers could assert the Fifth Amendment as a defense to a prosecution for failure to file returns involving federal occupational and excise taxes on gambling. The Court reasoned that because of the pervasive criminal regulation of gambling, a claim of privilege in lieu of the returns would itself be incriminating. Unlike the occupational and excise tax returns involved in *Marchetti*, however, income tax returns are not directed at those who are inherently suspected of criminal activity. The majority of income tax filers do not incriminate themselves by disclosing their occupation. Garner thus lacked the valid Fifth Amendment reason recognized in *Marchetti* for failing to claim any privilege on his required income tax return.

It was also claimed that the threat of criminal punishment for failing to make a return compels a taxpayer to make incriminating disclosures rather than risk advancing the Fifth Amendment privilege improperly. This argument has some substance, because a taxpayer cannot obtain a preliminary judicial ruling on his claim of privilege before exposing himself to possible criminal liability. However, prior decisions establish that "as long as a valid and timely claim of privilege is available as a defense to a taxpayer prosecuted for failure to make a return, the taxpayer has not been denied a free choice to remain silent merely because of the absence of a preliminary judicial ruling on his claim."

Andresen v. Maryland, 427 U.S. 463 (1976)

Facts: State investigators obtained warrants to search specified business files of an attorney who was under investigation for false pretenses in connection with real estate settlement activities. Pursuant to the warrants, the investigators searched the attorney's law office files in his presence and discovered incriminating evidence. At his trial for the crime of false pretenses, the attorney moved to suppress that evidence on the grounds that it was obtained in violation of the Fourth and Fifth amendments. He argued that the search warrants failed to describe the items to be searched with the particularity required by the Fourth Amendment. In addition, he asserted that the search of personal business files violated his Fifth Amendment privilege against compulsory self-incrimination. The trial court denied the suppression motion and the attorney was convicted.

Question: Did the admission into evidence of the attorney's personal business files violate either the Fourth or the Fifth Amendment?

Decision: No. Opinion by Justice Blackmun. Vote: 7–2, Brennan and Marshall dissenting.

Reasons: The Fifth Amendment provides that "no person . . . shall be compelled in any criminal case to be a witness against himself." The purpose of that provision is to prevent the state from compelling a defendant to incriminate himself through his own testimony or personal records. The discovery and evidentiary use of the attorney's files in this case, however, lacked any element of compulsion.

The records seized contained statements that [the attorney] had voluntarily committed to writing. The search for and seizure of these records were conducted by law enforcement personnel. Finally, when these records were introduced at trial, they were authenticated by a handwriting expert, not by [the attorney]. Any compulsion of [the attorney] to speak, other than the inherent psychological pressure to respond at trial to unfavorable evidence, was not present....

Accordingly, we hold that the search of an individual's office for business records, their seizure, and subsequent introduction into evidence does not offend the Fifth [Amendment].

The Fourth Amendment claim rests on the argument that the breadth of the descriptive terms in the search warrants violated the particularity requirement. The particularity requirement is designed to prevent the state from conducting exploratory rummaging of a person's belongings. The challenged search warrants were "for the most part ... models of particularity." But they all contained a phrase seeming to authorize a search for evidence of any crime unknown. It is apparent from its context in the language of the warrant, however, that the term *crime* referred only to the crime of false pretenses in connection with the sale of a particular lot. That interpretation of the warrant precludes any claim that it was unconstitutionally broad.

United States v. Mandujano, 425 U.S. 564 (1976)

Facts: A defendant was charged with perjuring himself before a federal grand jury. Before the grand jury questioning commenced, he was informed by the prosecutor of his constitutional right to refuse to answer self-incriminating questions. At trial, the defendant moved to suppress his grand jury statements, conceded to be false, on the ground that although he was the target of the investigation the government failed to provide full *Miranda* warnings. (In *Miranda* v. *Arizona*, 384 U.S. 436 [1966], the Court concluded that before interrogating a suspect held in police custody, the Fifth Amendment required that he be informed, *inter alia*, of his constitutional right to remain silent and that any statements made could be used against him in court.) The district court granted the motion to suppress.

Question: Must *Miranda* warnings be provided to a grand jury witness who is also the target of its investigation?

Decision: No. Plurality opinion by Chief Justice Burger. Vote: 8–0, Brennan, Marshall, Stewart, and Blackmun concurring. Stevens did not participate.

Reasons: Even assuming that *Miranda* warnings were required, the suppression motion was erroneously granted. The defendant's assumed right to such warnings does not entitle him to commit perjury and then successfully claim that prosecution for that crime was constitutionally barred. The permissible method of challenging the constitutionality of the grand jury questioning would have been to have answered all questions truthfully and thereafter assert the Fifth Amendment privilege against self-incrimination as a defense to any subsequent derivative criminal prosecutions.

The claim that *Miranda* warnings were required in this case must also be rejected. "Those warnings were aimed at the evils seen by the Court as endemic to police interrogation. . . . [They] sought to negate the 'compulsion' thought to be inherent in police station interrogation." Grand jury questioning, in contrast, does not occur in such an inherently coercive environment.

> To extend [*Miranda*] concepts to questioning before a grand jury inquiring into criminal activity under the guidance of a judge is an extravagant expansion never remotely contemplated by this Court in *Miranda*; the dynamics of constitutional interpretation do not compel constant extension of every doctrine announced by the Court.

The Court reserved decision on whether a prosecutor is constitutionally required to inform a witness before a grand jury of his constitutional right to refuse to answer self-incriminating questions.

Beckwith v. *United States*, 425 U.S. 341 (1976)

Facts: A taxpayer under investigation for criminal tax fraud was interrogated in his home by agents of the Internal Revenue Service (IRS). He agreed to answer questions after being informed of his Fifth Amendment right to remain silent and the possibility that his statements could be used against him in a criminal prosecution. Prior to trial for tax fraud, the taxpayer unsuccessfully moved to suppress all statements made to the revenue agents on the ground that he had not received the warnings mandated by *Miranda* v. *Arizona*, 384 U.S. 436 (1966). The taxpayer argued that the complexity of the tax structure and the confusion among taxpayers about the civil and criminal functions of the IRS placed him under "psychological constraints" tantamount to physical custody during his interrogation.

Question: Must *Miranda* warnings be provided to a suspect during a noncustodial interrogation to render his statements constitutionally admissible in a subsequent criminal prosecution?

Decision: No. Opinion by Chief Justice Burger. Vote: 7–1, Brennan dissenting. Stevens did not participate.

Reasons: The rationale of *Miranda* was that the compulsion in-herent in custodial surroundings required that certain warnings be provided a suspect before interrogation to ensure that his statements were voluntary. In situations, as here, where interrogation does not occur in an inherently coercive atmosphere, the *Miranda* warnings are not required. Statements obtained by government agents during interrogation, however, are excludable as evidence if made involun-tarily because of certain tactics used by the agents. In determining the voluntariness issue, the fact that warnings of some type were given or omitted would be relevant.

Paul v. Davis, 424 U.S. 693 (1976)

Facts: To alert local merchants to possible shoplifters, two chiefs of police distributed a flyer containing the photographs and names of numerous persons who had been arrested for shoplifting and who were characterized as "active shoplifters." The flyer included one person, Davis, against whom the shoplifting charge had been dropped. Davis filed a federal civil rights suit against the police officers under 42 U.S. Code 1983, alleging that his characterization as an active shoplifter in the flyer deprived him of liberty protected by the Fourteenth Amendment without due process of law. He asserted that the criminal characterization would inhibit his use of business establishments for fear of being suspected of shoplifting and appre-hended and would seriously impair his future employment oppor-tunities. The police officers moved to dismiss the suit on the ground that Davis failed to allege any deprivation of liberty protected by the Constitution.

Question: Did the allegations of damage to Davis's reputation state a claim under 42 U.S. Code 1983?

Decision: No. Opinion by Justice Rehnquist. Vote: 5–3, Bren-nan, Marshall, and White dissenting. Stevens did not participate.

Reasons: Section 1983 authorizes suits against state officers who have violated a person's constitutional rights. The allegations in this case appear to state a "classical claim for defamation actionable in the courts of virtually every State." Davis, however, has attempted to transform his state defamation claim into a constitutional claim merely because the defendants happen to be state officials. If that view were accepted, a person arrested by law enforcement officers who announce that they believe such person to be responsible for a particular crime in order to calm the fears of an aroused populace, presumably obtains a claim against such officers under section 1983. . . . [I]t would [also] be difficult to see why the survivors of an innocent bystander mistakenly shot by a policeman or negligently killed by a sheriff driving a government vehicle, would not have claims equally cognizable under section 1983.

Davis's interpretation of section 1983

would seem almost necessarily to result in every legally cognizable injury which may have been inflicted by a state official acting under "color of law" establishing a violation of the Fourteenth Amendment.

Earlier Supreme Court decisions have not recognized reputation as an independent liberty or property interest protected by the Constitution from infringement by state officials. These decisions generally establish that liberty or property interests "attain constitutional status by virtue of the fact that they have been initially recognized and protected by state law." In this case, Davis's interest in reputation enjoys no such status under state law. "Rather [it] is simply one of a number which the State may protect against injury by virtue of its tort law, providing a forum for vindication of those interests by means of damages action."

The claim that the use of the flyer to publicize Davis's arrest record violated a constitutional right of privacy also lacks merit. Recognized constitutional interests in privacy concern very different matters "relating to marriage, procreation, contraception, family relationships, and child rearing and education."

Imbler v. Pachtman, 424 U.S. 409 (1976)

Facts: Imbler's state murder conviction was ultimately overturned in a federal habeas corpus proceeding on the grounds that the state prosecutor knowingly used false testimony and suppressed evidence favorable to Imbler at the murder trial. Imbler then sued the state prosecutor for damages under 42 U.S. Code 1983 for alleged deprivations of his constitutional rights.[13] The federal district court dismissed the suit on the ground that a public prosecutor is absolutely

---

[13] The Supreme Court has held that a prosecutor's knowing use of false testimony (Napue v. Illinois, 360 U.S. 264 [1959]) or suppression of requested evidence favorable to the accused in a criminal case (Brady v. Maryland, 373 U.S. 83 [1963]) violates constitutional due process.

immune from civil liability under section 1983 for acts performed in connection with prosecutorial duties.

Question: Is a public prosecutor absolutely immune from a civil suit for damages under section 1983 for acts intimately associated with the judicial phase of the criminal process?

Decision: Yes. Opinion by Justice Powell. Vote: 8–0. Stevens did not participate.

Reasons: On its face, section 1983 authorizes a civil suit for damages against every person who acts under color of state law to deprive another of a constitutional right. In *Tenney* v. *Brandhove,* 341 U.S. 367 (1951), however, the Court concluded that section 1983 was not intended to abrogate longstanding common-law tort immunities enjoyed by public officials for reasons of public policy. In *Pierson* v. *Ray,* 386 U.S. 547 (1967), the Court held that section 1983 did not destroy the common-law absolute immunity of judges from civil damage suits brought on account of acts committed within their judicial jurisdiction. These decisions establish that the determination of whether immunity exists under section 1983 requires consideration of "the immunity historically accorded the relevant official at common law and the interests behind it."

At common law, a prosecutor is aboslutely immune from suits for malicious prosecution. This immunity derives from a "concern that harassment by unfounded litigation would cause a deflection of the prosecutor's energies from his public duties, and the possibility that he would shade his decisions instead of exercising the independence of judgment required by his public trust." Similar concerns justify conferring absolute immunity on prosecutors under section 1983. The threat of a damage judgment under that section would constrain the prosecutor in his choice of trial strategy and use of witnesses and might thereby reduce the likelihood of accurately determining guilt or innocence. In addition, merely defending the potentially numerous lawsuits under that statute would divert a prosecutor's energy and attention from his pressing duty of enforcing the criminal law. Finally, posttrial procedures to determine whether an accused received a fair trial should not be "blurred by even the subconscious knowledge that a . . . decision in favor of the accused might result in the prosecutor being called upon to respond in damages for his error or mistaken judgment."

The Court left open the question of whether similar reasons of public policy would justify protecting a prosecutor from section 1983 damage suits for acts performed "in the role of an administrator or investigative officer rather than that of advocate."

Rizzo v. Goode, 423 U.S. 362 (1976)

Facts: Under 42 U.S. Code 1983, several individuals and community organizations brought class actions against the mayor of Philadelphia, the city managing director, and the police commissioner, alleging unconstitutional mistreatment by police officers. The district court found approximately twenty instances of unconstitutional police action during a year. It also found, however, that the named defendants had no official policy to violate the legal or constitutional rights of the plaintiffs. Nevertheless, the court concluded that the frequency of police misconduct was sufficiently high to justify an injunction compelling the defendants to adopt a comprehensive program for dealing adequately with civilian complaints in accordance with detailed guidelines that it suggested. While observing that plaintiffs had no constitutional right to such improved police procedures, the court reasoned that its order was a necessary first step in attempting to prevent future abuses.

Question: Was the injunctive order of the district court proper?

Decision: No. Opinion by Justice Rehnquist. Vote: 5–3, Blackmun, Brennan, and Marshall dissenting. Stevens did not participate.

Reasons: The injunction was unwarranted for a combination of three reasons. First, the controversy between the named plaintiffs and the defendants was insufficiently concrete to make out a "case" within the permissible jurisdiction of federal courts under Article III of the Constitution. The alleged claims of injury were based upon what one of a small, unnamed minority of policemen might do to plaintiffs in the future because of that unknown policeman's perception of departmental disciplinary procedures. Under *O'Shea* v. *Littleton,* 414 U.S. 488 (1975), that alleged injury is too attenuated to confer standing upon plaintiffs to challenge police disciplinary procedures.

Second, the twenty instances of misconduct commited by a few policemen over a year (in a city of 3 million with 7,500 policemen) did not establish a persistent pattern of constitutional violations encouraged or supported by the defendants. The injunction was issued against defendants, who themselves violated no constitutional rights, to prevent future violations by policemen. Section 1983 authorizes injunctive relief only against those who are directly implicated in a constitutional violation.

Third, principles of federalism require that federal courts avoid interference with the internal governance of state or local agencies absent compelling circumstances. The injunctive order of the district court significantly revised the internal procedures of the Philadelphia police department in contravention of this precept.

Hampton v. *United States*, 425 U.S. 484 (1976)

Facts: At his trial for unlawful distribution of heroin, the defendant testified that the drug was supplied by a government informer. He unsuccessfully requested that the jury be instructed that if his testimony was believed, then acquittal was required as a matter of law. The defendant argued that constitutional due process would prohibit his conviction if the government had supplied the illegal drug that was used in the subsequent unlawful sale. The defendant conceded that he was predisposed to distribute heroin illegally and that the government did not implant this criminal design in his mind.

Question: Was the defendant entitled to the requested instruction to the jury?

Decision: No. Plurality opinion by Justice Rehnquist. Vote: 5–3, Brennan, Marshall, and Stewart dissenting. Stevens did not participate.

Reasons: In *United States* v. *Russell*, 411 U.S. 423 (1973), the Court ruled that the defense of entrapment could never be based on government misconduct if the defendant was predisposed to commit the crime charged. *Russell* also stated, however, that principles of due process might bar a conviction if the conduct of law enforcement agents was sufficiently outrageous.

The plurality opinion then proceeded to undermine the continuing vitality of that statement by concluding:

> The limitations of [constitutional due process] come into play only when the government activity in question violates some protected right of the *defendant*. . . . If the police engage in illegal activity in concert with a defendant beyond the scope of their duties the remedy lies, not in freeing the equally culpable defendant, but in prosecuting the police under the applicable provisions of state or federal law. [Emphasis in original.]

The Court asserted that a defendant predisposed to commit an offense had no constitutional right to prevent government agents from supplying the illegal drug necessary for its actual commission.

Criminal Law: Rights of the Accused

The controversial decisions of the Court in death penalty cases generally reflected its mixed rulings in significant cases concerning the rights of the accused. In *Gregg* v. *Georgia*, 428 U.S. 153 (1976), the Court upheld the constitutionality of the death penalty if imposed pursuant to strict procedural safeguards. In *Woodson* v. *North Carolina*, 428 U.S. 280 (1976), however, the Court held that a broad mandatory death penalty statute violates the prohibitions of the Eighth and Fourteenth amendments against "cruel and unusual" punishments.

In nine other cases important to criminal defendants, the Court ruled in their favor three times. It held that a plea of guilty is involuntary unless the defendant is informed of all elements of the crime to which he pled (*Henderson* v. *Morgan*, 426 U.S. 637 [1976]), that a suspect's silence after arrest cannot be used against him at trial (*Doyle* v. *Ohio*, 426 U.S. 610 [1976]), and that statements of witnesses cannot be withheld from a defendant under the Jencks Act as constituting a lawyer's "work product" (*Goldberg* v. *United States*, 425 U.S. 94 [1976]).

The government prevailed in two cases that could have substantially reduced a state's discretion in shaping its system of criminal trials. The Court rejected the claim that the use of nonlawyer judges in misdemeanor cases with a right to a trial *de novo* before a lawyer judge violated due process (*North* v. *Russell*, 427 U.S. 328 [1976]). The Court also upheld the constitutionality of a "two-tier" system of trial courts offering only a judge trial at the first stage but a trial *de novo* by jury at the second (*Ludwig* v. *Massachusetts*, 427 U.S. 618 [1976]).

The Court decisively rejected claims that the double jeopardy clause prohibits the retrial of a defendant who requested and obtained a mistrial (*United State* v. *Dinitz*, 424 U.S. 600 [1976]), that a prosecutor's failure to disclose exculpatory evidence always mandates a new trial (*United States* v. *Agurs*, 427 U.S. 97 [1976]), and that a right to counsel attaches to summary court-martial proceedings (*Middendorf* v. *Henry*, 425 U.S. 25 [1976]).

Gregg v. *Georgia*, 428 U.S. 153 (1976)

Facts: Convicted of murder under Georgia law and sentenced to death, Gregg challenged the constitutionality of his sentence under the Eighth and Fourteenth amendments as "cruel and unusual punishment." Georgia provides detailed procedures to control discretion in imposing the death penalty.[14] It permits the death penalty for only six categories of crimes, including murder. Trials concerning these offenses are conducted pursuant to a bifurcated procedure with a separate hearing on the question of sentencing. At the sentencing hearing, evidence of any mitigating or aggravating circumstances may be submitted to the judge or jury, whichever is the sentencing authority. The sentencing authority is required to consider such evidence, including ten statutorily defined aggravating circumstances, in imposing sentence. A defendant convicted of murder cannot be sentenced to death unless the sentencing authority finds beyond a reasonable doubt and specifies the existence of at least one of the statutory aggravating circumstances.

All death sentences receive automatic and expeditious review by the Georgia Supreme Court. It is required to set aside a sentence of death upon finding that it was imposed under the influence of passion or prejudice, without evidentiary support for the statutory aggravating circumstances, or was excessive in light of sentences received by similar defendants who committed similar crimes. If the state supreme court affirms a death sentence, it must include in its decision reference to similar cases it has considered. In order to assist the review process, the trial judge is required to provide the supreme court with comprehensive information concerning the defendant, the crime, and the circumstances of the trial.

Gregg argued that the Eighth Amendment prohibits the imposition of the death penalty in any circumstances, and, alternatively, that the Georgia sentencing scheme permits the exercise of arbitrary and capricious discretion in imposing the death penalty in violation of *Furman* v. *Georgia*, 408 U.S. 238 (1972).

Question: Does imposing the death penalty for murder under Georgia law violate the Eighth and Fourteenth amendments?

Decision: No. Plurality opinion by Justices Stewart, Powell, and Stevens. Vote: 7–2, Burger, White, Blackmun, and Rehnquist concurring, Brennan and Marshall dissenting.

Reasons: The Eighth Amendment, applicable to the states by virtue of the due process clause of the Fourteenth Amendment, prohibits "cruel and unusual punishments." The contours of that prohibition are shaped by contemporary standards of decency and

---

[14] In Furman v. Georgia, 408 U.S. 238 (1972), the Court held that permitting juries to exercise unfettered discretion in imposing the death sentence violated the Fourteenth Amendment.

the basic principle that punishments should not be excessive. The excessiveness protection precludes the unnecessary infliction of pain or a punishment grossly disproportionate to the severity of the crime committed.

The legitimacy of the death penalty for murder has generally been accepted throughout the 200-year history of the United States. Both the Fifth and Fourteenth amendments implicity acknowledge its legitimacy by prohibiting the deprivation of life without due process. Moreover, since the 1972 decision in *Furman,* thirty-five states and the U.S. Congress have passed laws providing for the death penalty, and juries have imposed the death sentence on more than 400 persons under these statutes. These facts clearly establish that the death penalty for murder is not contrary to contemporary standards of decency.

Neither is the death penalty excessive. It purports to serve two principal social purposes: retribution and deterrence. Retribution is a legitimate purpose of criminal punishment. That purpose "is essential to an ordered society that asks its citizens to rely on legal processes rather than self-help to vindicate their wrongs." Capital punishment serves a retributive purpose by showing "society's moral outrage at particularly offensive conduct."

No convincing empirical evidence exists to support or refute the view that the death penalty deters crime. This complex factual issue, however, is properly resolved by legislative bodies.

> Considerations of federalism, as well as respect for the ability of a legislature to evaluate, in terms of its particular state the moral consensus concerning the death penalty and its social utility as a sanction, require us to conclude, in the absence of more convincing evidence, that the infliction of death as a punishment for murder is not without justification and thus is not unconstitutionally severe.

Finally, the punishment of death is not disproportionate to the crime of murder. Accordingly, "the death penalty is not a form of punishment that may never be imposed, regardless of the circumstances of the offense, regardless of the character of the offender, and regardless of the procedure followed in reaching the decision to impose it."

Furman, however, held that because the death penalty is unique in its finality, it could not be imposed under procedures "that created a substantial risk that it would be inflicted in an arbitrary and capricious manner." Such a risk is created if the sentencing authority lacks comprehensive information concerning both the character of the defendant and the circumstances of the crime. This type of information will generally be available only if a bifurcated trial procedure is used, with a separate sentencing hearing. The risk of arbitrariness is also minimized if the sentencing authority is provided clear standards for evaluating the information relevant to the sentencing decision. Thus, the constitutional concerns of *Furman* can be met by providing the sentencing authority with adequate information and guidance as to whether a death sentence is warranted.

The challenged Georgia sentencing procedures satisfy the *Furman* concerns. A separate sentencing hearing is held where evidence of any aggravating or mitigating circumstances is permitted. The discretion of the sentencing authority is limited by the requirement that it find the existence beyond a reasonable doubt of at least one of the ten statutory aggravating circumstances before imposing the death sentence. The aggravating circumstances, moreover, focus the sentencing authority's attention on both the circumstances of the crime and the character of the defendant. For example, it is an aggravating circumstance under Georgia law that the crime was committed in the course of another felony, for money, upon a peace or judicial officer, in a particularly heinous way, or in a manner endangering the lives of several persons, or by an offender with a prior conviction for a capital felony. Georgia's scheme of appellate review of death sentences provides additional safeguards against arbitrariness and caprice.

> In short, Georgia's new sentencing procedures require as a prerequisite to the imposition of the death penalty, specific jury findings as to the circumstances of the crime or the character of the defendant. Moreover to guard further against a situation comparable to that presented in *Furman*, the Supreme Court of Georgia compares each death sentence with the sentences imposed on similarly situated defendants to ensure that the sentence of death in a particular case is not disproportionate. . . . [T]hese procedures . . . satisfy the concerns of *Furman*.

The Court rejected the argument that unconstitutional discretion remained under Georgia law because of the lack of standards to guide a prosecutor in the decision whether to prosecute a capital offense or to guide the executive in the decision whether to grant clemency to a person sentenced to death. It stressed that *Furman* dealt only with the exercise of sentencing discretion regarding persons already convicted of a capital offense.

In the companion cases of *Proffitt* v. *Florida*, 428 U.S. 242 (1976), and *Jurek* v. *Texas*, 428 U.S. 262 (1976), the Court sustained the constitutionality of the death-sentencing procedures established under Florida and Texas law as applied to individuals convicted of murder. The Florida procedures closely resemble those upheld in *Gregg*. There is a separate sentencing hearing where any evidence relevant to sentencing may be offered. An advisory jury is directed to consider whether any of eight statutory aggravating factors outweigh any of seven mitigating factors in determining whether to recommend a death sentence. The ultimate sentencing decision rests with the trial judge, who must consider the same factors as the advisory jury. He can ignore a jury recommendation of life imprisonment only if the facts clearly and unmistakably warrant a death sentence. The Florida Supreme Court automatically reviews a death sentence to ensure that similar results are reached in similar cases.

The Texas law upheld in *Jurek* limits capital homicides to intentional and knowing murders committed in five situations: murder of a police officer or fireman, murder committed in the course of specified serious felonies, murder committed for remuneration, murder committed while escaping from a penal institution, and murder of a prison employee by a prison inmate. A death sentence is imposed for such crimes only if a jury, in a separate sentencing hearing, finds beyond a reasonable doubt that the accused deliberately caused the death of the victim, would probably continue to commit violent criminal acts constituting a threat to society, and acted unreasonably in response to the provocation, if any, by the victim. Texas also provides expedited judicial review of all death sentences.

Woodson v. North Carolina, 428 U.S. 280 (1976)

Facts: A North Carolina statute imposes a mandatory death penalty on persons convicted of first-degree murder, defined to include a broad category of homicidal offenses. A defendant sentenced under that statute challenged its constitutionality on the ground that it violated the Eighth Amendment prohibition of "cruel and unusual punishments," applicable to the states by virtue of the due process clause of the Fourteenth Amendment.

Question: Does the North Carolina mandatory death penalty statute violate the Eighth and Fourteenth amendments?

Decision: Yes. Plurality opinion by Justices Stewart, Powell, and Stevens. Vote: 5–4, Brennan and Marshall concurring, Burger, White, Blackmun, and Rehnquist dissenting.

Reasons: As noted in *Gregg* v. *Georgia*, 428 U.S. 172 (1976), the constitutional prohibition against cruel and unusual punishments is substantially defined by contemporary standards of decency. Evidence of such standards can be gleaned from "history, and traditional usage, legislative enactments, and jury determinations." This evidence shows that contemporary American society rejects imposition of a mandatory death sentence for all persons convicted of a specified offense.

Since adoption of the Eighth Amendment, in 1791, both Congress and the states have generally narrowed the category of capital offenses and expanded the discretion of the sentencing authority in determining whether to impose a death sentence. This trend was stimulated in large part because jurors refused to convict in capital cases if they believed death to be an inappropriate sentence for the accused. "The consistent course charted by the state legislatures and by Congress since the middle of the past century demonstrates that the aversion of jurors to mandatory death penalty statutes is shared by society at large."

It is true that after the 1972 decision in *Furman* v. *Georgia*, 408 U.S. 238,[15] several states, including North Carolina, enacted mandatory death penalty statutes. These statutes, however, do not reflect a "renewed societal acceptance of mandatory death sentencing." Rather, they seem to have resulted from a misinterpretation of *Furman* to require a mandatory death penalty or none at all.

> North Carolina's mandatory death penalty statute for first-degree murder departs markedly from contemporary standards respecting the imposition of the punishment of death and thus cannot be applied consistently with the Eighth and Fourteenth Amendments' requirement that the State's power to punish "be exercised within the limits of civilized standards."

In addition, the mandatory death penalty statute contravenes the holding in *Furman* that a death sentence cannot constitutionally be imposed without standards. Historically, juries operating under discretionary statutes have imposed the death sentence for first-degree murder infrequently. It is thus reasonable to assume that many juries will acquit defendants in first-degree murder cases under North Carolina law for the purpose of sparing their lives. This fact makes the mandatory death penalty statute defective under *Furman* because no standards guide the jury in its determination of "which first-degree murderers shall live and which shall die."

---

[15] There the Court held unconstitutional statutes providing juries with unfettered discretion in determining whether to impose a death sentence.

Finally, the North Carolina statute is constitutionally tainted because it fails to allow a full consideration of the defendant's character and the circumstances of the crime in imposing the death sentence.

> [I]n capital cases the fundamental respect for humanity underlying the Eighth Amendment . . . requires consideration of the character and record of the individual offender and the circumstances of the particular offense as a constitutionally indispensable part of the process of inflicting the penalty of death.
>
> This conclusion rests squarely on the predicate that the penalty of death is qualitatively different from a sentence of imprisonment, however long. Death, in its finality, differs more from life imprisonment than a 100-year prison term differs from one of only a year or two. Because of that qualitative difference, there is a corresponding difference in the need for reliability in the determination that death is the appropriate punishment in a specific case.

In a companion case, *Roberts* v. *Louisiana*, 428 U.S. 325 (1976), the Court struck down a Louisiana mandatory death penalty statute on the authority of *Woodson*. The Louisiana statute mandated the death penalty for five categories of homicide if the jury found that the defendant had "a specific intent to kill or to inflict great bodily harm."

Henderson v. *Morgan*, 426 U.S. 637 (1976)

Facts: On the advice of counsel, a defendant pleaded guilty to second-degree murder and was sentenced. He subsequently obtained federal habeas corpus relief on the ground that the plea of guilty was involuntary because entered without his knowledge that intent to cause death was an element of the murder charge. The district court found that neither counsel nor court ever advised the defendant of this element of second-degree murder. Accordingly, it ruled that the plea was involuntarily and thus unconstitutionally entered because the defendant lacked knowledge as to the elements of the crime to which he pled. The court of appeals affirmed.

Question: Was the defendant's plea of guilty involuntary and thus unconstitutional?

Decision: Yes. Opinion by Justice Stevens. Vote: 7–2, Rehnquist and Burger dissenting.

Reasons: A plea of guilty is not voluntary in the sense that it constitutes an intelligent admission of a crime unless the defendant has actual notice and knowledge of the elements of that crime. In this case, the defendant was never informed, through indictment, advice of counsel or court, or otherwise, that intent to cause death was an element of second-degree murder. There was no proof of this element either by stipulation of defense counsel or by voluntary admission by the defendant. "In these circumstances it is impossible to conclude that his plea to the unexplained charge of second-degree murder was voluntary."

Doyle v. Ohio, 426 U.S. 610 (1976)

Facts: Under arrest for unlawfully selling drugs, two suspects after receiving *Miranda* warnings exercised their constitutional rights to remain silent.[16] At trial, these defendants testified to an exculpatory story. On cross-examination, the prosecutor, over timely objection of the defense counsel, was permitted to impeach the credibility of the defendants through questions relating to their postarrest silence. The prosecutor sought to show that such silence was wholly inconsistent with the trial testimony of the defendants which provided an exculpatory explanation for the suspicious circumstances leading to their arrest. The defendants sought review of their convictions on the theory that the use of their postarrest silence to impeach their credibility violated the due process clause of the Fourteenth Amendment.

Question: Did the challenged prosecutor's questioning violate the due process clause?

Decision: Yes. Opinion by Justice Powell. Vote: 6–3, Stevens, Blackmun, and Rehnquist dissenting.

Reasons: Miranda requires that before custodial interrogation may commence, the police must warn a suspect, *inter alia,* of his rights to remain silent and to retained or appointed counsel.

> Silence in the wake of these warnings may be nothing more than the arrestee's exercise of these *Miranda* rights. Thus, every post-arrest silence is insoluby ambiguous because of

---

[16] In Miranda v. Arizona, 384 U.S. 436 (1966), the Court held, *inter alia,* that a suspect held in police custody must be informed of his constitutional right to remain silent before interrogation could be constitutionally commenced.

what the State is required to advise the person arrested.
. . . Moreover, while it is true that the *Miranda* warnings
contain no express assurance that silence will carry no
penalty, such assurance is implicit to any person who receives
the warnings. In such circumstances, it would be funda-
mentally unfair and a deprivation of due process to allow
the arrested person's silence to be used to impeach an explanation subsequently offered at trial.

Goldberg v. *United States*, 425 U.S. 94 (1976)

Facts: Under the Jencks Act, 18 U.S. Code 3500, after a witness
called by the United States in a criminal prosecution has testified on
direct examination, the defendant has a right to obtain any "statement" made by that witness in the possession of the United States if
it relates to the subject matter of the testimony of the witness. In
a mail fraud prosecution, the government possessed notes taken by
a government attorney during a pretrial interview with a government
witness. After the witness had testified, the defendant moved to
obtain the interview notes under the Jencks Act on the theory that
they constiuted a "statement" of the witness. The district court denied
the motion on the ground that the notes were the "work product"
of government counsel and thus exempt from production under the
act.

Question: Is a statement otherwise producible under the Jencks
Act exempted from production if it constitutes a lawyer's "work
product"?

Decision: No. Opinion by Justice Brennan. Vote: 9–0.

Reasons: "[N]othing in the Jencks Act or its legislative history . . .
excepts from production otherwise producible statements on the
ground that they constitute 'work product' of Government lawyers."
It is argued, however, that when a statement by a witness has been
prepared by government attorneys, compelling its disclosure would
undermine the policies behind the work-product doctrine: protection
of a lawyer's mental impressions, personal beliefs, trial strategy, and
legal conclusions. But none of this information falls within the scope
of a statement by a witness, thereby rendering it producible. The
interview notes at issue in this case would constitute a producible
statement only in the event that they were read back to the government witness and he adopted or approved them.

North v. *Russell*, 427 U.S. 328 (1976)

Facts: Under Kentucky state law, certain small cities are authorized to use nonlawyers as police court judges in the initial trial of misdemeanor cases. A defendant may appeal as of right from any police court decision and obtain a trial *de novo* in a court where all judges are lawyers. Convicted of drunken driving by a nonlawyer police judge, North sought state habeas corpus relief, claiming a denial of constitutional rights of due process and equal protection. He argued that due process precluded his trial by a nonlawyer judge and that equal protection prohibited the state from permitting lay judges to preside in small cities but not large ones.

Question: Does the Kentucky system for utilizing nonlawyers as police judges violate either the due process or equal protection clauses of the Fourteenth Amendment?

Decision: No. Opinion by Chief Justice Burger. Vote: 6–2, Stewart and Marshall dissenting. Stevens did not participate.

Reasons: The crucial fact in the Kentucky system is the right of the defendant to appeal as of right and obtain a new trial in a court presided over by lawyer judges. Although uncounseled defendants may be unaware of their rights to appeal, "we . . . assume that police court judges in Kentucky recognize their obligation to inform all convicted defendants . . . of their unconditional right to a trial *de novo* and of the necessity that an 'appeal' be filed within 30 days in order to implement that right."

Several substantial interests justify authorization by the state of nonlawyer judges in police courts located in small communities. The state judiciary is increasingly burdened. Speedy and relatively inexpensive adjudication, often in the interest of both the defendant and the state, can be obtained in police courts.

> Moreover, state policy takes into account that it is a convenience to those charged to be tried in or near their own community, rather than travel to a distant court where a law-trained judge is provided, and to have the option, as here, of a trial after regular business hours.

Finally, a defendant can obtain a prompt trial *de novo* by pleading guilty in the police court.

In the absence of significant countervailing interests of the defendant, Kentucky's use of nonlawyer police judges does not violate due process.

The equal protection challenge is equally unavailing. The use of nonlawyer judges only in relatively small cities was rationally based on the facts that lawyers are more available in larger cities, larger cities have greater financial resources to provide better qualified court personnel, and the volume of judicial business in large cities requires lawyer judges to ensure efficiency and expedition in court operations.

Ludwig v. Massachusetts, 427 U.S. 618 (1976)

Facts: Massachusetts has a two-tier system of trial courts for certain misdemeanors and felonies. A person charged with such a crime is tried initially in the lower tier by a judge and has no opportunity for a jury trial. If convicted, the defendant may appeal to the second tier and obtain a trial *de novo* by jury. The defendant may effectively avoid trial in the lower tier by admitting certain facts tantamount to a plea of guilty and thereby promptly obtain a jury trial *de novo*. A defendant may suffer adverse collateral consequences from conviction in the lower tier, however, such as revocation of parole or of his driver's license. A defendant convicted of a motor vehicle offense under the two-tier system challenged its constitutionality, claiming that it violated both his right to jury trial and the double jeopardy clause of the Fifth Amendment.

Question: Does the Massachusetts two-tier system of trial courts for certain crimes offend either the Sixth Amendment right to jury trial or the double jeopardy clause?

Decision: No. Opinion by Justice Blackmun. Vote: 5–4, Stevens, Brennan, Stewart, and Marshall dissenting.

Reasons: The Sixth Amendment, as applicable to the states through the due process clause of the Fourteenth Amendment, requires a state to afford a defendant a trial by jury in any prosecution where the sentence may exceed six months' imprisonment. Under the two-tier trial court system of Massachusetts, a defendant can obtain a trial by jury, but only after submitting to a bench trial in the lower tier. It is argued that requiring trial in the first tier unconstitutionally burdens the right to jury trial in three ways.

First, the defendant is required to bear the financial cost of an additional trial and may lose wages for the duration.

Although these burdens are not unreal and although they may, in an individual case, impose a hardship, we conclude that they do not impose an unconstitutional burden on the exercise of the right to a trial by jury. In Massachusetts, the accused may enjoy his right to trial by jury expeditiously by invoking the above-described procedure of "admitting sufficient findings of fact." He, therefore, need not pursue, in any real sense, a defense at the lower tier.

Second, the defendant is potentially subject to a harsher sentence if he obtains a jury trial *de novo* in the second tier. However, "due process is violated only by the vindictive imposition of an increased sentence. The Court in *Colten* [v. *Kentucky*, 407 U.S. 104 (1972)] held that the danger of such sentencing does not inhere in the two-tier system."

Third, there are adverse psychological and physical effects that attend the delay in obtaining a jury trial under the two-tier system. However,

> it is nearly always true that an accused may obtain a faster adjudication of his guilt or innocence by waiving a jury trial even in those States where he may have one in the first instance. No one has seriously charged, however, that the fact that trials by jury are not scheduled so quickly as trials before a judge impermissibly burdens the constitutional right to trial by jury. Finally we are uncertain whether the delay in obtaining a jury trial is increased by the *de novo* procedure or decreased. [The defendant] has not presented any evidence to show that there is a greater delay in obtaining a jury in Massachusetts than there would be if the Commonwealth abandoned its two-tier system.

Accordingly, the Court concluded that the two-tier court system of Massachusetts placed no unfair or excessive burdens on the exercise of the right to a jury trial.

The double jeopardy claim rested on the theory that the *de novo* trial procedure exposes the defendant to criminal prosecution twice for the same crime. It has been the settled law for eighty years, since *United States* v. *Ball*, 163 U.S. 662 (1896), however, that the double jeopardy clause does not bar a state from retrying a defendant who has succeeded in overturning his initial conviction. Since only the defendant can trigger a second trial under the Massachusetts two-tier system by appealing a conviction in the lower tier, *Ball* clearly permits the second prosecution to proceed.

United States v. *Dinitz*, 424 U.S. 600 (1976)

Facts: In a criminal trial, the trial judge expelled the lead defense counsel for repeated misconduct during the opening statement. The judge then ruled that he would consider three alternative courses of action: He would issue a stay of the trial pending application to the court of appeals to review the propriety of the expulsion, continue the trial with co-counsel representing the defendant, or declare a mistrial to permit the defendant to obtain other counsel. On motion by the defendant, the trial judge adopted the last alternative. Before his second trial, however, the defendant moved to dismiss the charges against him on the ground that a retrial would violate the double jeopardy clause of the Fifth Amendment.

Question: Was the retrial constitutionally barred by the double jeopardy clause?

Decision: No. Opinion by Justice Stewart. Vote: 6–2, Brennan and Marshall dissenting. Stevens did not participate.

Reasons: The double jeopardy clause generally protects a defendant against repeated prosecutions for the same offense. However, the Court has long recognized certain exceptions to this general rule when a mistrial is declared. If the defendant did not request or consent to the mistrial, a retrial is constitutionally barred unless there was a "manifest necessity" for the mistrial, or the "ends of public justice would otherwise be defeated." This strict standard reflects the strong interests of the defendant in choosing whether to have a particular tribunal complete his trial. When the defendant requests a mistrial, however, that interest disappears. Moreover,

> when judicial or prosecutorial error seriously prejudices a defendant, he may have little interest in completing the trial and obtaining a verdict from the first jury. The defendant may reasonably conclude that a continuation of the tainted proceeding would result in a conviction followed by a lengthy appeal and, if a reversal is secured, by a second prosecution. [Under *United States* v. *Ball*, 163 U.S. 662 (1896), the double jeopardy clause permits a retrial if a conviction is set aside by the trial judge or reversed on appeal.]

Accordingly, a defendant's request for a declaration of mistrial may advance objectives similar to those served by the double jeopardy clause: avoidance of the anxiety, expense, and delay occasioned by multiple prosecutions. Thus, absent bad faith conduct by the trial judge or prosecutor intended to provoke such action, the double jeopardy clause is no barrier to the retrial of a defendant who requests a mistrial.

United States v. *Agurs*, 427 U.S. 97 (1976)

Facts: On trial for second-degree murder, the defendant claimed to have acted in self-defense. The evidence disclosed that the victim had been carrying two knives shortly before the killing, including the murder weapon used by the defendant. After conviction, the defendant moved for a new trial on the ground that the prosecution failed to disclose voluntarily the fact that the victim had a prior criminal record that would have given further evidence of his violent character. The district court denied the motion. It reasoned that the trial provided clear and uncontradicted evidence of the victim's character and that the prior conviction would have been of marginal evidentiary value at best. The court of appeals reversed. It held that the prior conviction was material evidence and that its nondisclosure required a new trial because its evidentiary use might have resulted in a different verdict.

Question: Did the prosecutor's failure to disclose the victim's prior conviction justify the grant of a new trial?

Decisions: No. Opinion by Justice Stevens. Vote: 7–2, Marshall and Brennan dissenting.

Reasons: The Court has imposed a duty on prosecutors to disclose exculpatory evidence to the defendant in various circumstances. In *Mooney* v. *Holohan*, 294 U.S. 103 (1935), the Court held that a prosecutor's knowing use of perjured testimony violates due process and requires the reversal of a conviction "if there is any reasonable likelihood that the false testimony could have affected the judgment of the jury." This strict sanction is imposed because the unconstitutional action involves both prosecutorial misconduct and a "corruption of the truth-seeking function of the trial process."

In *Brady* v. *Maryland*, 373 U.S. 83 (1963), the Court held that a prosecutor's pretrial failure to disclose exculpatory evidence that was material and specifically requested by the defendant violated due process and required a new trial.

This case is unlike *Mooney* or *Brady*, the Court reasoned, because the failure to disclose involved no prosecutorial misconduct and no request for disclosure was made. Because a prosecutor has no "constitutional duty routinely to deliver his entire file to defense counsel, we cannot consistently treat every nondisclosure as though it were error." Of course, "there are situations in which evidence is obviously of such substantial value to the defense that elementary fairness requires it to be disclosed even without a specific request." But where the materiality of exculpatory evidence is questionable, a prosecutor's failure to disclose it voluntarily constitutes an error of constitutional magnitude only if it creates a reasonable doubt as to the defendant's guilt.

> This means that the omission must be evaluated in the context of the entire record. If there is no reasonable doubt about guilt whether or not the additional evidence is considered, there is no justification for a new trial. On the other hand, if the verdict is already of questionable validity, additional evidence of relatively minor importance might be sufficient to create a reasonable doubt.

Middendorf v. Henry, 425 U.S. 25 (1976)

Facts: Under the Uniform Code of Military Justice (UCMJ), a serviceman lacks any right to counsel in a summary court-martial proceeding. Summary courts-martial are generally used to punish minor UCMJ offenses and may impose maximum sentences of thirty days' confinement at hard labor and a loss of pay and rank. The presiding officer at the summary court-martial acts as judge, factfinder, prosecutor, and defense counsel. He must inform the accused of the charges and the name of the accuser, call all witnesses desired by the accused, and permit the accused to cross-examine witnesses. The accused must consent to trial by summary court-martial, or the case will be either dismissed or referred to a special or general court-martial. Although the accused generally enjoys a right to counsel at special or general courts-martial, the punishments authorized in such proceedings substantially exceed those permissible in summary courts-martial.

Several servicemen brought suit attacking the constitutionality of the summary court-martial procedures on the ground that the failure to grant an accused the right to counsel violated both the Sixth Amendment guarantee of counsel in criminal cases and the Fifth Amendment right of due process.

Question: Is the failure to provide a right to counsel in summary courts-martial unconstitutional?

Decision: No. Opinion by Justice Rehnquist. Vote: 5–3, Brennan, Stewart, and Marshall dissenting. Stevens did not participate.

Reasons: The Sixth Amendment right to counsel extends to "criminal prosecutions." Although a summary court-martial conviction may result in imprisonment, that fact alone does not make the proceeding criminal. The Court, for example, concluded in *In re Gault*, 387 U.S. 1 (1967), that a juvenile court proceeding which could result in confinement was not "criminal" within the meaning of the Sixth Amendment. In addition, summary courts-martial are distinguishable from traditional civilian criminal trials in several important respects. They occur within the military community; the offenses tried generally have no civilian counterpart and carry little popular opprobrium; the penalties which may be imposed are limited; and the proceedings lack an adversarial quality, since the presiding officer must thoroughly and impartially inquire into both sides of the matter to assure that the interests of both the government and the accused are protected. Accordingly, a summary court-martial is not a "criminal prosecution" for purposes of the Sixth Amendment.

The Fifth Amendment due process claim also lacks merit. The requirements of due process in a proceeding depend upon a balancing of the interests of the individual against those of the government. The presence of counsel in a summary court-martial would

> turn a brief, informal hearing which may be quickly convened and rapidly concluded into an attenuated proceeding which consumes the resources of the military to a degree which Congress could properly have felt to be beyond what is warranted by the relative insignificance of the offense being tried. Such a lengthy proceeding is a particular burden to the armed forces because virtually all the participants, including the defendant and his counsel, are members of the military whose time may be better spent than in possibly protracted disputes over the imposition of discipline.

The interest of the accused in having counsel present may be realized by exercising his option to be tried by special or general court-martial rather than by summary court-martial. Although exercising that option might subject the accused to greater penalties, similar unhappy choices must frequently be made by civilian criminal defendants. Thus, due process does not justify "overturn[ing] the congressional determination that counsel is not required in summary courts-martial."

Ristiano v. *Ross*, 424 U.S. 589 (1976)

Facts: A black man was charged with violent crimes against a white security guard. A state trial judge denied a motion to question potential jurors specifically as to racial prejudice during *voir dire*, in addition to questioning them as to general bias or prejudice. After conviction, the defendant sought habeas corpus relief on the ground that the denial violated his right to a fair trial as guaranteed by constitutional due process.

Question: Did the trial judge's refusal to question potential jurors specifically about racial prejudice deny the defendant's constitutional right to a fair trial?

Decision: No. Opinion by Justice Powell. Vote: 6–2, Brennan and Marshall dissenting. Stevens did not participate.

Reasons: In *Ham* v. *South Carolina*, 409 U.S. 524 (1973), the Court recognized that in some highly inflammatory cases "an impermissible threat to the fair trial guaranteed by due process is posed by a trial court's refusal to question prospective jurors specifically about racial prejudice during *voir dire*." *Ham*, however, did not establish a general constitutional requirement that such questions be asked where crimes of violence between races are involved. The circumstances in this case did not "suggest a significant likelihood that racial prejudice might infect [the defendant's] trial." Accordingly, "the trial judge acted within the Constitution in determining that the demands of due process could be satisfied by his more generalized but thorough inquiry into the impartiality of the veniremen."

The Court added, however, that generally it would be wiser for state courts to propound questions concerning racial prejudice at the request of the defendant. Under its supervisory power, moreover, the Court would have required such action by a federal court in the circumstances of this case.

Abortion

In *Planned Parenthood of Central Missouri* v. *Danforth*, 428 U.S. 52 (1976), the Court expanded the constitutional right of women to obtain abortions initially established by *Roe* v. *Wade*, 410 U.S. 113 (1973). The Court struck down provisions of a Missouri law requiring spousal or parental consent in certain circumstances to make an abortion lawful. It also rejected a legislative finding that after twelve weeks of pregnancy abortions performed by the saline amniocentesis method are deleterious to maternal health.

The Court permitted physicians to assert the constitutional rights of their indigent patients by attacking a state statute restricting Medicaid reimbursement to abortions obtained for medical reasons (*Singleton* v. *Wulff*, 428 U.S. 106 [1976]). This holding marked a clear departure from recent decisions of the Court in which the requirement of standing was applied strictly.[17]

The abortion decisions of the Burger Court differ in some respects from its general philosophy and approach in other areas of constitutional law. The Burger Court has generally declined to recognize new constitutional claims not closely tied to some express constitutional provision.[18] *Roe,* in contrast, established a constitutional right to an abortion derived from inexplicit concepts of privacy implicit in several constitutional provisions. The Burger Court has generally paid great deference to legislative judgment in deciding constitutional claims.[19] *Planned Parenthood,* in contrast, closely scrutinized a legislative finding relating to maternal health. In its use of standing to deny certain plaintiffs access to federal courts, the Burger Court has sought to reduce judicial intervention in the governing process.[20] *Singleton,* in contrast, increases the opportunity for judicial intervention in the regulation of abortions.

The public controversy created by the abortion decisions of the Court has generated numerous proposals in Congress for a constitutional amendment that would overturn these holdings.[21] In addition, federal legislation has been enacted which increases the barriers to obtaining an abortion, especially by indigent persons.[22] The continuing intensity of views surrounding the abortion issue was reflected in

---

[17] See, for example, Warth v. Seldin, 422 U.S. 490 (1975); United States v. Richardson, 418 U.S. 166 (1973); Schlesinger v. Reservists Committee to Stop the War, 418 U.S. 208 (1973); Linda R. S. v. Richard P., 410 U.S. 614 (1972).

[18] See, for example, San Antonio Independent School District v. Rodriguez, 411 U.S. 1 (1972); Lindsey v. Normet, 405 U.S. 56 (1972).

[19] See Gregg v. Georgia, 428 U.S. 153 (1976); Weinberger v. Salfi, 422 U.S. 749 (1975).

[20] In dismissing a suit for lack of standing in United States v. Richardson, 418 U.S. 166 (1973), the Court stated: "In a very real sense, the absence of any particular individual or class to litigate these claims gives support to the argument that the subject matter is committed to the surveillance of Congress, and ultimately to the political process. Any other conclusion would mean that the Founding Fathers intended to set up something in the nature of an Athenian democracy or a New England town meeting to oversee the conduct of the National Government by means of lawsuits in federal courts."

[21] See S. J. Res. 6, 10, 11, 91, 94th Congress, 1st session (1975).

[22] 42 U.S. Code 300a-7 prohibits a court from requiring an individual or institution to assist in performing abortions, if contrary to religious beliefs or moral convictions, simply because the individual or institution receives financial benefits under certain federal medical programs. 42 U.S. Code 2996f(b)(8) prohibits the use of funds made available by the Legal Services Corporation to provide legal assistance regarding litigation which seeks to procure a nontherapeutic abortion. Section 209 of the HEW Appropriation Act of 1977 prohibits the use of Medicaid funds for the performance of an abortion unless the life of the mother would be endangered by childbirth.

the 1976 Democratic primary elections. Candidate Ellen McCormack campaigned almost exclusively on an anti-abortion platform and raised sufficient financial support to qualify for approximately $250,000 in federal matching funds.

Planned Parenthood of Central Missouri v. *Danforth*, 428 U.S. 52 (1976)

Facts: Two Missouri-licensed physicians and Planned Parenthood, a not-for-profit Missouri corporation, brought suit challenging the constitutionality of several provisions of the Missouri abortion statute on the ground, *inter alia*, that they interfered with a mother's right to obtain an abortion. Under the challenged provisions:

- A mother could lawfully obtain an abortion for nonmedical reasons only if the fetus lacked viability, defined as "that stage of fetal development when the life of the unborn child may be continued indefinitely outside the womb by natural or artificial life-supportive systems."
- During the first twelve weeks of pregnancy, an abortion would be unlawful if the woman failed to certify in writing that her consent to the abortion was informed and voluntary, failed to obtain her spouse's consent, or, if the woman was an unmarried minor, failed to obtain the consent of one parent.
- After twelve weeks of pregnancy, abortions performed by the saline amniocentesis method are prohibited.
- Health facilities and physicians performing abortions are required to make certain reports and maintain certain records relating to the abortions they perform.
- A physician performing an abortion is subject to criminal prosecution and civil damages for failing to exercise his professional skills to preserve the life of the fetus.

The federal district court upheld the constitutionality of all the challenged provisions except for the imposition of criminal penalties on physicians who failed to seek to preserve the life of an aborted fetus.

Question: Are the challenged provisions of the Missouri abortion statute unconstitutional?

Decision: Yes, except for the requirements concerning record keeping and reporting and written consent by the woman. Opinion by Justice Blackmun. Vote: 5–4, Burger, Stevens, White, and Rehnquist dissenting in part.

Reasons: In *Roe* v. *Wade*, 410 U.S. 113 (1973), the Court held that a woman's constitutional right of privacy protects her decision whether or not to obtain an abortion. Specifically, the Court concluded that during the first trimester of pregnancy, the state could not regulate the abortion decision. From that point until the fetus becomes viable, the state may, under *Roe*, prescribe abortion procedures reasonably designed to protect maternal health. After viability, "a point purposefully left flexible for professional determination, and dependent upon developing medical skill and technical ability, the State may regulate an abortion to protect the life of the fetus and even may proscribe abortion except where it is necessary, in appropriate medical judgment, for the preservation of the life or health of the mother." The challenged provisions must be tested against the underlying reasoning of *Roe*.

The definition of viability. The physicians contended that a specified number of weeks must be fixed by statute as the point of viability in order to satisfy *Roe*. *Roe* recognized, however, that

> viability was a matter of medical judgment, skill, and technical ability. . . . [I]t is not the proper function of the legislature or the courts to place viability . . . at a specific point in the gestation period. The time when viability is achieved may vary with each pregnancy, and the determination of whether a particular fetus is viable is, and must be, a matter for the judgment of the responsible attending physician.

Missouri's statutory definition of viability reflects this fact and is therefore not unconstitutional.

The woman's consent. Missouri requires a woman to certify in writing that her decision to terminate a pregnancy during the first twelve weeks is both informed and voluntary. The purpose of this requirement is to ensure that the frequently stressful decision to obtain an abortion is not the product of coercion. It does not unconstitutionally interfere with a woman's decision to obtain an abortion. The state has a legitimate interest in assuring that such a decision is made with full awareness of its significance and consequences.

The spouse's consent. Missouri generally prohibits abortions during the first twelve weeks of pregnancy unless the written consent of the spouse is obtained. This provision is tantamount to permitting a father to veto a mother's decision to obtain an abortion unilaterally during this period. *Roe* held that the state itself was constitutionally forbidden from exercising such power. It clearly follows that the state cannot "delegate" unilateral veto authority, even to the spouse, to prevent an abortion during the first trimester of pregnancy.

> It seems manifest that, ideally, the decision to terminate a pregnancy should be one concurred in by both the wife and her husband. No marriage may be viewed as harmonious or successful if the marriage partners are fundamentally divided on so important and vital an issue. But it is difficult to believe that the goal of fostering mutuality and trust in a marriage, and of strengthening the marital relationship and the marriage institution, will be achieved by giving the husband a veto power exercisable for any reason whatsoever or for no reason at all. . . . Since it is the woman who physically bears the child and who is the more directly and immediately affected by the pregnancy, as between the two, the balance weighs in her favor.

Parental consent. During the first twelve weeks of pregnancy, Missouri generally requires unmarried minors to obtain the consent of one parent as a condition to obtaining an abortion. The purpose of this requirement is to assure the protection of minors and to safeguard the authority of the family relationship. Its effect, however, is to make the wishes of the parents superior to those of the minor.

> [T]he State may not impose a blanket provision . . . requiring the consent of a parent or person *in loco parentis* as a condition for abortion of an unmarried minor during the first 12 weeks of her pregnancy. Just as with the requirement of consent from the spouse, so here, the State does not have the constitutional authority to give a third party an absolute, and possibly arbitrary, veto over the decision of the physician and his patient to terminate the patient's pregnancy, regardless of the reason for withholding the consent.

It is unlikely that family harmony and unity would be promoted by providing a parent with absolute authority to prevent a minor from obtaining an abortion that she and her physician think appropriate.

In a related case, *Bellotti* v. *Baird*, 428 U.S. 132 (1976), the Court indicated that a state might constitutionally require an unmarried minor to obtain a court determination that she is capable of giving informed consent before terminating a pregnancy without parental consent.

Saline amniocentesis. On the basis of detailed legislative findings that the technique is deleterious to maternal health, Missouri prohibits the use of saline amniocentesis as a method of abortion after the first trimester of pregnancy. Approximately 70 percent of abortions in the United States are performed in this way after this initial period of pregnancy. *Roe* held that after the first trimester of pregnancy the state could regulate the abortion procedure in ways reasonably related to protecting maternal health. The prohibition of the saline amniocentesis method, however, fails to meet the reasonable relationship requirement.

The use of this method is an accepted medical procedure, safer than other methods not barred by Missouri. It is commonly used nationally and safer with regard to maternal mortality than childbirth. Its proscription is "an unreasonable or arbitrary regulation designed to inhibit, and having the effect of inhibiting, the vast majority of abortions after the first twelve weeks. As such, it does not withstand constitutional challenge."

Record keeping. The challenged record-keeping requirements are designed to obtain statistics on abortions in furtherance of medical knowledge and to assure that abortions are lawfully performed. Information gathered and maintained under these provisions is confidential and can be used only for statistical purposes. Certain records may be inspected by public health officers. The record-keeping provisions do not impose an illegitimate regulatory burden on the abortion decision. While perhaps approaching permissible constitutional limits, the challenged record-keeping provisions serve to promote maternal health without impairing the physician-patient confidential relationship. As such, they pass constitutional scrutiny.

Preservation of the fetus. Missouri imposes criminal liability on a physician who fails to use his professional skills to preserve the life or health of a fetus, whatever the stage of pregnancy. That provision is unconstitutional under *Roe* which prohibits the state from preventing abortions until the stage of viability.

Singleton v. *Wulff*, 428 U.S. 106 (1976)

Facts: Missouri participates in the federal Medicaid program, under which the federal government subsidizes qualifying state plans for medical assistance to the needy. A Missouri statute prohibits the use of Medicaid funds to pay for abortions obtained for nonmedical reasons. Two Missouri-licensed physicians brought suit in federal district court challenging the constitutionality of that prohibition on the ground, *inter alia*, that it violated their patients' rights of privacy. The plaintiffs alleged that they had performed and would continue to perform abortions for persons eligible for Medicaid payments and that

Missouri had refused them Medicaid payments for abortions performed for nonmedical reasons. The suit was dismissed for lack of standing.

Question: Did the physicians have standing to challenge the constitutionality of Missouri's prohibition against the use of Medicaid funds to pay for non-medically related abortions?

Decision: Yes. Plurality opinion by Justice Blackmun. Vote: 5–4, Stevens concurring, Powell, Burger, Stewart, and Rehnquist dissenting.

Reasons: In order to obtain standing, a plaintiff must allege some concrete injury caused by the conduct or law at issue and also be a proper proponent of the legal rights asserted. In this case, the physician-plaintiffs clearly satisfied the concrete injury test:

> Their complaint and affidavits . . . allege that they have performed and will continue to perform operations for which they would be reimbursed under the Medicaid program, were it not for the limitation of reimbursable abortions to those that are "medically indicated." If the physicians prevail in their suit to remove this limitation, they will benefit, for they will then receive payment for the abortions.

Whether the physicians were appropriate parties to advance the constitutional rights of their patients is a more difficult question. Ordinarily a plaintiff can assert only his own constitutional rights. The Court has departed from this rule in the past, however, when a special relationship exists between the litigant and the third party whose constitutional rights he seeks to advance. This relationship generally involves two factual elements.

> The first is the relationship of the litigant to the person whose right he seeks to assert. If the enjoyment of the right is inextricably bound up with the activity the litigant wishes to pursue, the court at least can be sure that its construction of the right is not unnecessary in the sense that the right's enjoyment will be unaffected by the outcome of the suit. Furthermore, the relationship between the litigant and the third party may be such that the former is fully, or very nearly, as effective a proponent of the right as the latter. . . . The other factual element . . . is the ability of the third party to assert his own right. . . . If there is some genuine obstacle to such assertion . . . the third party's absence from court loses its tendency to suggest that his right is not truly at stake, or truly important to him, and the party who is in court becomes by default the right's best available proponent.

Both factual elements were present in this case. The constitutional rights of impecunious women to obtain non-medically related abortions cannot be enjoyed unless physicians are paid for providing such services. Moreover, a physician is intimately involved in the decision to have an abortion and is well qualified to litigate the question of state interference with that decision.

There may also be obstacles to a woman's assertion of her own constitutional right to an abortion:

> [S]he may be chilled from such assertion by a desire to protect the very privacy of her decision from the publicity of a court suit. A second obstacle is the imminent mootness, at least in the technical sense, of any individual woman's claim. Only a few months, at the most, after the maturing of the decision to undergo an abortion, her right thereto will have been irrevocably lost, assuming, as it seems fair to assume, that unless the impecunious woman can establish Medicaid eligibility she must forgo abortion. . . . For these reasons, we conclude that it generally is appropriate to allow a physician to assert the rights of women patients as against governmental interference with the abortion decision.

Freedom of Speech, Press, and Association

The Court established some significant First Amendment principles in the nine important cases it decided this term concerning freedom of speech, press, and association. It handed down landmark decisions concerning government regulation of the financing of political campaigns (*Buckley* v. *Valeo*, 424 U.S. 1 [1976]), and judicial gag orders (*Nebraska Press Association* v. *Stuart*, 427 U.S. 539 [1976]).

The decision of the Court in *Virginia State Board of Pharmacy* v. *Virginia Citizens Consumer Council*, 425 U.S. 748 (1976), threatens the validity of a host of government controls on so-called commercial speech. The 1942 case of *Valentine* v. *Chrestensen*, 316 U.S. 52, had been interpreted by many as standing for the proposition that commercial speech is excluded from First Amendment protection.[23] In *Bigelow* v. *Virginia*, 421 U.S. 809 (1975), however, the Court decisively rejected that interpretation and concluded that validity of government regulation of commercial speech depended on a balancing of the First Amendment interests advanced by the speech against the

---

[23] There the Court upheld a New York statutory prohibition against commercial advertising by handbill, circular, or otherwise, on any street.

public interest allegedly served by the regulation.[24] In applying that balancing test in *Virginia State Board of Pharmacy*, the Court struck down a statute prohibiting licensed pharmacists from advertising the prices of prescription drugs. Significantly, the Court found a strong First Amendment interest in the dissemination of price information because of its importance to the effective operation of the free enterprise system. It also rejected the claim that the public interest in maintaining high professional standards justified the prohibition against price advertising because alternative means were available to achieve that goal.

Numerous state and local laws prohibit or substantially restrict price advertising by certain professionals, such as lawyers, doctors, dentists, accountants, architects, and engineers. All such laws interfere with the strong First Amendment interest in the public dissemination of price information recognized in *Virginia State Board of Pharmacy*. That decision also suggests strongly that this interference cannot be justified by the public interest in maintaining high professional standards. It is difficult to perceive any other public interest that might justify the infringement of First Amendment interests created by prohibiting price advertising by particular professions.[25] Some claim that the prohibitions are necessary to avoid misleading the public, but that evil is easily prevented by making false or misleading advertising unlawful.

First Amendment protections were reduced in *Hudgens* v. *NLRB*, 424 U.S. 507 (1976). There the Court reversed its holding in *Food Employees* v. *Logan Valley Plaza*, 391 U.S. 308 (1968), that a privately owned shopping center was prohibited under the First Amendment from excluding labor picketing from its premises. That overruling was foreshadowed in *Lloyd Corp.* v. *Tanner*, 407 U.S. 551 (1972).[26]

In seeking to prevent urban blight, several cities have used zoning ordinances to control the location of businesses offering so-called adult entertainment. Some cities, such as Boston, have sought to con-

---

24 In *Bigelow*, the Court held that the First Amendment prohibited a Virginia prosecution of a newspaper owner for carrying advertisements informing Virginia residents where legal abortions could be obtained in New York.

25 In Semler v. Oregon State Board of Dental Examiners, 294 U.S. 608 (1935), the Court upheld a prohibition against price advertising by dentists that was attacked under the due process and equal protection clauses of the Fourteenth Amendment and the obligation-of-contracts clause of Article 1, section 10, of the Constitution. The Court did not specifically address any First Amendment issues.

26 *Lloyd* declined to grant First Amendment protection to the distribution of handbills protesting the Vietnam War on the premises of a privately owned shopping center.

centrate all such businesses in a particular area. Other cities, such as Detroit, have used zoning to ensure a dispersal of offerings of adult entertainment in the belief that concentration increases crime and depresses property values. In *Young* v. *American Mini Theaters*, 427 U.S. 50 (1976), the Court upheld the constitutionality of Detroit zoning ordinances requiring the dispersal of adult theaters or bookstores. Rejecting the claim that the ordinances violated the First Amendment, Justice Stevens made clear that political speech commands greater protection than the exhibition of erotic materials.

The Court has generally viewed with disfavor any licensing scheme to regulate speech protected by the First Amendment. They generally offer a dangerous opportunity for discrimination against unpopular speech or speakers. In addition, these schemes operate to some extent as a prior restraint on free speech, an evil that the First Amendment was specifically designed to prevent.[27] In *Hynes* v. *Mayor and Council of Borough of Oradell*, 425 U.S. 610 (1976), the Court avoided the prior-restraint issue in straining to find ambiguities in an ordinance requiring a license for political and charitable door-to-door canvassing and solicitation and in thus holding it unconstitutionally vague.

Justice White wrote, in *Cox Broadcasting Corp.* v. *Cohn*, 420 U.S. 469 (1975), that this "century has experienced a strong tide running in favor of the so-called right of privacy." Concern with the interest of privacy has stimulated Congress to pass the Privacy Act.[28] It was also one reason that the Court refused, in *Gertz* v. *Welch*, 418 U.S. 323 (1974), to extend the so-called actual-malice rule of *New York Times* v. *Sullivan*, 376 U.S. 254 (1964),[29] to defamation suits brought by private individuals against the press. This term, in *Time Inc.* v. *Firestone*, 424 U.S. 448 (1976), the Court expanded its protection of privacy interests in holding that *Time* magazine lacked the protection of the actual-malice rule in a defamation suit brought by Mary Firestone that attacked a false report of the grounds of her divorce from the wealthy industrialist Russell Firestone.

Historically, the Court has been reluctant to interfere with the operations of the military.[30] In recent years, the Court has concluded that the First Amendment offers less protection to servicemen than to

---

[27] See Near v. Minnesota, 283 U.S. 697 (1931).

[28] P.L. 93-579.

[29] There the Court held that, under the First Amendment, a defamation suit brought by a public official against the press could not succeed absent clear and convincing proof that a false statement of fact was published with actual malice.

[30] See, for example, Korematsu v. United States, 323 U.S. 214 (1944).

civilians[31] and that federal courts should generally abstain from interfering in court-martial proceedings.[32] This term the Court rejected the claims of Dr. Benjamin Spock and other political activists that they were unconstitutionally denied access to the Fort Dix Military Reservation in seeking to distribute political campaign literature and hold political meetings (*Greer* v. *Spock*, 424 U.S. 828 [1976]).

The Court threatened the existence of numerous systems of political patronage throughout the country by its decision in *Elrod* v. *Burns*, 425 U.S. 909 (1976). There the Court concluded that First Amendmend rights of free speech and association prohibit the discharge of non-policy-making government employees because of their political affiliation. The plurality opinion of the Court suggests that the First Amendment also prohibits government hiring on a partisan political basis or requirements that government employees contribute to a particular political party.[33]

Buckley v. *Valeo*, 424 U.S. 1 (1976)

Facts: A presidential candidate, a United States senator, a potential campaign contributor, and several other plaintiffs brought suit challenging the constitutionality of the central provisions of the Federal Election Campaign Act of 1971, as amended in 1974. The challenged provisions provided as follows:

- *Limitations on contributions.* Individual contributions are limited to $1,000 per candidate per election, with an overall annual limitation of $25,000 in campaign contributions; independent expenditures by individuals and groups "relative to a clearly identified candidate" are limited to $1,000 annually; political committees are limited to $5,000 per candidate per election.

- *Limitations on expenditures.* Campaign expenditures by candidates for federal office are generally limited to (a) $70,000 per primary or general election for the House of Representatives, (b) 8 cents per voter in a Senate primary election and 12 cents per voter in the general election, and (c) $10 million for seeking the presidential nomination and $20 million in the general election

---

[31] Parker v. Levy, 417 U.S. 733 (1973).
[32] See Schlesinger v. Councilman, 420 U.S. 738 (1975); McLucas v. DeChamplain, 421 U.S. 21 (1975).
[33] The incumbent party in Indiana routinely requires more than 7,000 state employees to contribute 2 percent of their paychecks to party coffers. See *Washington Post*, August 27, 1976.

campaign; national political party convention expenditures are limited to $2 million; candidates for the House, Senate, or presidency may expend from their personal resources a maximum of $25,000, $35,000, and $50,000, respectively.

- *Reporting and disclosure of contributions and expenditures.* The name and address of each individual contributing in excess of $10 must be reported and, if the contribution exceeds $100, must be publicly disclosed together with his occupation and principal place of business; individual expenditures in excess of $100 must be similarly disclosed.

- *Public financing of presidential elections.* Presidential primary elections are subsidized from the public treasury. In the general election, major parties are entitled to $20 million, minor parties (those whose candidate received at least 5 percent but less than 25 percent of the votes in the preceding election) are entitled to a lesser amount that is based on voter support, and other parties receive no subsidy. A candidate in a presidential primary is entitled to receive federal "matching" funds if he receives more than $5,000 in private contributions coming from twenty different states (counting only the first $250 of each contribution). Once these conditions are satisfied, the candidate receives one dollar in federal money for each privately raised dollar, disregarding the amount of any private contribution exceeding $250.

- *Federal Election Commission.* The Federal Election Commission (FEC) with a majority of members selected by the Congress, is established to administer and enforce the act.

The major theory of the plaintiffs' suit was that the substantive portions of the act violated the First Amendment freedoms of speech and association or invidiously discriminated against nonincumbent candidates and minor parties in contravention of the due process clause of the Fifth Amendment. The challenge to the FEC rested on the theory that its members were unconstitutionally appointed. Plaintiffs contended that under Article II, section 2 of the Constitution, only the President may appoint (with the advice and consent of the Senate) officers to administer and enforce federal statutes.

Question: Are the challenged provisions of the Federal Election Campaign Act constitutional?

Decision: Yes, except for the limitations on expenditures and the method of appointing members of the Federal Election Commission. Per curiam opinion. Vote: 6–2, Brennan, Stewart, and Powell supporting the entire opinion, Marshall dissenting as to the limitations on personal expenditures by candidates, Blackmun dissenting as to the limitations on contributions, Rehnquist dissenting as to the provisions concerning public funding of elections, Burger dissenting as to the limitations on contributions, public funding, and reporting and disclosure provisions, White dissenting as to the limitations on expenditures. Stevens did not participate.

Reasons: The Court reasoned as follows:

Limitations on contributions. A major purpose of the First Amendment is to protect political expression so that political and social changes desired by the people may be achieved through the electoral process. Political speech relating to candidates for public office is thus entitled to the broadest First Amendment protection.

> A restriction on the amount of money a person or group can spend on political communication during a campaign necessarily reduces the quantity of expression by restricting the number of issues discussed, the depth of their exploration, and the size of the audience reached. This is because virtually every means of communicating ideas in today's mass society requires the expenditure of money.

Accordingly, political contributions and expenditures are inextricably a part of political speech and are therefore entitled to the shelter of the First Amendment.

The freedom of individuals to associate with others to advance political beliefs or particular parties or candidates is also guaranteed by the First Amendment. The $1,000 limitation on individual contributions restricts both the exercise of this right and the freedom of political speech.

Two weighty societal interests justify these kinds of restrictions, however. First, it is a proper purpose to attempt to avoid the appearance or the actuality of corruption resulting from large individual financial contributions.

> Under a system of private financing of elections, a candidate lacking immense personal or family wealth must depend on financial contributions from others to provide the resources necessary to conduct a successful campaign. . . . To the extent that large contributions are given to secure political *quid pro quo*s from current and potential office holders, the integrity of our system of representative democracy is undermined.

Second, the public perception of improper influence flowing from large financial contributions may seriously erode confidence in the system of representative government.

The Court emphasized, that the $1,000 limitation on contributions does not substantially restrict political speech or association. A contributor remains free in any event to express his own views.

> A contribution serves as a general expression of support for the candidate and his views, but does not communicate the underlying basis for the support. . . . At most, the size of the contribution provides a very rough index of the intensity of the contributor's support. . . . A limitation on the amount of money a person may give to a candidate or campaign organization thus involves little direct restraint on his political communication.

In addition, there was no showing that the limitation on contributions would have any drastically adverse effects upon the funding of campaigns. Their overall effect is merely "to require candidates and political committees to raise funds from a greater number of persons and to compel people who would otherwise contribute amounts greater than the statutory limits to expend such funds on direct political expression."

Finally, there is no evidence to support the claim that the $1,000 limitation on contributions invidiously discriminates against challengers on the theory that incumbents begin most campaigns with a substantial political advantage. The record reveals that many challengers are able to raise substantial sums and a significant number outspend their incumbent rivals. "To be sure, the limitations may have a significant effect on particular challengers or incumbents, but the record provides no basis for predicting that such adventitious factors will invariably and invidiously benefit incumbents as a class."

Accordingly, "the weighty interests served by restricting the size of financial contributions to political candidates are sufficient to justify the limited effect upon First Amendment freedoms caused by the $1,000 contribution ceiling."

The act excludes from the definition of contributions volunteer services and certain related expenses up to $500 incurred on behalf of a candidate. These provisions are a constitutionally acceptable means of "encouraging citizen participation in political campaigns while continuing to guard against the corrupting potential of large financial contributions to candidates."

The overall ceiling of $25,000 on annual individual contributions is also constitutional. It does limit the number of candidates and committees with which an individual may associate himself through financial support.

But this quite modest restraint upon protected political activity serves to prevent evasion of the $1,000 contribution limitation by a person who might otherwise contribute massive amounts of money to a particular candidate through the use of unearmarked contributions to political committees likely to contribute to that candidate, or huge contributions to the candidate's political party.

Limitations on expenditures. The expenditure ceilings of the act impose "direct and substantial restraints on the quantity of political speech." The $1,000 ceiling on independent expenditures "relative to a clearly identified candidate" applies to all individuals who are neither candidates nor owners of institutional press facilities and to all other groups, except political parties and campaign organizations. This limitation touches First Amendment interests and is enforceable through criminal sanctions. Accordingly, the doctrine of unconstitutional vagueness requires that the phrase *relative to* be narrowly construed, to apply "only to expenditures for communications that in express terms advocate the election or defeat of a clearly identified candidate for federal office."

The $1,000 ceiling is nevertheless unconstitutional. It imposes a severe restraint on the quantity and diversity of political speech. The countervailing governmental interests are limited. The ceiling fails to prevent corruption or its appearance because unlimited amounts may be expended by persons or groups that do not in express terms advocate the election or defeat of a candidate. Moreover, the danger of real or apparent corruption is not as great with independent expenditures as it is with large campaign contributions. These expenditures may provide little or no assistance to a candidate's campaign. "The absence of prearrangement and coordination of an expenditure with the candidate or his agent . . . alleviates the danger that expenditures will be given as a *quid pro quo* for improper commitments."

It is argued, however, that the interest of the government in equalizing the relative ability of individuals or groups to influence the outcome of elections justifies the $1,000 ceiling.

But the concept that government may restrict the speech of some elements of our society in order to enhance the relative voice of others is wholly foreign to the First Amendment, which was designed "to secure 'the widest possible dissemination of information from diverse and antagonistic sources,' and 'to assure unfettered interchange of ideas for the bringing about of political and social changes desired by the people.' "

The $50,000, $35,000, and $25,000 limitations on personal and family expenditures imposed respectively on candidates for president, senator, and representative substantially restrain the First Amendment right of a candidate to advocate his own election. "[I]t is of particular importance that candidates have the unfettered opportunity to make their views known so that the electorate may intelligently evaluate [their] personal qualities and their positions on vital public issues before choosing among them on election day."

The interest of the government in avoiding actual or apparent corruption is not advanced by the restrictions on a candidate's personal expenditures. Indeed, the use of personal funds reduces outside influences upon a candidate. Any interest in equalizing the relative financial resources of competing candidates is insufficient to justify the limitations on personal expenditures by a candidate. "[T]he First Amendment simply cannot tolerate [such] restriction[s] upon the freedom of a candidate to speak without legislative limit on behalf of his own candidacy."

The limitations on overall campaign expenditures by candidates seeking nomination for election and election to federal office are also unconstitutional. While restricting political speech, the limitations on expenditures do not alleviate the potentially corrupting influence of large contributions. In addition, any interest in equalizing the financial resources and opportunities of candidates through limitations on expenditures is not sufficiently substantial to justify the restrictions. There is no assurance that each candidate will be capable of raising the maximum permitted amount, and candidates lacking initial recognition of their names may be handicapped by the limits.

It was argued, nevertheless, that the government has a legitimate interest in reducing the costs, alleged to be skyrocketing, of political campaigns through ceilings on expenditures. But

> the First Amendment denies government the power to determine that spending to promote one's political views is wasteful, excessive, or unwise. In a free society ordained by our Constitution it is not the government but the people— individually as citizens and candidates and collectively as associations and political committees—who must retain control over the quantity and range of debate on public issues in a political campaign.

Reporting and disclosure requirements. The reporting and disclosure requirements were attacked as overbroad insofar as they are applicable to candidates from minor parties and independent candidates and in their application to contributions as small as $10 or $100. Generally speaking, the act requires that each contribution in excess of $10 be reported to the FEC. Each contribution or independent expenditure in excess of $100 must be publicly disclosed along with identifying details about the contributor. In theory, these requirements could seriously impinge on rights of association and belief protected by the First Amendment. The knowledge of an individual's campaign contributions can reveal much about his political activities, associations, and beliefs. Public disclosure of contributions could thus deter some individuals who might otherwise contribute. Disclosure may also expose contributors to harassment or retaliation by political opponents.

Three weighty interests of government, however, are advanced by public disclosure. First, disclosure provides the electorate with information about the identities of a candidate's financial supporters and the way his campaign money is spent.

> It allows voters to place each candidate in the political spectrum more precisely than is often possible solely on the basis of party labels and campaign speeches. The sources of a candidate's financial support also alert the voter to the interests to which a candidate is most likely to be responsive and thus facilitate predictions of future performance in office.
>
> Second, disclosure requirements deter actual corruption and avoid the appearance of corruption by exposing large contributions and expenditures to the light of publicity. . . .
>
> Third . . . record-keeping, reporting, and disclosure requirements are an essential means of gathering the data necessary to detect violations of the contribution limitations.

The potential damage caused by disclosure to the associational interests of minor parties and their members and to the supporters of independent candidates could be significant. These movements are likely to have an insubstantial financial base that could be fatally eroded if contributors feared reprisal for their support. Since the record fails to show that these potential harms are likely to be realized by disclosure, however, and there exists a substantial public interest in its favor, the claim that the disclosure requirements violate the First Amendment associational freedoms of these plaintiffs lacks merit.

Compelled disclosure of contributors to minor parties would be unconstitutional if there was shown a

> reasonable probability that [it would] subject them to threats, harassment or reprisals from either government officials or

private parties. The proof may include . . . specific evidence of past or present harassment of members due to their associational ties, or of harassment directed against the organization itself. . . . New parties that have no history upon which to draw may be able to offer evidence of reprisals and threats directed against individuals or organizations holding similar views.

The disclosure requirements imposed upon independent individual expenditures which expressly advocate a particular election result are constitutionally permissible. They advance the informational interest of the electorate in the range of a candidate's supporters. It is "a reasonable and minimally restrictive method of furthering First Amendment values by opening the basic processes of our federal election system to public view."

The $10 and $100 reporting and disclosure thresholds were attacked on the ground that they lack a substantial nexus with the interests of government that are advanced by the reporting and disclosure requirements. It was argued that these amounts are too low to attract the attention of the candidate or have a corrupting influence. But the Constitution does not compel Congress to adopt the highest reasonable threshold: "The line is necessarily a judgmental decision, best left in the context of this complex legislation to congressional discretion. We cannot say, on this bare record, that the limits designated are wholly without rationality."

Public financing of presidential election campaigns. The primary and general presidential elections and the nominating conventions of national parties are subsidized from general revenues at a maximum level equal to the number of individual taxpayers who authorize a payment of $1 for such purposes on their income tax returns. To be eligible for matching funds for presidential primary campaigns, a candidate must pledge not to exceed the overall $10 million expenditure ceiling and various subceilings applicable in the various states. In the general presidential election, a candidate is eligible for a public subsidy only if he agrees to the $20 million limitation on expenditures.

It was argued that the public subsidies are unconstitutional because they are contrary to the general welfare in violation of Article I, section 8, of the Constitution, inconsistent with the First Amendment, and invidiously discriminatory against minor and new parties in violation of due process. The Court found all these claims meritless.

The general welfare clause is a grant, not a limitation, of congressional power. Restrictions on the exercise of that power must be found elsewhere in the Constitution. Congress was legislating for the general welfare in providing for public subsidies "to reduce the deleterious influence of large contributions on our political process, to facilitate communication by candidates with the electorate, and to free candidates from the rigors of fund raising."

The public subsidies do not abridge First Amendment freedoms. Rather, they serve "to facilitate and enlarge public discussion and participation in the electoral process, goals vital to a self-governing people."

Finally, the subsidies advance substantial government interests without unfairly burdening the political opportunities of minor parties or candidates. With regard to general elections, a party must receive at least 5 percent of the vote to qualify for a subsidy equal to only a percentage of the subsidies given to the major parties. These provisions, however, reflect a constitutionally appropriate accommodation between the needs and strengths of major and minor parties.

> Since the Presidential elections of 1856 and 1860, when the Whigs were replaced as a major party by the Republicans, no third party has posed a credible threat to the two major parties in Presidential elections. Third parties have been completely incapable of matching the major parties' ability to raise money and win elections. Congress . . . thus was justified in providing both major parties full funding and all other parties only a percentage of the major-party entitlement.

Identical treatment of all parties would also be contrary to the strong public interest in avoiding the proliferation of splinter parties.

Consideration of the electoral prospects of nonmajor parties in the absence of public financing, moreover, makes it apparent that the general election funding plan does not place these parties at a disadvantage. Whereas major parties accepting public funds must comply with a ceiling on spending, minor parties ineligible for public financing can spend unlimited amounts. The position of minor parties that receive public funds is also improved. Public funding for major-party candidates replaces private contributions entirely; public funding supplements private contributions for minor-party candidates, since they may solicit private contributions up to the applicable spending limit. Accordingly, "the general election funding system does not work an invidious discrimination against candidates of nonmajor parties."

The public financing of the nominating conventions of national parties is constitutional under the basic reasoning sustaining general election funding. There is a strong government interest in eliminating private contributions as the sole financial support for such conventions. In addition, nonmajor parties ineligible for the public subsidy are not bound by a $2 million ceiling on expenditures and may solicit private contributions for their conventions without the restriction of the $1,000 limit on contributions applicable to candidates.

Public funding for presidential primaries was claimed to be unconstitutional because it is not extended to candidates failing to run in primaries and because the eligibility formula increases the influence of wealth on the electoral process. The first claim lacked merit, the Court reasoned, because Congress could rationally conclude that abuses springing from private contributions were improbable in political campaigns in which a candidate was seeking to obtain a place on the state ballot through petition drives. Assistance to such candidates, moreover, might foster frivolous candidacies, splinter parties, and unrestrained factionalism.

Contrary to the assertion of the second claim, the primary matching fund provisions enhance the importance of small contributions. Only the first $250 of each contribution is eligible for matching. The candidates with lesser fund-raising capabilities, moreover, profit most from the matching provisions. Eligibility for matching funds is conditioned upon acceptance of a spending limit, so that such candidates can increase their spending in relation to spending by candidates capable of raising large private funds. Accordingly, the primary matching fund provisions are constitutional.

The Federal Election Commission. The FEC is vested with the primary responsibility for administering and enforcing the act. It receives and discloses statements of contributions and expenditures, is authorized to prescribe rules and regulations and enforce civil violations through litigation, and may render advisory opinions interpreting the act which, if followed in good faith, immunize an individual from criminal prosecution. The commission also determines the eligibility of candidates for public subsidies.

The authority of the commission is lodged in six members. Two each are appointed by the President, the speaker of the House of Representatives, and the president pro tempore of the Senate. All six must be confirmed by a majority of both houses of Congress.

It was argued that vesting the FEC with wide-ranging rule-making and enforcement authority violates the constitutional principle of separation of powers because a majority of its members are appointed by Congress. Article II, section 2, clause 2 of the Constitution (the appointments clause) provides in pertinent part: "[The President] shall nominate, and by and with the Advice and Consent of the Senate, shall appoint . . . all other Officers of the United States, whose Appointments are not . . . otherwise provided for [in the

Constitution], and which shall be established by Law." That clause also authorizes Congress to vest the appointment of "inferior" officers in the President alone, courts of law, or heads of departments.

The appointments clause is part of a carefully balanced constitutional scheme providing for a separation of powers between the executive, legislative, and judicial branches. The purpose of the separation was to prevent any single branch from exercising a controlling influence over another branch and thereby endangering liberties. The appointments clause is designed in part to prevent the legislative branch from exercising a dominant influence over the executive function of law enforcement through the power of appointments. Its application to "Officers of the United States" as properly interpreted includes "any appointee exercising significant authority pursuant to the laws of the United States." Members of the FEC are clearly officers under the appointments clause because they exercise substantial enforcement and administrative authority under the Federal Election Campaign Act. Since Congress lacks authority to appoint such officers under the clause, the exercise of enforcement and administrative authority by the FEC is unconstitutional. Because it is a legislatively appointed body, the commission may exercise authority only insofar as it relates to a valid legislative power. Under the act, this would include the receipt and disclosure of campaign finance information and investigation of campaign law violations.

Following its practice in apportionment and voting rights cases, however, the Court stayed its judgment for thirty days insofar as it held unconstitutional the enforcement and administrative authority of the commission. During that time, Congress would have "an opportunity to reconstitute the Commission by law or to adopt other valid enforcement mechanisms without interrupting enforcement of the provisions the Court sustains."

Nebraska Press Association v. *Stuart*, 427 U.S. 539 (1976)

Facts: A crime of multiple murder committed in a small Nebraska town attracted widespread coverage by local, regional, and national newspapers, and by radio and television stations. After arrest, the suspect (Simants) made a confession to law enforcement officers. At the request of the prosecutor and defense counsel, the trial judge entered a broad gag order to prevent pretrial publicity that might endanger the right of the accused to a trial by an impartial jury. The order generally prohibited the press from publicly disseminating any prejudicial information concerning Simants, including confessions, whether or not presented in open court. Several press and broadcast associations appealed the order, claiming that it constituted a prior restraint on publication in violation of the First Amendment protection of a free press. The Nebraska Supreme Court narrowed the gag order to prohibit reporting before trial of only three matters: the existence and nature of any confessions or admissions made by the defendant to law enforcement officers; any confessions or admissions made to any third parties, except members of the press; and other facts strongly implicative of the accused. As so modified, the Nebraska Supreme Court held that the order was a constitutionally permissible compromise between the protection of a free press and the defendant's right to be tried by an impartial jury.

Question: Did the modified gag order violate the First Amendment guarantee of a free press?

Decision: Yes. Opinion by Chief Justice Burger. Vote: 9–0.

Reasons: The due process clause of the Fourteenth Amendment guarantees a defendant a right to trial by an impartial jury in all state criminal cases. In most cases, pretrial publicity does not threaten this right. When it does, however, the trial judge possesses a variety of means to minimize the threat. The case can be continued or transferred to a different venue permeated with less publicity. Prosecutors, defense counsel, and their assistants can be enjoined from commenting on the case. Prospective jurors can be questioned at length about possible bias. The gag order against the press in this case was issued before use of any of these other means was considered.

It has been established since *Near* v. *Minnesota,* 283 U.S. 697 (1931), that any prior restraint against the press presumptively violates the First Amendment.

> The thread running through [*Near* and subsequent] cases is that prior restraints on speech and publication are the most serious and the least tolerable infringement on First Amendment rights. A criminal penalty or a judgment in a defamation case is subject to the whole panoply of protections afforded by deferring the impact of the judgment until all avenues of appellate review have been exhausted. Only after judgment has become final, correct or otherwise, does the law's sanction become fully operative.
>
> A prior restraint, by contrast and by definition, has an immediate and irreversible sanction. If it can be said that a threat of criminal or civil sanctions after publication "chills" speech, prior restraint "freezes" it at least for the time.

The factor of timeliness is important because delayed news is often unread news.

The Court found it unnecessary in this case to determine whether the First Amendment absolutely forbids the imposition of any gag order against the press in a criminal trial. It was clear that the challenged gag order imposed by the Nebraska Supreme Court lacked sufficient justification to overcome the presumption of unconstitutionality that attaches to prior restraints. First, the trial judge failed to consider whether the effects of pretrial publicity on the selection of impartial jurors could be mitigated in other ways. Second, the order itself was of questionable efficacy in stemming pretrial publicity because it could not generally apply to publishers outside the territorial jurisdiction of the issuing court. Moreover, the absence of news concerning the trial would undoubtedly cause, in a small town, the spreading of rumors that could have prejudicial effects on the judgment of prospective jurors. Third, the order barred the reporting of statements in open court. The First Amendment gives the press absolute freedom to report anything that transpires in the courtroom.

> Our analysis ends as it began, with a confrontation between prior restraint imposed to protect one vital constitutional guarantee and the explicit command of another that the freedom to speak and publish shall not be abridged. We reaffirm that the guarantees of freedom of expression are not an absolute prohibition under all circumstances, but the barriers to prior restraint remain high and the presumption against its use continues intact. We hold that, with respect to the order entered in this case prohibiting reporting or commentary on judicial proceedings held in public, the barriers have not been overcome.

Virginia State Board of Pharmacy v. *Virginia Citizens Consumer Council, Inc.*, 425 U.S. 748 (1976)

Facts: Several drug consumers attacked the constitutionality of a Virginia statute that prohibited licensed pharmacists from advertising the prices of prescription drugs. The consumers successfully claimed before a three-judge federal district court that the prohibition violated their First Amendment rights to receive information concerning drug prices.

Question: Does Virginia's prohibition against prescription drug price advertising violate the First Amendment rights of prescription drug consumers to receive information?

Decision: Yes. Opinion by Justice Blackmun. Vote: 7–1, Rehnquist dissenting. Stevens did not participate.

Reasons: It was first necessary to consider whether drug consumers can assert a First Amendment right to receive price information through advertising, even assuming that pharmacists do enjoy a corollary right to so advertise. It is clear that past decisions such as *Lamont* v. *Postmaster General*, 381 U.S. 301 (1965), and *Kleindienst* v. *Mandel*, 408 U.S. 753 (1972), establish that freedom of speech protects both a right of communication as well as a right to receive the content of that communication. Accordingly, if the First Amendment protects advertising of prescription prices by Virginia pharmacists, then it protects a reciprocal right of drug consumers to receive that advertising.

It was first argued that price advertising constitutes "commercial speech" and is thus unprotected by the First Amendment under *Valentine* v. *Chrestensen*, 316 U.S. 52 (1942). There the Court upheld a New York statutory prohibition against advertising by handbill, by circular, or otherwise, on any street. It reasoned that although such a broad proscription could not validly be applied to all communication, when limited to "purely commercial speech" it violated no First Amendment rights. Subsequent decisions, however, have severely eroded the "commercial speech" doctrine so casually erected in *Valentine*. They have established that speech does not lose First Amendment protection either because money is paid for its dissemination, or because it is sold for a profit, or because it involves a solicitation to purchase. The controlling question with regard to the advertising at issue was whether it was so removed from the exposition of ideas and from " 'truth, science, morality, and acts in general, in its diffusion of liberal sentiments on the administration of Government' " that it lacks any First Amendment protection. The answer was no.

The pharmacist has a legitimate economic interest in price advertising. The consumer has a significant interest in obtaining information about drug prices. "When drug prices vary as strikingly as they do, information as to who is charging what becomes more than a convenience. It could mean the alleviation of physical pain or the enjoyment of basic necessities." There is also a public interest in the free flow of commercial information. Such information advances the working of our free enterprise system in which resources are allocated in large measure through numerous private economic decisions.

Against these substantial individual and societal interests must be weighed the interest of the state in maintaining a high degree of professionalism among licensed pharmacists. It was claimed that price advertising would cause pharmacists to offer lower quality service in attempting to maximize profits and would damage the professional image of pharmacists.

> The strength of these [and other] proffered justifications is greatly undermined by the fact that high professional standards, to a substantial extent, are guaranteed by the close regulation to which pharmacists in Virginia are subject. . . . Virginia is free to require whatever professional standards it wishes of its pharmacists. . . . But it may not do so by keeping the public in ignorance of the entirely lawful terms that competing pharmacists are offering.

The Court specifically reserved decision on whether bans against the advertising of certain professional services of almost infinite variety, such as medical or legal services, might be justified because of a greater possibility of confusion and deception than exists in connection with the sale of standardized products such as drugs.

Hudgens v. NLRB, 424 U.S. 507 (1976)

Facts: Striking union warehouse employees picketed their employer's retail shoe store located in a large privately owned suburban shopping center. After being threatened by the owner of the shopping center with arrest for criminal trespass, the picketers departed. The union filed an unfair labor practice charge against the owner with the National Labor Relations Board (NLRB), alleging that exclusion of the picketers by the owner constituted an interference with the right of employees to strike under section 7 of the National Labor Relations Act. A decision by the board upholding the charge was affirmed by a court of appeals. It reasoned that under *Lloyd Corp. v. Tanner*, 407 U.S. 551 (1972), the First Amendment protected the right of employees to picket in the privately owned mall if other locations less intrusive upon property rights were either unavailable or ineffective. (In *Lloyd*, the Court held that a privately owned shopping center could constitutionally prohibit the distribution on its property of handbills protesting the Vietnam War, at least if adjacent public streets and sidewalks were available for the distribution of handbills. In *Food Employees v. Logan Valley Plaza*, 391 U.S. 308 [1968], the Court held that employees had a First Amendment right to picket on a privately owned shopping center if the picketing concerned a labor dispute with one of the center's lessees and if other practical alternatives to effective picketing were unavailable. The *Lloyd* decision was distinguishable from *Logan Valley* because the prohibited distribution of handbills did not concern a lessee of the shopping center and because of the ready availability of other effective locations for the activity.)

Question: Should the *Logan Valley* decision be expressly overruled in light of the *Lloyd* decision?

Decision: Yes. Opinion by Justice Stewart. Vote: 6–2, Marshall and Brennan dissenting. Stevens did not participate.

Reasons: The First Amendment protects free speech only against abridgment by the goverment. In *Marsh* v. *Alabama*, 326 U.S. 501 (1946), however, the Court concluded that a so-called company town should be treated as a municipality for First Amendment purposes. Consequently, the *Marsh* Court held that a company town could not restrict the distribution of literature on its sidewalks. *Logan Valley* extended the *Marsh* doctrine to privately owned shopping centers, at least insofar as the picketing activity concerned a business located in the center and the picketing could not be effectively carried out elsewhere. The *Lloyd* decision, although distinguishable from *Logan Valley*, adopted a rationale wholly inconsistent with the *Logan Valley* result. It expressly rejected the argument accepted in *Logan Valley* that a large, privately owned shopping center should be treated as the functional equivalent of a municipality under the First Amendment. To retain the holding in *Logan Valley*, moreover, would make the protection of First Amendment rights dependent on the content of the speech at issue. That result would be inconsistent with the well-established First Amendment doctrine that the government may not discriminate in the regulation of expression on the basis of its content. Accordingly, *Logan Valley* was overruled and the case was remanded to the NLRB to consider the unfair labor charge uninfluenced by First Amendment considerations.

Young v. *American Mini Theatres*, 427 U.S. 50 (1976)

Facts: Detroit adopted "Anti-Skid Row" zoning ordinances in 1972 to prohibit the location of "adult" theaters or bookstores within 500 feet of a residential area or within 1,000 feet of two "regulated uses." Those uses included such businesses as hotels, beer or billiard halls, pawnshops, and shoeshine parlors. The term *adult* was defined as a primary emphasis on the exhibition of films or sale of books that describe or relate to specified sexual activities or anatomical areas. The purpose of the ordinances was to stem the concentrated growth of such establishments that were found to attract an undesirable quantity and quality of transients, affect property values adversely, cause an increase in crime, especially prostitution, and encourage residents and businesses to move elsewhere. Two operators of adult motion picture theaters brought suit attacking the constitutionality of the ordinances, contending that they were unconstitutionally vague, an invalid prior restraint on constitutionally protected expression, and in violation of the equal protection clause of the Fourteenth Amendment because they classified theaters on the basis of the content of their exhibitions. The district court rejected the contentions. Relying primarily on *Police Department of Chicago v. Mosley*, 408 U.S. 92 (1971), the court of appeals reversed, upholding the equal protection argument.

Question: Are the Detroit zoning ordinances unconstitutional?

Decision: No. Opinion by Justice Stevens. Vote: 5–4, Stewart, Brennan, Marshall, and Blackmun dissenting.

Reasons: The vagueness challenge to the ordinances had two parts. First, it was claimed that the amount of sexual activity sufficient to characterize an exhibition as adult was uncertain. In addition, the ordinances were attacked for failing to specify the procedures for obtaining a waiver from its restrictions. The theater operators in this case did not suffer because of these alleged deficiencies, however. They neither applied for a waiver nor doubted the characterization of their theaters as adult. To advance First Amendment values by preventing any chilling effect on free speech that an unconstitutionally vague statute might engender, the Court has on occasion permitted a litigant to assert the First Amendment rights of others. This exception to traditional rules of standing, however, is not justified "if the statute's deterrent effect on legitimate expression is not 'both real and substantial' and if the statute is 'readily subject to a narrowing construction by the state courts.'"

The challenged ordinances were unlikely to have a significant deterrent effect, because most films can be readily characterized as adult or not. In areas of uncertainty, the ordinances lent themselves to a narrowing construction by the state judiciary.

> Since there is surely a less vital interest in the uninhibited exhibition of material that is on the border line between pornography and artistic expression than in the free dissemination of ideas of social and political significance, and since the limited amount of uncertainty in the statute is easily susceptible of a narrowing construction, we think this is an inappropriate case in which to adjudicate the hypothetical claims of persons not before the Court.

The Court rejected the claim that the ordinances were an unconstitutional prior restraint on free speech. The ordinances did not impose restrictions on the number of adult books or theaters available to the public but only on their locations. Such restrictions are inherent in commercial zoning schemes and provide no basis for their invalidation.

The equal protection claim rested on the premise that the government may not select a particular type of protected First Amendment communication for regulatory treatment on the basis of its content. The Court has held on numerous occasions, however, that the degree of First Amendment protection that certain speech enjoys depends significantly on its content or the circumstances in which it is uttered. But these decisions also clearly establish that the government must remain neutral in its regulation of communication—that is, the regulation cannot differentiate on the basis of the "social, political, or philosophical message" intended to be communicated.

> Moreover, even though we recognize that the First Amendment will not tolerate the total suppression of erotic materials that have some arguably artistic value, it is manifest that society's interest in protecting this type of expression is of a wholly different, and lesser, magnitude than the interest in untrammeled political debate. . . . Whether political oratory or philosophical discussion moves us to applaud or to despise what is said, every schoolchild can understand why our duty to defend the right to speak remains the same. But few of us would march our sons and daughters off to war to preserve the citizen's right to see "Specified Sexual Activities" exhibited in the theaters of our choice. Even though the First Amendment protects communication in this area from total suppression, we hold that the State may legitimately use the content of these materials as the basis for placing them in a different classification from other motion pictures.

Detroit's substantial interest in preserving the character of its neighborhoods and preventing urban blight clearly justified its decision to avoid concentration of adult theaters through exercise of its zoning authority. "[T]he city must be allowed a reasonable opportunity to experiment with solutions to admittedly serious problems."

Hynes v. Mayor and Council of Borough of Oradell, 425 U.S. 610 (1976)

Facts: A New Jersey municipality enacted an ordinance regulating certain types of political and charitable door-to-door canvassing and solicitation. It required "any person desiring to canvass, solicit or call from house to house for a recognized charitable . . . or political campaign or cause" to provide advance notice to the local police department in writing for identification purposes only. A candidate for the New Jersey state assembly and three registered voters brought suit challenging the constitutionality of the ordinance on the ground that it infringed their First Amendment rights of free speech and political association. In rejecting the claim, the Supreme Court of New Jersey held that the ordinance was a legitimate exercise of the municipality's police power, designed to reduce crime and fears about strangers wandering from door to door. It concluded that the requirement of advance notice was so easily satisfied that it offended no First Amendment interests.

Question: Is the challenged ordinance unconstitutional?

Decision: Yes. Opinion by Chief Justice Burger. Vote: 7–1, Rehnquist dissenting. Stevens did not participate.

Reasons: Past decisions of the Court have established that a municipality may seek to protect its citizens from crime and undue annoyance by regulating house-to-house soliciting and canvassing. These cases have also established, however, that such regulation must be pursuant to "a narrowly drawn ordinance, that does not vest in municipal officials the undefined power to determine what messages residents will hear" in order to avoid a conflict with the First Amendment. In addition, the regulation must be sufficiently specific so that men of common intelligence can understand its coverage and commands. The challenged ordinance was too vague to satisfy this due process requirement of precision.

The ordinance failed to explain what is a "recognized charitable cause." It could include charities exempt from federal taxation, or those recognized by a community agency, or by a municipal official. Likewise, there was no explanation of what is meant by a political cause. The ordinance also failed to specify what must be done to comply with the requirement that advance notice be given. It is unclear what information must be provided to the police department to constitute adequate identification. This vagueness lends the ordinance to arbitrary enforcement by the police, the type of vice condemned by the Court in *Lovell* v. *Griffin,* 303 U.S. 444 (1938), and *Schneider* v. *State,* 308 U.S. 147 (1939).

Time Inc. v. *Firestone*, 424 U.S. 448 (1976)

Facts: Russell Firestone, a member of a wealthy industrial family, sought a divorce from his wife, Mary, in Florida state court on grounds of extreme cruelty and adultery. After a lengthy trial, during which the wife held a few press conferences, the divorce was granted. The final judgment of the court mentioned marital infidelity, but was otherwise obscure as to the reason for its decision. (The Florida Supreme Court ultimately concluded that the divorce was improperly granted for lack of domestication or attachment to the home, a ground not recognized in Florida law.) A few weeks after the decision of the trial court, *Time* magazine published an item in its "Milestones" section which asserted, *inter alia*, that the Firestones' divorce was granted on grounds of extreme cruelty and adultery. Mary Firestone then brought a libel suit against *Time* in Florida state court alleging that adultery was not the basis of the divorce decree. Without finding that *Time* was either negligent or malicious in publishing the "Milestones" item, a jury awarded Mary Firestone $100,000 for personal humiliation and mental anguish. The verdict was affirmed by the Florida Supreme Court over the claim of *Time* that it violated the First Amendment protection of a free press. *Time* unsuccessfully argued that liability for publishing the defamatory falsehood concerning Mary Firestone could not be constitutionally upheld unless the publication was made with "actual malice." *Time* asserted that this conclusion was mandated either because Mary Firestone was a public figure as defined by *Gertz* v. *Welch*, 418 U.S. 323 (1974), or because the falsehood concerned an interpretation of judicial proceedings. (In *Curtis Publishing Co.* v. *Butts*, 388 U.S. 130 [1967], the Court held that the First Amendment prohibits a public figure from recovering damages against the press for a defamatory falsehood absent proof that the publication was made with actual malice, that is, with knowledge that it was false or with reckless disregard of whether it was false or not.)

Question: Was the verdict of the jury unconstitutional under the First Amendment because not based upon a finding of actual malice?

Decision: No. Opinion by Justice Rehnquist. Vote: 5–3, Brennan, White, and Marshall dissenting. Stevens did not participate.

Reasons: In *Gertz* v. *Welch*, the Court concluded that a public figure for purposes of the First Amendment generally has

> especial prominence in the affairs of society. Some occupy positions of such persuasive power and influence that they

are deemed public figures for all purposes. . . . [Others] have thrust themselves to the forefront of particular public controversies in order to influence the resolution of the issue involved.

Here, Mary Firestone lacked any prominent role in the affairs of society, except perhaps the society of Palm Beach. She also did not thrust herself into the forefront of any public controversy to influence its resolution. Resort to the legal process to obtain a divorce is obligatory. Accordingly, Firestone was not a public figure for the purpose of determining the constitutional protection afforded *Time's* report of the factual and legal basis for her divorce.

The argument that the actual-malice rule should be extended to all reports of judicial proceedings was rejected for similar reasons. Such reports may generally contain information advancing First Amendment values. But "there appears little reason why . . . individuals should substantially forfeit that degree of protection which the law of defamation would otherwise afford them simply by virtue of their being drawn into a courtroom."

Time also contended that its "Milestones" item should be protected by the actual-malice rule because it was a rational interpretation of an ambiguous court decision. An unclear court decree, however, does not license a publisher to adopt among several conceivable interpretations the one most damaging to an involved individual. A publisher has a duty to determine whether its interpretation of a court judgment is factually correct.

Gertz, nevertheless, established that a publisher may not be held liable for defamatory statements concerning private individuals absent proof of his negligence. In this case, there was no finding by either a jury or a judge that *Time* was negligent in publishing the "Milestones" item asserting that adultery was a ground for the Firestones' divorce. Accordingly, the case was remanded to the Florida Supreme Court to determine whether or not *Time* was negligent.

Greer v. *Spock*, 424 U.S. 828 (1976)

Facts: Benjamin Spock, the 1972 presidential candidate of the People's Party, was denied access to the Fort Dix Military Reservation for the purpose of distributing campaign literature and holding a meeting to discuss election issues with service personnel and their dependents. Other persons were barred from entering Fort Dix to distribute literature because they had previously done so without obtaining the approval of military authorities there. Spock and the would-be distributors of leaflets challenged the constitutionality of their respective exclusions from Fort Dix on the ground that First Amendment rights of free speech and association were thereby infringed. The Fort Dix military authorities justified their action under army regulations which prohibited, on the base, speeches and demonstrations of a partisan political nature, and the distribution of literature without the prior approval of the base commander. Under the latter regulation, approval could be withheld only if dissemination of the literature presented "a clear danger to the loyalty, discipline, or morale of troops at [the] installation."

Question: Did the exclusion from Fort Dix of Spock and those who wanted to distribute leaflets pursuant to army regulations violate the First Amendment?

Decision: No. Opinion by Justice Stewart. Vote: 6–2, Brennan and Marshall dissenting. Stevens did not participate.

Reasons: A major purpose of the Constitution is to provide for the common defense. The Court has on numerous occasions recognized "the special constitutional function of the military in our national life." The primary business of the military is to fight or be prepared to fight wars.

> [I]t is consequently the business of a military installation like Fort Dix to train soldiers, not to provide a public forum.
> A necessary concomitant of the basic function of a military installation has been "the historically unquestioned power of [its] commanding officer summarily to exclude civilians from the area of his command." . . . The notion that federal military reservations, like municipal streets and parks, have traditionally served as a place for free public assembly and communication of thoughts by private citizens is thus historically and constitutionally false.

Accordingly, Spock and the distributors of leaflets had no generalized constitutional right to make political speeches or distribute literature at Fort Dix. There was no evidence that the military authorities ever permitted a candidate to campaign there. This blanket prohibition against campaigning serves to insulate the military from both the reality and appearance of acting as a "handmaiden for partisan political causes or candidates." That policy is "wholly consistent with the American constitutional tradition of a politically neutral military establishment under civilian control." It violates no constitutional rights.

The Court rejected the challenge to the army regulation requiring the advance approval of the military commander before distributing literature at Fort Dix. That regulation authorized disapproval only if the literature would create a clear 'danger to the effective functioning of the troops at the installation. A publication cannot be barred simply because it is critical of government policies or officials. "There is nothing in the Constitution that disables a military commander from acting to avert what he perceives to be a clear danger to the loyalty, discipline, or morale of troops on the base under his command."

Elrod v. Burns, 425 U.S. 909 (1976)

Facts: After a Democrat was elected sheriff of Cook County, Illinois, he discharged several Republican non-civil-service employees working in the sheriff's office. It was the practice in Cook County that when the political affiliation of the sheriff changed, the new sheriff would replace non-civil-service employees with members of his own party. The Republicans brought suit against the Democratic sheriff, Mayor Richard Daley, and other defendants alleging that they were discharged solely because of their partisan political affiliation in violation of their First Amendment rights of free speech and association. The district court dismissed the suit for failure to state a claim.

Question: Did the discharged Republican employees state a claim for violation of First Amendment rights?

Decision: Yes. Plurality opinion by Justice Brennan. Vote: 5–3, Stewart and Blackmun concurring, Burger, Powell, and Rehnquist dissenting. Stevens did not participate.

Reasons: The Cook County sheriff's practice of dismissing employees because of their political affiliation reflects one aspect of the general practice of political patronage in the United States. This practice places restrictions on free speech and association. As a condition of maintaining their jobs, the discharged Republican employees would have been "required to pledge their political allegiance to the Democratic Party, work for the election of other candidates of the Democratic Party, contribute a portion of their wages to the Party, or obtain the sponsorship of a member of the Party, usually at the price of one of the first three alternatives."

In addition, a system of political patronage tilts the electoral process in favor of the incumbent party. Both current and prospective government employees are deterred from offering support to competing parties. "As government employment, state or federal, becomes more pervasive, the greater the dependence on it becomes, and therefore the greater becomes the power to starve political opposition by commanding partisan support, financial and otherwise."

Past decisions clearly establish that the type of burden placed on freedom of political belief and association by the Cook County sheriff's patronage practices can be constitutionally justified only by a compelling state interest. In addition, the burden on these First Amendment freedoms can be no broader than necessary to advance that interest.

One interest offered to justify the challenged patronage system was the need to ensure that public employees are both responsive to policy directives and motivated to work efficiently.

> We are not persuaded. The inefficiency resulting from the wholesale replacement of large numbers of public employees every time political office changes hands belies this justification. And the prospect of dismissal after an election in which the incumbent party has lost is only a disincentive to good work. . . . More fundamentally, however, the argument does not succeed because it is doubtful that the mere difference of political persuasion motivates poor performance; nor do we think it legitimately may be used as a basis for imputing such behavior.

In addition, the goal of efficient performance on a job can be ensured without restricting freedom of political beliefs by authorizing discharge of public employees for insubordination or poor work.

Responsiveness to new government policies can be achieved by narrowly limiting patronage dismissals to policy-making positions.

> Nonpolicymaking individuals usually have only limited responsibility and are therefore not in a position to thwart the goals of the in-party.
>
> No clear line can be drawn between policymaking and nonpolicymaking positions. While nonpolicymaking individuals usually have limited responsibility, that is not to say that one with a number of responsibilities is necessarily in a policymaking position. The nature of the responsibilities is critical. Employee supervisors, for example, may have many responsibilities, but those responsibilities may have only limited and well-defined objectives. An employee with responsibilities that are not well defined or are of broad scope more likely functions in a policymaking position. In determining whether an employee occupies a policymaking

position, consideration should also be given to whether the employee acts as an adviser or formulates plans for the implementation of broad goals.

The burden is on the state to prove that a particular employee occupies a policy-making position in order to justify his discharge for patronage reasons. In this case, that issue will be open on remand.

The third interest asserted to justify political patronage is the need to encourage participation in party politics and thereby invigorate the democratic process. However,

political parties existed in the absence of active patronage practice prior to the administration of Andrew Jackson, and they have survived substantial reduction in their patronage power through the establishment of merit systems.

Patronage dismissals thus are not the least restrictive alternative to achieving the contribution they may make to the democratic process.

Any contribution that patronage makes to the democratic process, moreover, is clearly outweighed by its substantial burdens on freedom of political belief and association.

Accordingly, a general practice of patronage dismissals violates the First Amendment, and the discharged Republicans thus stated a valid claim for relief.

Federalism

In *National League of Cities* v. *Usery*, 426 U.S. 833 (1976), the Court reversed its eight-year-old decision in *Maryland* v. *Wirtz*, 392 U.S. 183 (1968), and held that Congress lacked authority under the commerce clause to infringe upon state sovereignty by regulating the wages and hours of state and municipal employees. In *Hughes* v. *Alexandria Scrap Corp.*, 426 U.S. 794 (1976), the Court upheld the authority of states to prefer domestic over foreign businesses in their procurement or subsidization of goods and services. A contrary ruling would have jeopardized the constitutionality of several state laws permitting or requiring preference to in-state suppliers in the procurement of certain commodities.

National League of Cities v. *Usery*, 426 U.S. 833 (1976)

Facts: In 1974, purporting to act under its authority to regulate interstate commerce, Congress amended the minimum wage and overtime provisions of the Fair Labor Standards Act to cover almost all employees of states and their various political subdivisions. Several states, cities, and other plaintiffs brought suit attacking the constitutionality of the amendments, claiming that Congress lacked authority to regulate public employees in this fashion because it infringed state sovereignty. A three-judge federal district court dismissed the complaint.

Question: Did Congress have constitutional authority under the commerce clause to enact the 1974 amendments to the Fair Labor Standards Act?

Decision: No. Opinion by Justice Rehnquist. Vote: 5–4, Brennan, White, Marshall, and Stevens dissenting.

Reasons: It is well established that Congress possesses plenary authority to regulate private activity under the commerce clause, even activity that is purely intrastate, so long as it affects interstate or foreign commerce. There are other constitutional provisions, however, that establish affirmative limits to the exercise of congressional authority under the commerce clause. One such limit is the Tenth Amendment, which declares the constitutional policy that central attributes of state sovereignty are not to be impaired by the exercise of federal authority. "One undoubted attribute of state sovereignty is the States' power to determine the wages which shall be paid to those whom they employ in order to carry out their governmental functions, what hours those persons will work, and what compensation will be provided where these employees may be called upon to work overtime."

The complaint alleged that the 1974 amendments would impose substantial additional costs on the plaintiffs and would compel the termination of some programs. The amendments would also limit their ability to regulate pay scales and working hours.

> This congressionally imposed displacement of state decisions may substantially restructure traditional ways in which the local governments have arranged their affairs. . . . [The amendments would] significantly alter or displace the States' abilities to structure employer-employee relationships in such areas as fire prevention, police protection, sanitation, public health, and parks and recreation. These activities are typical of those performed by state and local governments in discharging their dual functions of administering the public law and furnishing public services. . . . If Congress may withdraw from the States the authority to make those fundamental employment decisions upon which their systems for

performance of these functions must rest, we think there would be little left of the States' "separate and independent existence." . . . We hold that insofar as the challenged amendments operate to directly displace the States' freedom to structure integral operations in areas of traditional governmental functions, they are not within the authority granted Congress by Art. I, § 8, cl. 3.

The Court added, however, that its decision would not preclude Congress from temporarily regulating wages of public employees to combat a national emergency as it did under the Economic Stabilization Act upheld in *Fry v. United States*, 421 U.S. 542 (1975).[34] But the Court concluded that its reasoning in *National League of Cities* compelled the overruling of *Maryland v. Wirtz*, 392 U.S. 183 (1968), which upheld application of the Fair Labor Standards Act to employees of public schools, hospitals, and institutions caring for the infirm or mentally ill.

Hughes v. Alexandria Scrap Corp. 426 U.S. 794 (1976)

Facts: To reduce environmental blight, Maryland subsidizes the removal and processing of abandoned automobiles. The state pays a "bounty" for the destruction, by a processor licensed under the statute, of any vehicle formerly titled in Maryland. A wrecker licensed under the statute shares in the bounty if he delivers an abandoned vehicle to the processor for scrapping. In order to avoid suits by owners claiming that their vehicles had not been abandoned, however, certain documentation proving clear title must be submitted by licensed processors to qualify for the bounty. Under a 1974 statutory amendment, a Maryland processor satisfies this requirement with regard to so-called hulks (vehicles more than eight years old and inoperable) by submitting a simple document that certifies the right of the seller to convey the hulk and the right of the processor to indemnification for any third-party claims arising from its destruction. (Such hulk indemnity agreements had long been an industry practice.) Non-Maryland hulk processors, however, are required to submit more burdensome documentation to qualify for the bounty. They must produce a certificate of title, a police certificate vesting title, a bill of sale from a police auction, or—in the case of licensed wreckers only—a wrecker's certificate.

---

[34] That act temporarily froze the wages of state and local employees as part of a general emergency measure to combat inflation that threatened the national economy.

Because it is easier to sign an indemnity agreement than to secure some form of documentation of a title, unlicensed suppliers of hulks channeled most of their business to Maryland processors after the 1974 amendment. That was because Maryland processors could claim a state bounty by submitting the indemnity agreement and thus offered higher prices for the hulks lacking documentation of titles than did foreign processors. A Virginia processor brought suit challenging the constitutionality of the amendment on the ground that it unduly burdened the flow of interstate commerce and arbitrarily discriminated against non-Maryland processors in violation of the equal protection clause of the Fourteenth Amendment.

Question: Is the 1974 amendment providing an easier method for Maryland processors to qualify for hulk bounties than for non-Maryland processors unconstitutional?

Decision: No. Opinion by Justice Powell. Vote: 6–3, Brennan, White, and Marshall dissenting.

Reasons: The constitutionality of the 1974 amendment under the commerce clause must be determined under the standards enumerated in *Pike* v. *Bruce Church, Inc.*, 397 U.S. 137 (1970). There the Court stated that whether a state-imposed burden on the flow of interstate commerce would be tolerated depended on "the nature of the local interest involved, and on whether it could be promoted as well with a lesser impact on interstate activities."

The practical effect of the 1974 amendment was to reduce the flow of hulks to non-Maryland processors. That is because bounties could be more easily claimed by Maryland processors, thereby allowing them to offer enhanced prices to unlicensed suppliers of hulks. However, the 1974 amendment did not create a burden on interstate commerce that was flourishing through natural market forces. Rather, the commerce in removal and processing of hulks existed only because Maryland chose to enter the market to subsidize these business operations. The commerce clause was intended to preclude a state from obstructing free-market forces, but not to prohibit its entry into the market as a purchaser on terms designed to enhance trade and business with its own citizens.

> We do not believe the Commerce Clause was intended to require independent justification for such action. Maryland entered the market for the purpose, agreed by all to be commendable as well as legitimate, of protecting the State's environment. As the means of furthering this purpose, it elected the payment of state funds—in the form of boun-

ties—to encourage the removal of automobile hulks from Maryland streets and junkyards. . . . [Under] the 1974 amendment . . . the financial benefit [was] channeled, in practical effect, to domestic processors. . . . [This tended to cause hulks in Maryland] to be processed inside the State rather than flowing to foreign processors. But no trade barrier of the type forbidden by the Commerce Clause, and involved in previous cases, impedes their movement out of State. . . . Nothing in the purposes animating the Commerce Clause forbids a State, in the absence of congressional action, from participating in the market and exercising the right to favor its own citizens over others.

The equal protection argument rested upon the premise that the 1974 amendment lacked rationality in its discrimination against non-Maryland processors. The purpose of the statute was to clear "Maryland's landscape of abandoned automobiles." It was rational for the state to assume that hulks delivered to Maryland processors were more likely to have been abandoned within Maryland than those delivered to foreign processors. The Constitution does not compel a state "to verify logical assumptions with statistical evidence." On the basis of the foregoing assumption, the 1974 amendment rested upon a rational and legitimate foundation. "[B]y making it easy for an in-State processor to receive bounties but difficult for an out-of-State processor to do so, [the amendment] tends to ensure that the State's limited resources are targeted to hulks abandoned inside Maryland as opposed to some contiguous State."

Racial Discrimination

In the 1960s, the country generally united behind legislative efforts to forbid discrimination against blacks on the basis of race. This general consensus was promoted by dramatic, nationally publicized confrontations between civil rights marchers and government authorities in such places as Birmingham and Selma. It resulted in the enactment of such landmark legislation as the Civil Rights Act of 1964,[35] the Voting Rights Act of 1965,[36] and the Fair Housing Title of the Civil Rights Act of 1968.[37] The primary moral basis of these

[35] P.L. 88-351. The House approved the legislation by a vote of 290-130 and the Senate by a vote of 73-27.
[36] P.L. 89-110. The House approved the legislation by a vote of 328-74 and the Senate by a vote of 79-18.
[37] P.L. 90-284, Title VIII, 42 U.S. Code 3601, et seq. The House approved the legislation by a vote of 250-172 and the Senate by a vote of 71-20.

laws was the belief that blacks should have an equal opportunity with other citizens to obtain employment, to vote, and to lease or purchase housing. This belief was and is widely shared.

The 1970s have brought more difficult legal issues relating to race. Many derive from what are popularly characterized as affirmative action programs or decrees. In seeking to overcome the adverse effects of past racial discrimination, these programs and court orders have given preference to blacks over whites in such areas as employment,[38] admission to professional schools,[39] and voting power.[40] In formulating desegregation decrees, the federal courts have sought to involve school districts which themselves were uninvolved in the creation of racially segregated schools.[41] These cases frequently raise the basic question of whether it is constitutional or otherwise lawful to "penalize" innocent persons to overcome the injurious effects of unlawful racial discrimination practiced by others, even when the beneficiaries of the program have personally suffered no discrimination. Both legal scholars and the public are sharply divided on this question.

In recent decisions, the Court struck down an interdistrict busing order to remedy school segregation and an order seeking to maximize black voting power to remedy an annexation alleged to be unlawful.[42] This term the Court rejected the claim that the Voting Rights Act requires the drawing of electoral districts to ensure that blacks are elected in proportion to their share of population (*Beer v. United States*, 425 U.S. 130 [1976]). It also indicated that racial discrimination in public housing cannot be remedied by forcing municipalities uninvolved in the unlawful conduct to offer increased housing opportunities for blacks (*Hills v. Gautreaux*, 425 U.S. 284 [1976]). But in *Franks v. Bowman Transportation Co.*, 424 U.S. 747 (1976), the Court construed the Civil Rights Act of 1964 to authorize the award of retroactive seniority status to black applicants who had been unlawfully denied employment. *Franks*, however, specifically reserved decision on the question whether an innocent employee adversely affected by such relief might also obtain compensatory relief from his

---

[38] See Adcox v. Caddo Parish School Bd, 11 FEP Cases 1312 (W.D. La. 1974).

[39] Compare Alevy v. Downstate Medical Center, 348 N.E. 2d 537 (N.Y. 1976) (upholding such preferences), with Bakke v. Regents of the University of California, 45 U.S.L.W. 2179 (Calif., September 16, 1976) (holding such preferences unconstitutional), certiorari granted, 45 U.S.L.W. 3555 (1977).

[40] City of Richmond v. United States, 376 F. Supp. 1344 (E.D. Va.), reversed, 422 U.S. 358 (1975).

[41] Buchanan v. Evans, 393 F. Supp. 428 (D. Del.) affirmed, 423 U.S. 963 (1975).

[42] Milliken v. Bradley, 418 U.S. 717 (1974); City of Richmond v. United States, 422 U.S. 358 (1975).

employer. A lower federal court has concluded that under Title VII of the 1964 Civil Rights Act, a male employee who is denied promotion on the basis of sex because of an affirmative action plan designed to remedy past discrimination against women may recover damages against his employer.[43]

In a nationally publicized case, the Court interpreted a century-old civil rights statute to prohibit private schools from refusing to admit black children on account of race (*Runyon v. McCrary*, 427 U.S. 160 [1976]). The Court also ruled that the statute protected whites as well as blacks from private acts of racial discrimination (*McDonald v. Santa Fe Trail Transportation Co.*, 427 U.S. 273 [1976]). That decision brought a sharp dissent from Justice White, who observed that under the Court's reasoning, a former white slaveholder would have had a claim for damages against a former black slave for refusing to contract with him on account of race.

In an important employment case, the Court ruled that a public employer does not violate the Constitution simply by using tests that operate to disqualify a disproportionate percentage of blacks in the hiring process (*Washington v. Davis*, 426 U.S. 229 [1976]). It held that a purpose or intent to discriminate on the basis of race must be proved.

Beer v. *United States*, 425 U.S. 130 (1976)

Facts: Section 5 of the Voting Rights Act generally prohibits any covered state or political subdivision from changing any voting law in effect on November 1, 1964, unless either the U.S. attorney general or the U.S. District Court for the District of Columbia finds that the change has neither the purpose nor the effect of abridging the right to vote on account of race. The city of New Orleans, 55 percent white and 45 percent black, reapportioned its councilmanic districts after the 1970 census. The city retained its general plan adopted in 1954 of electing seven councilmen from five single-member districts with two at-large seats. The reapportionment plan marginally improved black voting power by producing black population majorities in two districts and a black voting population majority in one. New Orleans sought approval of its plan under section 5 of the Voting Rights Act in federal district court. Approval was denied on the

---

[43] McAleer v. American Telephone and Telegraph, Civ. Action No. 75-2049 (D.D.C. 1976). An out-of-court settlement for $14,000—$7,500 for McAleer and $6,500 for his attorney—was ultimately made. *Washington Post*, September 15, 1976.

grounds that two at-large seats were retained without a compelling government interest to justify a departure from single-member districts, and the single-member districts were not drawn to permit blacks to elect councilmen in proportion to their share of either population or registered voters.

Question: Did the New Orleans reapportionment plan violate section 5 of the Voting Rights Act?

Decision: No. Opinion by Justice Stewart. Vote: 5–3, Brennan, Marshall, and White dissenting. Stevens did not participate.

Reasons: Section 5 applies only to proposed changes in voting procedures. Because the at-large seats have existed without change since 1954, their retention was not subject to the preclearance procedures of section 5.

The legality of the single-member districts must be determined with an understanding of the purpose behind section 5, which is to "insure that no voting-procedure changes would be made that would lead to a retrogression in the position of racial minorities with respect to their effective exercise of the electoral franchise."

Accordingly, a legislative reapportionment which improves the voting power of racial minorities can never abridge the right to vote within the meaning of section 5. The New Orleans reapportionment plan of 1970 clearly improved the position of black voters compared with the 1961 plan, in which none of the councilmanic districts contained a clear black majority of registered voters. The district court thus erred in finding that the plan violated section 5.

Hills v. *Gautreaux*, 425 U.S. 284 (1976)

Facts: A federal appeals court held that the United States Department of Housing and Urban Development (HUD) had acted unconstitutionally in providing financial assistance and sanctioning a racially discriminatory public housing program operated by the Chicago Housing Authority (CHA). The CHA was found to have unconstitutionally selected public housing sites to avoid the placement of black families in white neighborhoods. The appeals court also ruled that in fashioning an appropriate remedy for the unconstitutional conduct of HUD and CHA, the district court had authority to compel HUD to seek increased public housing outside the limits of Chicago if necessary to disestablish the segregated public housing system within the city. It rejected the view that *Milliken* v. *Bradley*,

418 U.S. 717 (1974), limited the remedial authority of the district court to the city of Chicago, since the racially discriminatory acts were committed there and solely against residents of the city.

Question: Does the district court possess authority to order HUD to seek increased public housing opportunities outside the boundaries of Chicago to remedy the unconstitutional acts of the department committed within the city?

Decision: Yes. Opinion by Justice Stewart. Vote: 8–0. Stevens did not participate.

Reasons: In *Milliken* v. *Bradley,* the Court concluded that a school desegregation remedy must be restricted to the district responsible for the segregation except in very limited circumstances. A cross-district remedy is proper only if the racially discriminatory acts of one district have been a "substantial cause" of segregation in the other. The rationale of *Milliken* was that in the absence of an interdistrict violation or effect, a nonoffending unit of local government cannot be restructured in a remedial decree to overcome the constitutional violation of another unit. *Milliken,* however, did not establish "a *per se* rule that federal courts lack authority to order parties found to have violated the Constitution to undertake remedial efforts beyond the municipal boundaries of the city where the violation occurred."

In this case, ordering HUD to take action beyond the boundary lines of Chicago would be consistent with *Milliken* because both HUD and CHA have authority to operate outside the city limits. Such relief would not necessarily entail coercion of those government units not involved with the unconstitutional conduct of HUD and CHA. HUD's discretion in funding particular housing proposals and contracting for low-income housing directly with private owners and developers can be directed toward fostering increased housing opportunities in the Chicago metropolitan area without preempting the power of local governments. A metropolitan remedial decree ordering HUD to exercise its discretion in this manner

> would not consolidate or in any way restructure local governmental units. [It] would neither force suburban governments to submit public housing proposals to HUD nor displace the rights and powers accorded local government entities under federal or state housing statutes or existing land use laws. The order would have the same effect on the suburban governments as a discretionary decision by HUD to use its statutory powers to provide . . . alternatives to the

racially segregated Chicago public housing system created by CHA and HUD.

Postscript: On June 7, 1976, HUD agreed with counsel for the Gautreaux plaintiffs to undertake an areawide pilot project intended to house approximately 400 plaintiff-class families in existing housing pursuant to the existing section 8 housing program of HUD. The purpose of the project is to develop information that would assist the federal district court and the litigants in devising relief throughout the metropolitan area.

Franks v. *Bowman Transportation Co.,* 424 U.S. 747 (1976)

Facts: A federal district court found that a certain group of black applicants were denied employment by the Bowman Transportation Company because of race in violation of Title VII of the Civil Rights Act of 1964. In determining what remedial relief should be granted, however, the district court refused to award the applicants seniority status retroactive to the date of their individual applications to Bowman. The court of appeals affirmed the denial of retroactive seniority on the ground that such relief was barred by section 703(h) of Title VII.

Question: Were the black applicants improperly denied retroactive seniority status under Title VII?

Decision: Yes. Opinion by Justice Brennan. Vote: 5–3, Burger, Powell, and Rehnquist dissenting. Stevens did not participate.

Reasons: Section 703(h) generally permits an employer to use a bona fide seniority or merit system as a basis for setting pay or other conditions of employment. The legislative history of that provision clearly shows that a primary purpose was to legitimize seniority systems existing on its effective date, even though they perpetuated the effects of earlier discrimination. But "[t]here is no indication . . . that section 703(h) was intended to modify or restrict relief otherwise appropriate once an illegal discriminatory practice occurring after the effective date of the Act is proved." The court of appeals thus erred in concluding that section 703(h) barred the award of seniority relief to the black applicants in this case.

The propriety of retroactive seniority must be determined under section 706(g) of Title VII. That provision authorizes federal courts to remedy unlawful employment discrimination by ordering "such affirmative action as may be appropriate, which may include . . . reinstatement or hiring of employees, with or without back pay . . . , or any other relief as the court deems appropriate." A central purpose of this remedial authority is to place the victim of unlawful employment discrimination in as good a position as he would have been in the absence of discrimination. With regard to victims of racial discrimination in hiring, the make-whole purpose of section 706(g) will presumptively be achieved by, *inter alia*, "slotting the victim in that position in the seniority system that would have been his had he been hired at the time of his application." This is because seniority status is enormously important in the allocation of employment benefits and the determination of employment rights under collective bargaining agreements.

An award of retroactive seniority status under section 706(g), however, may not be appropriate in all circumstances. The district court possesses equitable discretion to deny such relief for reasons "which, if applied generally, would not frustrate [the] central statutory purposes [of Title VII] of eradicating discrimination throughout the economy and making persons whole for injuries suffered through past discrimination." (Quoting *Albemarle Paper Co.* v. *Moody*, 422 U.S. 405, at 421 [1975].) This standard, however, denies a district court the discretion to reject a retroactive seniority award solely because it may prejudice the economic interests of other employees. That reason, if applied generally, would frustrate the make-whole objective of Title VII.

The Court thus remanded the case for a determination of whether special circumstances justified a departure from the presumption in favor of retroactive seniority relief under section 706(g). It specifically reserved decision on the question of whether an innocent employee adversely affected by such relief might also obtain compensatory relief from the discriminating employer or union.

Runyon v. McCrary, 427 U.S. 160 (1976)

Facts: Two private schools, each with an enrollment of approximately 200 students, advertised publicly for additional students. In response to the advertisements, the parents of two black children sought their admission at the schools. Admission was denied solely because of the children's race. The parents, suing on behalf of their children, brought a class action against the private schools alleging that their refusal to admit black children solely on account of race violated 42 U.S. Code 1981. That section provides that "all persons . . . shall have the same right . . . to make and enforce contracts . . .

as is enjoyed by white citizens." The district court sustained the section 1981 claims of the parents, enjoined the schools from discriminating against applicants on the basis of race, and awarded the parents and children damages for the embarrassment, humiliation, and mental anguish they suffered. The court of appeals affirmed.

Question: Did the private schools violate section 1981 in excluding qualified children solely because they are black?

Decision: Yes. Opinion by Justice Stewart. Vote: 7–2, White and Rehnquist dissenting.

Reasons: The Court has previously interpreted section 1981 to prohibit racial discrimination in the making and enforcing of private contracts in *Johnson* v. *Railway Express Agency*, 421 U.S. 454 (1975), and *Tillman* v. *Wheaton-Haven Recreation Association*, 410 U.S. 431 (1973). The racial exclusion practiced by the private schools in this case constitutes "a classic violation of section 1981." The schools refused to contract for the provision of educational services to black children solely because of race.

It was argued, however, that application of section 1981 in these circumstances violates constitutional rights of freedom of association and privacy and a parent's right to direct the education of his children. The First Amendment protection of freedom of association permits parents to educate their children in schools *teaching* the desirability of racial segregation. But the Constitution places no value and affords no protection to the *practice* of private racial discrimination.

Past Supreme Court decisions have recognized the constitutional rights of parents to educate their children in private schools meeting state educational requirements. They fail, however, to support the claim that parents have constitutional rights to educate their children in private, racially segregated schools.

Finally, no constitutional right of privacy is undermined by application of section 1981 to private schools. The Court reasoned that

> a person's decision whether to bear a child and a parent's decision concerning the manner in which his child is to be educated may fairly be characterized as exercises of familial rights and responsibilities [and thus of constitutional rights to privacy]. But it does not follow that because government is largely or even entirely precluded from regulating the child-bearing decision, it is similarly restricted by the Constitution from regulating the implementation of parental decisions concerning a child's education.

McDonald v. *Santa Fe Trail Transportation Co.*, 427 U.S. 273 (1976)

Facts: Two white employees were dismissed by their employer for misappropriating property. They brought suit under 42 U.S. Code 1981 and Title VII of the Civil Rights Act of 1964 alleging that their dismissals were racially discriminatory because a black employee charged with the same misconduct was retained. Section 1981 provides that "all persons . . . shall have the same right . . . to make and enforce contracts . . . as is enjoyed by white citizens." Title VII prohibits the discharge of "any individual" on account of race. The district court dismissed the suit on the ground that neither section 1981 nor Title VII protects white persons against racial discrimination. The court of appeals affirmed.

Question: Do both Title VII and section 1981 protect white employees from discharge solely on account of race?

Decision: Yes. Opinion by Justice Marshall. Vote: 9–0 on the Title VII question and 7–2 regarding section 1981, White and Rehnquist dissenting.

Reasons: On its face, Title VII prohibitions are not limited to discrimination against members of any particular race. In addition, the Equal Employment Opportunity Commission, charged with enforcing Title VII, has interpreted it "to proscribe racial discrimination in private employment against whites on the same terms as racial discrimination against nonwhites." Uncontradicted legislative history supports that interpretation. Accordingly, a white employee is protected under Title VII from a racially motivated discharge by private employers. This protection does not lapse simply because the employee may have committed a serious criminal offense against his employer.

Section 1981 also affords white employees a remedy against racial discrimination in private employment. In *Johnson* v. *Railway Express Agency*, 421 U.S. 454 (1975), the Court concluded that section 1981 protects black employees from private racial discrimination. The language of the statute provides some justificaion for excluding its application to white employees because it speaks in terms of ensuring all persons the same contractual rights "as is enjoyed by white citizens." The legislative history, however, clearly establishes that it was intended to protect white persons from private racial discrimination to the same extent as nonwhites.

Washington v. *Davis*, 426 U.S. 229 (1976)

Facts: To select among applicants for participation in its pre-employment police training program, the District of Columbia police department administers a test designed to measure verbal ability, vocabulary, reading, and comprehension. That test (Test 21) is used generally by the United States Civil Service Commission in selecting applicants for employment throughout the federal government. Applicants scoring below a minimum level on Test 21 are excluded from the training program and are thus disqualified for employment as police officers. Black applicants who failed Test 21 brought suit challenging its legality both under the due process clause of the Fifth Amendment and under federal statutes 5 U.S. Code 3304 and 42 U.S. Code 1981. They claimed that because a greater percentage of black applicants failed the test than white applicants, the test was racially discriminatory and contrary to due process, unless it was an accurate predictor of job performance. The statutory claims rested upon the same theory. The district court found that Test 21 was not culturally slanted to favor whites and was reasonably related to success in the police training program. It noted further that since 1969 the percentage of new black police force recruits approximated the percentage of blacks within the territory in which the department had recruited. On the basis of these facts, the district court rejected the plaintiffs' claims.

The court of appeals reversed, relying on *Griggs* v. *Duke Power Co.,* 401 U.S. 424 (1971).[44] It reasoned that the disproportionate impact of Test 21 on blacks was sufficient to establish a constitutional violation, absent proof that the test was an adequate predictor of job performance in addition to predicting success in the training program.

Quesion: Does Test 21 violate either constitutional due process or federal statutes?

Decision: No. Opinion by Justice White. Vote: 7–2, Brennan and Marshall dissenting.

Reasons: The court of appeals erroneously applied the legal standards established in *Griggs* v. *Duke Power Co.,* a case involving

---

[44] There the Court interpreted Title VII of the Civil Rights Act of 1964 to prohibit a private employer's use of tests that operated to disqualify a disproportionate percentage of blacks from employment unless the tests demonstrably measured job performance.

Title VII of the 1964 Civil Rights Act, to resolve the constitutional issue. Past decisions "have not embraced the proposition that a law or other official act, without regard to whether it reflects a racially discriminatory purpose, is unconstitutional *solely* because it has a racially disproportionate impact." (Emphasis in original.) On the contrary, they have established that proof of a racially discriminatory purpose is necessary to justify constitutional condemnation of a law or official practice under the due process or equal protection clause. Of course, an improper purpose can often be inferred from a law's disproportionate impact on blacks. But disproportionate impact, "standing alone, . . . does not trigger the rule . . . that racial classifications are to be subjected to the strictest scrutiny and are justifiable only by the weightiest of considerations."

In this case, the facts did not warrant inference of a racially discriminatory purpose behind Test 21 simply because of its disproportionate effect on black applicants. The Court found the test to be neutral on its face and to serve the valid purpose of seeking to upgrade communicative abilities that are important for police work. The police department had made affirmative and generally successful efforts to hire blacks. These facts might be insufficient to sustain a challenge to the test under Title VII, which requires demonstrable proof of a relation to job performance for any test having a racially disproportionate impact. But "we are not disposed to adopt this more rigorous standard for the purposes of applying the Fifth and the Fourteenth Amendments in cases such as this."

The statutory claims were also properly rejected by the district court. The provisions of 42 U.S. Code 1981 and 5 U.S. Code 3304 regarding standards of job relatedness and the corresponding standards of Title VII were assumed to be identical. Under these standards, an employment test that disproportionately disqualifies blacks can be sustained only if professional validation studies prove that it is a reasonable predictor of successful job performance. The district court found that Test 21 adequately predicted success in the police recruit training course, without determining its relevance to job performance. The court of appeals erred in concluding that the job-relatedness requirement could be satisfied only by proving a direct relation between performance on Test 21 and actual job performance. The "more sensible construction of the job relatedness requirement" is that proof of a valid relationship between Test 21 and the training program was sufficient.

Pasadena City Board of Education v. Spangler, 427 U.S. 424 (1976)

Facts: In 1970, a federal district court held that the Pasadena school system was unconstitutionally segregated. The court ordered that any desegregation plan submitted by the board of education include provisions ensuring that no elementary or secondary school have a majority of minority students in the school year commencing in September 1970. The court also retained jurisdiction over the suit to monitor implementation of desegregation plans regarding school personnel, school construction, and student assignments. In 1974, the board of education petitioned the district court, *inter alia*, to eliminate its "no majority of any minority" requirement concerning pupil assignments and to terminate its jurisdiction over the case. In denying the motion, the district court stated that its 1970 remedial order "meant . . . that at least during my lifetime there would be no majority of any minority in any school in Pasadena."

Question: Did the district court err in failing to eliminate its "no majority of any minority'" requirement concerning student assignments?

Decision: Yes. Opinion by Justice Rehnquist. Vote: 6–2, Marshall and Brennan dissenting. Stevens did not participate.

Reasons: In *Swann* v. *Board of Education,* 402 U.S. 1 (1971), the Court stated that in formulating desegregation decrees a particular degree of racial balance is a permissible "starting point" but cannot be an "inflexible requirement." There is no substantive constitutional right to attend a school with a particular racial mix. Accordingly, the district court violated the mandate of *Swann* "in enforcing its [1970] order so as to require annual readjustment of attendance zones so that there would not be a majority of any minority in any Pasadena public school."

It is important to note that this case did not involve a desegregation plan to be implemented a step at a time and thus be incomplete at its inception. Nor did the plan call for particular revisions of attendance zones for particular schools. The district court also found that the required annual modifications in attendance zones needed to comply with the no-majority-of-any-minority requirement were not caused by "white flight" traceable to the desegregation decree itself.

The 1970 approved desegregation plan was

> designed to obtain racial neutrality in the attendance of students at Pasadena's public schools. No one disputes that the

initial implementation of this plan accomplished *that* objective. That being the case, the District Court was not entitled to require the School District to rearrange its attendance zones each year so as to ensure that the racial mix desired by the court was maintained in perpetuity. For having once implemented a racially neutral attendance pattern in order to remedy the perceived constitutional violations on the part of the defendants, the District Court had fully performed its function of providing the appropriate remedy for previous racially discriminatory attendance patterns. [Emphasis in original.]

Federal Courts and Procedure

Alexis de Tocqueville wrote in 1835 that "Americans have the strange custom of seeking to settle any political or social problem by a lawsuit instead of using the political process as do people in most other countries."[45] That "strange custom" today threatens to overwhelm the federal judiciary.

In his 1976 year-end report on the condition of the federal judiciary, Chief Justice Burger cited the following figures:

- In fiscal 1975, 160,000 new cases were filed in federal district courts, or 402 cases per judgeship, "an unrealistic number for one judge." The comparable figure in 1970 was only 317 cases per judgeship.
- Through procedural efficiencies and longer hours, the average disposition per judgeship in 1975 was 371 cases, up 27 percent from 292 in 1970. Nevertheless, the enormous increase in filings during that period resulted in an increase in the number of cases per judgeship awaiting disposition from 285 to 371.
- In 1968, 282 appeals per circuit judgeship were filed; in 1975, the figure was 515.
- In 1968, 6,615 cases awaited disposition in the eleven courts of appeals, and as of July 1, 1975, the number was 12,128.

On the basis of a 1976 survey of judgeship needs, the Judicial Conference of the United States has recommended the creation of 106 additional federal district judgeships and 16 additional appellate judgeships. In urging Congress to act on an earlier request for fewer judgeships, the chief justice noted: "The Judicial Conference and the judges can do nothing more, except wait on Congress and urge

---

45 *Democracy in America* (New York: Alfred A. Knopf, Vintage Books, 1957), p. 290.

prompt action. Action taken in 1976 on 1972 needs and projected needs is hardly a reasonable response."

The problem of the existing federal caseload is exacerbated by the requirements of the Speedy Trial Act of 1974 (P.L. 93–619). For the year beginning July 1, 1976, the act requires the government to file an information or indictment against a person within 60 days after arrest or service of summons. Ten days are permitted from indictment or information to arraignment. Trial must commence within 180 days of arraignment. These times will be reduced annually until they become 30, 10, and 60 days on July 1, 1979. Many fear that the trial of civil suits will be intolerably delayed on account of the Speedy Trial Act if the federal caseload is not substantially reduced.

Federal district courts are obtaining some relief through the increasing use of federal magistrates.[46] Under 28 U.S. Code 636(b) district courts may assign magistrates any duties "not inconsistent with the Constitution and laws of the United States." In fiscal 1975, magistrates disposed of 255,061 matters that would otherwise have required the attention of a federal judge. There are now approximately 150 full-time magistrates. This term, in *Mathews* v. *Weber*, 423 U.S. 261 (1976), the Court held that magistrates could be authorized to review initially all social security benefit cases.

Many have charged in recent years that the federal judiciary has become too much involved in the oversight of the environment, schools, prisons, police departments, mental health institutions, and other areas of legislative or executive concern.[47] Opposition to such intimate involvement rests on at least two grounds. In areas of public health and safety, some argue that the courts lack sufficient scientific knowledge to decide intelligently important issues related to subjects such as nuclear power, disturbance to the ozone layer, or food additives. To remedy this alleged defect, a task force of the Presidential Advisory Group on Anticipated Advances in Science Technology has proposed the establishment of a "science court" composed of impartial scientists to conduct inquiries into conflicting scientific claims in an effort to determine the facts.[48]

Others have opposed an "activist" federal judiciary on the ground that unelected and independent judges should be reluctant to interfere with the majoritarian political process. In recent years, the

---

[46] Full-time magistrates are appointed by the several federal district courts for a term of eight years (28 U.S. Code 631). A statute expanding the jurisdiction of magistrates was recently enacted (P.L. 94-577).

[47] See "The Power of Our Judges," *U.S. News and World Report*, January 19, 1976, p. 29.

[48] See *Science*, August 20, 1976, p. 653.

Supreme Court has indicated some sympathy with that view by narrowly construing jurisdictional statutes[49] and erecting a barrier to federal courts through an expansive application of the requirement of standing.[50]

Justice Powell recently stated that the present Court, in contrast to the Warren Court, "mindful of preserving the vitality of the democratic process, may be more deferential to legislative judgments, it is more likely to give some weight to federalism, and it is more conventional in demanding compliance with jurisdictional and standing requirements."[51]

This term the Court generally validated Powell's observation in holding that a federal district court lacked pendent jurisdiction over a state law claim asserted in conjunction with federal claims premised upon 42 U.S. Code 1983 (*Aldinger v. Howard*, 427 U.S. 1 [1976]) and that indigents lacked standing to challenge an Internal Revenue Service ruling relaxing the requirements for hospital services to the poor in order to qualify as a tax-exempt charitable organization (*Simon v. Eastern Kentucky Welfare Rights Organization*, 426 U.S. 26 [1976]). The Court refused, however, to permit a district judge to decline jurisdiction over a suit removed from state court on the ground that his civil docket was too crowded (*Thermtron Products, Inc. v. Hermansdorfer*, 423 U.S. 336 [1976]). And, as discussed in the section on abortion, the Court relaxed standing requirements for asserting a mother's constitutional right to an abortion (*Singleton v. Wulff*, 428 U.S. 106 [1976]).

Mathews v. *Weber*, 423 U.S. 261 (1976)

Facts: Pursuant to the Federal Magistrates Act, 28 U.S. Code 636(b), a federal district court adopted a policy of initially referring all social security benefit cases to United States magistrates. The magistrates review the administrative record developed by the Department of Health, Education and Welfare (HEW), hear oral argument, and prepare a recommended decision as to whether the administrative determination is supported by substantial evidence. (In reviewing

---

[49] See Zahn v. International Paper Co., 414 U.S. 291 (1973); Johnson v. Mississippi, 421 U.S. 213 (1975).

[50] See, for example, Warth v. Seldin, 422 U.S. 490 (1975); United States v. Richardson, 418 U.S. 166 (1974); Bangor Punta Operations, Inc. v. Bangor and Aroostook R.R. Co., 417 U.S. 703 (1974); O'Shea v. Littleton, 414 U.S. 488 (1974).

[51] See address of Justice Lewis F. Powell, "Report on the Court," American Bar Association Labor Law Section meeting, August 11, 1976.

social security decisions under 42 U.S. Code 405[g], the district court may only consider the pleadings and administrative record. Findings of fact by HEW must be accepted if supported by substantial evidence.) The parties may object to the recommendations of the magistrate. The district judge then makes an independent decision, and he may request additional oral argument from the parties. In a suit seeking judicial review of a Medicare determination, HEW objected to referral of the matter to a magistrate on grounds that it violated Rule 53(b) of the Federal Rules of Civil Procedure (FRCP) and was unauthorized by section 636(b).

Question: Is the challenged policy of initially referring all social security benefit cases to magistrates authorized by 28 U.S. Code 636(b)?

Decision: Yes. Opinion by Chief Justice Burger. Vote: 8–0. Stevens did not participate.

Reasons: Section 636(b) provides that: "Any district court of the United States . . . may establish rules pursuant to which any . . . United States magistrate . . . may be assigned within the territorial jurisdiction of such court such . . . duties as are not inconsistent with the Constitution and laws of the United States." That section was designed to increase the overall efficiency of the federal judiciary, which was struggling under heavy caseloads. Under the challenged policy,

> the magistrate may do no more than propose a recommendation. . . . The district judge is free to follow it or wholly to ignore it, or, if he is not satisfied, he may conduct the review in whole or in part anew. The authority—and the responsibility—to make an informed, final determination, . . . remains with the judge.
>
> The magistrate's limited role in this type of case nonetheless substantially assists the district judge in the performance of his judicial function, and benefits both him and the parties. A magistrate's review helps focus the Court's attention on the relevant portions of what may be a voluminous record, from a point of view as neutral as that of an Article III judge. Review also helps the Court move directly to those legal arguments made by the parties that find some support in the record. Finally, the magistrate's report puts before the district judge a preliminary evaluation of the cumulative effect of the evidence in the record, to which the parties may address argument, and in this way narrows the dispute.

That type of preliminary review function is within the contemplation of section 636(b).

It was argued that the magistrate, in accepting referral of all social security benefit cases, functions as a special master. This automatic referral was thus claimed to violate Rule 53(b) of the FRCP, which requires that "reference to a master shall be the exception and not the rule" and made "only upon a showing that some exceptional need requires it." That rule also requires that the findings of fact by a master be accepted by the court unless clearly erroneous. "Under the reference in this case, however, the judge remains free to give the magistrate's recommendation whatever weight the judge decides it merits. It cannot be said, therefore, that the magistrate acts as a special master in the sense that either Rule 53 or the Federal Magistrates Act uses that term." It was nevertheless maintained that the magistrate will act as a master *de facto* because his recommendation will be automatically accepted in every case. "We categorically reject the suggestion that judges will accept, uncritically, recommendations of magistrates."

Aldinger v. *Howard*, 427 U.S. 1 (1976)

Facts: After dismissal from her county job without a hearing, Aldinger brought suit in federal district court under 42 U.S. Code 1983[52] alleging a violation of her constitutional rights. Aldinger named as defendants a county official, his wife, county commissioners, and the county itself. Jurisdiction over the section 1983 claim was invoked under 28 U.S. Code 1343(3). The district court was alleged to have pendent jurisdiction over additional claims against the parties under state law.

The district court dismissed the section 1983 claim against the county. The dismissal was required by *Moor* v. *County of Alameda*, 411 U.S. 693 (1973), and *City of Kenosha* v. *Bruno*, 412 U.S. 507 (1973), which held that section 1983 has no application to a city or county. The claims against the county under state law were also dismissed on the theory that the absence of any independent federal jurisdiction over the county precluded the exercise of pendent jurisdiction by the district court.

Question: Did the district court have pendent jurisdiction over the state law claims against the county under section 1343(3)?

---

[52] Section 1983 makes unlawful the deprivation of constitutional rights under color of state law.

Decision: No. Opinion by Justice Rehnquist. Vote: 6–3, Marshall, Brennan, and Blackmun dissenting.

Reasons: The question of pendent jurisdiction in this case did not concern the litigation of additional state *claims* between parties with respect to whom independent federal jurisdiction existed. Rather, it involved the question whether pendent jurisdiction can be used to implead an additional *party* over which independent federal jurisdiction is lacking. The answer requires consideration of the scope of federal judicial power over cases and controversies under Article III of the Constitution.

In *United Mine Workers v. Gibbs*, 383 U.S. 715 (1966), the Court held that if substantial federal and state claims between parties grow out of a "common nucleus of operative fact" so that the plaintiff would normally be expected to assert both types of claims in one lawsuit, then pendent jurisdiction can constitutionally extend to the claims made under state law. *Gibbs*, however, did not specifically address the issue of whether its holding should also apply when pendent jurisdiction is used to seek the joinder of additional parties rather than claims. When federal jurisdiction already exists over a defendant, it is not unfair to require an answer to a state law claim stemming from a common nucleus of fact. Joining both claims in one lawsuit also serves judicial economy.

> But it is quite another thing to permit a plaintiff, who has asserted a claim against one defendant with respect to which there is federal jurisdiction, to implead an entirely different defendant on the basis of a state law claim over which there is no independent basis of federal jurisdiction, simply because his claim against the first defendant and his claim against the second defendant "derive from a common nucleus of operative fact." . . . True, the same considerations of judicial economy would be served insofar as plaintiff's claims "are such that he would ordinarily be expected to try them all in one judicial proceeding." . . . But the addition of a completely new party would run counter to the well-established principle that federal courts, as opposed to state trial courts of general jurisdiction, are courts of limited jurisdiction marked out by Congress.

The last-mentioned fact is especially significant in the context of this lawsuit, in which federal jurisdiction derives from section 1983 claims. In excluding counties from the coverage of that statute, Congress expressed a policy against federal pendent jurisdiction over such defendants under section 1343(3), at least when premised on a common nucleus of fact forming the basis of section 1983 claims against others.

> Resolution of a claim of pendent party jurisdiction . . . calls for careful attention to the relevant statutory language. . . . [W]e think a fair reading of the language used in section 1343, together with the scope of section 1983, requires a holding that the joinder of a municipal corporation, like the county here, for purposes of asserting a state law claim not within federal diversity jurisdiction, is without the statutory jurisdiction of the district court.

The Court concluded by observing that

> the question of pendent party jurisdiction is "subtle and complex," and we believe that it would be as unwise as it would be unnecessary to lay down any sweeping pronouncement upon the existence or exercise of such jurisdiction. Two observations suffice for the disposition of the type of case before us. If the new party sought to be impleaded is not otherwise subject to federal jurisdiction, there is a more serious obstacle to the exercise of pendent jurisdiction than if parties already before the court are required to litigate a state law claim. Before it can be concluded that such jurisdiction exists, a federal court must satisfy itself not only that Art. III permits it, but that Congress in the statutes conferring jurisdiction has not expressly or by implication negated its existence.

Simon v. Eastern Kentucky Welfare Rights Organization, 426 U.S. 26 (1976)

Facts: Under the Internal Revenue Code, 26 U.S. Code 501(c)(3), a nonprofit hospital is accorded favorable tax treatment[53] if it is "organized and operated exclusively for . . . charitable purposes." In 1956, the Internal Revenue Service (IRS) issued a ruling generally defining what requirements a nonprofit hospital must satisfy to qualify as a charitable organization under section 501(c)(3). One requirement was that the hospital serve indigents without cost or at reduced rates to the extent that its finances permitted. In 1969, the IRS modified its ruling to remove this requirement and to permit a nonprofit hospital to qualify under section 501(c)(3) if it offered only emergency care to indigents without cost.

---

[53] Among other benefits, such hospitals are exempt from income taxation, and their benefactors may deduct from their income the amounts of their donations.

Several indigent persons and organizations composed of indigents sued the secretary of the Treasury and the commissioner of the Internal Revenue Service seeking to have the 1969 modification nullified on the grounds that it was unauthorized under section 501(c)(3) and was issued in violation of the Administrative Procedure Act. The complaint alleged that each individual plaintiff had been denied hospital services on account of indigency by hospitals that the defendants had decided were entitled to the tax benefits of section 501(c)(3). It further alleged that these denials were "encouraged" by the tax benefits that the defendants had unlawfully granted. The district court and court of appeals denied the motion of the defendants to dismiss the complaint on the ground that the plaintiffs lacked standing to sue.

Question: Did the plaintiffs lack standing to sue?

Decision: Yes. Opinion by Justice Powell. Vote: 8-0. Stevens did not participate.

Reasons: Article III of the Constitution limits the jurisdiction of federal courts to "actual cases or controversies. . . . The concept of standing is part of this limitation." It requires that the plaintiff allege "an injury to himself that is likely to be redressed by a favorable decision." Otherwise, the alleged dispute cannot fairly be characterized as a concrete "case" under Article III.

The plaintiff organizations are dedicated to promoting access of the poor to health services. It was established in *Sierra Club* v. *Morton,* 405 U.S. 727 (1972), however, that an organization's abstract concern with a subject is not a substitute for the concrete-injury requirement of Article III. Since the plaintiff organizations alleged no concrete injury to themselves, they can establish standing only as representatives of individual members who suffered such injury. Accordingly, standing was established in this suit only if the individual plaintiffs or members of the organizations were alleged to have suffered the requisite injury caused by the asserted illegal action of the defendants in according tax-exempt status to certain not-for-profit hospitals.

The complaint did allege actual injury to the indigent plaintiffs in the denial of hospital services solely because of indigency. "It is purely speculative," however, whether the denials were caused by the 1969 modified tax ruling or whether they resulted "from decisions made by the hospitals without regard to the tax implications." It is equally speculative whether a favorable decision for the plaintiffs would increase the availability of hospital service to them. Hospitals might choose to forgo favorable tax treatment under section 501(c)(3) to avoid the financial costs of providing the uncompensated services that the plaintiffs seek to require. Accordingly, the plaintiffs lacked standing for failing to establish either that their asserted injuries were the consequence of the challenged action of the defendants, or that the requested relief would redress those injuries.

Thermtron Products, Inc. v. *Hermansdorfer*, 423 U.S. 336 (1976)

Facts: Two citizens of Kentucky filed suit in a Kentucky state court against an Indiana corporation seeking damages for injury arising from an automobile accident. The Indiana corporation had the case removed to a Kentucky federal district court pursuant to 28 U.S. Code 1441. (Section 1441 authorizes such removal by a defendant if the case filed in state court could have been brought initially in federal district court. The state suit at issue here, between residents of diverse states and involving more than $10,000 in controversy, could have been filed originally in federal district court pursuant to 28 U.S. Code 1332.) The district court remanded the case to state court on the ground that it could not try the suit in the foreseeable future because its civil docket was so crowded. The defendant's appeal of the remand order was denied by the court of appeals on the ground that 28 U.S. Code 1447(d) prohibited review of such orders.

Question: Did the federal district court improperly remand the case to state court?

Decision: Yes. Opinion by Justice White. Vote: 5–3, Rehnquist, Burger, and Stewart dissenting. Stevens did not participate.

Reasons: 28 U.S. Code 1447(c) authorizes a federal district court to remand a case to the state court if it was "removed improvidently and without jurisdiction." Section 1447(d) forbids appellate review of remand orders issued pursuant to section 1447(c). The remand order at issue here, however, was made for reasons unmentioned in section 1447(c).

> The determining factor was the District Court's heavy docket, which [it] thought would unjustly delay plaintiffs in going to trial on the merits of their action. This consideration . . . is plainly irrelevant . . . to the question whether [the case] was removed "improvidently and without jurisdiction." . . .
> Removal of cases from state courts has been allowed since the First Judiciary Act, and the right to remove has never been dependent on the state of the federal court's docket. It is indeed unfortunate if the judicial manpower provided by

Congress in any district is insufficient to try with reasonable promptness the cases properly filed in or removed to that court in accordance with the applicable statutes.

The district court thus exceeded its authority in remanding on grounds not permitted by section 1447(c). Accordingly, section 1447(d) did not bar appellate review, since its prohibition is triggered only when a trial judge purports to remand a case on the ground that it was removed "improvidently and without jurisdiction."

Government Employment

There are at present approximately 11.2 million civilian federal, state, and municipal employees. That figure constitutes approximately 18.4 percent of total employment in the United States. In 1955, the comparable figures were 5.7 million and 13.1 percent. The increased size and importance of government employment has doubtless contributed in part to an increase in litigation over the rights of government employees. This term, the decisions of the Court generally reflected a reluctance to interfere with the employment practices of state and local governments.

In *McCarthy* v. *Philadelphia Civil Service Commission*, 424 U.S. 645 (1976), the Court upheld the constitutionality of a residency requirement for municipal employees. In light of *McCarthy*, many cities have imposed or are considering imposing such residency requirements in the belief that it will assist their depressed local economies.[54]

The Court also retreated from the spirit of recent decisions in which a property or liberty interest in government employment entitled to protection under the due process clause of the Fourteenth Amendment was recognized.[55] It ruled that neither constitutionally protected property or liberty interests were involved in the discharge of a policeman for reasons alleged to be false and stigmatizing (*Bishop* v. *Wood*, 426 U.S. 341 [1976]).

The authority of government to establish grooming standards and a mandatory retirement age for policemen was upheld in *Kelley* v. *Johnson*, 425 U.S. 238 (1976), and *Massachusetts Board of Retirement* v. *Murgia*, 427 U.S. 307 (1976). In addition, the Court held that the discharge of striking teachers by a school board involved in triggering the strike did not violate constitutional due process (*Horton-*

---

[54] See Neal R. Peirce, " 'Work Here, Live Here' Rules: An Overdue Reform," *Washington Post*, August 30, 1976.

[55] See Board of Regents v. Roth, 408 U.S. 564 (1972); Perry v. Sindermann, 408 U.S. 593 (1972).

ville Joint School District No. 1 v. *Hortonville Education Association,* 426 U.S. 482 [1976]).

Government employees won a victory in *Fitzpatrick* v. *Bitzer,* 427 U.S. 445 (1976). There the Court upheld the constitutionality of a federal statute authorizing federal courts to award money damages and attorneys' fees in suits brought by state employees against a state to redress discrimination in employment on the basis of race, color, religion, sex, or national origin. The Court rejected the claim that the Eleventh Amendment barred such relief.

McCarthy v. Philadelphia Civil Service Commission, 424 U.S. 645 (1976)

Facts: A Philadelphia fireman's employment was terminated because he moved his residence outside the city to New Jersey in violation of an ordinance requiring municipal employees to reside in Philadelphia. The fireman brought suit challenging the constitutionality of the residency requirement on the ground that it violated his right of interstate travel.

Question: Can municipalities constitutionally impose a city residency requirement on their employees?

Decision: Yes. Per curiam opinion. Vote: 9–0.

Reasons: In prior decisions involving welfare benefits and the right to vote, *durational* residency requirements were held violative of the constitutional right of interstate travel. However, no decision has questioned conditioning entitlement to these rights or municipal employment on satisfying an appropriately defined and uniformly applied bona fide residency requirement. The challenged Philadelphia ordinance making residence a condition of city employment involves that kind of bona fide continuing residency requirement.

Bishop v. Wood, 426 U.S. 341 (1976)

Facts: Discharged without a hearing, a city policeman brought suit claiming a procedural due process right to a pretermination hearing. He argued that the due process clause of the Fourteenth Amendment protected both his "property" interest in continued employment and his "liberty" interest in avoiding any stigma that would attach to his discharge. The property interest of the policeman was asserted to derive from a city ordinance that classified him as a "permanent employee."

The district court interpreted the ordinance to authorize the termination of permanent employees "at will," so long as the dischargee is provided written reasons for the action if he so requests. It thus concluded that the policeman lacked any constitutionally cognizable property interest in continued employment. The claim to a liberty interest was rejected because the adverse reasons for discharge of the policeman were provided orally and exclusively to him. The court of appeals affirmed.

Question: Did the discharge of the policeman implicate any property or liberty interests protected by the due process clause of the Fourteenth Amendment?

Decision: No. Opinion by Justice Stevens. Vote: 5–4, Brennan, White, Marshall, and Blackmun dissenting.

Reasons: In *Board of Regents* v. *Roth*, 408 U.S. 564 (1972), the Court concluded that property interests protected by the due process clause derive not from the Constitution but from an independent source such as state law "that support claims of entitlement to [certain] benefits." In this case, state law does not support the policeman's claim of entitlement to a pretermination hearing because it authorized his discharge at will. Accordingly, the discharge did not deprive him of a constitutionally protected property interest.

The claim of a deprivation of a liberty interest is equally without foundation. In *Roth*, the Court held that the failure of a state college to retain an untenured teacher, of itself, did not violate any liberty interest in seeking future employment. "This same conclusion applies to the discharge of a public employee whose position is terminable at the will of the employer when there is no public disclosure of the reasons for the discharge."

It was claimed, nonetheless, that since adverse reasons for the discharge that were alleged to be false were provided to the policeman during pretrial discovery, he would be stigmatized in the absence of a judicial hearing to clear his good name. But since these communications occurred after the discharge for which the policeman sought redress, "it surely cannot provide retroactive support for his claim."

> The federal court is not the appropriate forum in which to review the multitude of personnel decisions that are made daily by public agencies. We must accept the harsh fact that numerous individual mistakes are inevitable in the day-to-day administration of our affairs. The United States Constitution cannot feasibly be construed to require federal judicial review for every such error. In the absence of any claim that

the public employer was motivated by a desire to curtail or to penalize the exercise of an employee's constitutionally protected rights, we must presume that official action was regular and, if erroneous, can best be corrected in other ways. The Due Process Clause of the Fourteenth Amendment is not a guarantee against incorrect or ill-advised personnel decisions.

Kelley v. *Johnson,* 425 U.S. 238 (1976)

Facts: A policeman challenged the constitutionality of police department regulations establishing grooming standards. The regulations governed the style and length of hair and the wearing of sideburns, mustaches, beards, and wigs. A federal district court sustained the challenge, reasoning that choice of personal appearance is a type of "liberty" protected by the Fourteenth Amendment and that the police department failed to establish any public need for the standards sufficient to justify intrusions on that liberty. The police department claimed that the grooming standards promoted esprit de corps within the department and made policemen more readily identifiable by the public.

Question: Are the challenged police department regulations establishing grooming standards unconstitutional?

Decision: No. Opinion by Justice Rehnquist. Vote: 6–2, Brennan and Marshall dissenting. Stevens did not participate.

Reasons: Past decisions provide little guidance on whether matters of personal appearance involve liberty interests protected by the Fourteenth Amendment. Assuming an affirmative answer, however, the policeman's claim was nevertheless rejected.

A state or political subdivision has an interest as an employer in regulating the conduct of its employees which differs significantly from the powers it possesses in relation to the citizenry in general. In *Civil Service Commission* v. *Letter Carriers,* 413 U.S. 548 (1973), and *Broadrick* v. *Oklahoma,* 413 U.S. 601 (1973), the Court found constitutional justification for comprehensive restrictions on the political activity of both federal and state employees. This case involving grooming standards involved a far lesser invasion of any constitutionally protected liberty interests.

The promotion of safety of persons and property is unquestionably at the core of the State's police power, and virtually all state and local governments employ a uniformed police force to aid in the accomplishment of that purpose. Choice of organization, dress, and equipment for law enforcement personnel is a decision entitled to the same sort of presumption of legislative validity as are state choices designed to promote other aims within the cognizance of the State's police power.

The challenged grooming regulations, therefore, must be sustained if they are rationally connected to the promotion of safety of persons or property by the police department. The choice to impose grooming standards to promote uniformity of appearance

> may be based on a desire to make police officers readily recognizable to members of the public, or a desire for the *esprit de corps* which such similarity is felt to inculcate within the police force itself. Either one is a sufficiently rational justification for regulations so as to defeat [the policeman's] claim based on the liberty guaranty of the Fourteenth Amendment.

Massachusetts Board of Retirement v. *Murgia*, 427 U.S. 307 (1976)

Facts: A Massachusetts state law requires all uniformed state police officers to retire at the age of fifty. A retired officer who was admitted to be physically and mentally able to perform satisfactorily after the age of fifty brought suit attacking the constitutionality of the statute. He contended that the mandatory retirement requirement constituted invidious discrimination on the basis of age in contravention of the equal protection clause of the Fourteenth Amendment. A three-judge federal district court ruled in favor of the retired officer.

Question: Does the Massachusetts retirement statute for uniformed state police officers violate the equal protection clause?

Decision: No. Per curiam opinion. Vote: 7–1, Marshall dissenting. Stevens did not participate.

Reasons: The provision for mandatory retirement at the age of fifty must be sustained if it has a rational basis. *San Antonio Independent School District* v. *Rodriguez*, 411 U.S. 1 (1973), established that more vigorous equal protection scrutiny is required only if a legislative classification affects a "fundamental" right or operates to the special disadvantage of a "suspect class." The mandatory retirement provision involves neither situation.

The right of an individual to be employed by the government is not fundamental, and uniformed police officers over the age of fifty fail to qualify as a suspect class under *Rodriguez*. There the Court described a suspect class as one "saddled with such disabilities, or subjected to such a history of purposeful unequal treatment, or relegated to such a position of political powerlessness as to command extraordinary protection from the majoritarian political process."

The Court declined to hold that, in all instances, age should be considered a suspect classification.

> While the treatment of the aged in this Nation has not been wholly free of discrimination, such persons, unlike, say, those who have been discriminated against on the basis of race or national origin, have not experienced a "history of purposeful unequal treatment" or been subjected to unique disabilities on the basis of stereotyped characteristics not truly indicative of their abilities.

The choice of the age of fifty for mandatory retirement rationally furthers the state objective of ensuring that all its uniformed police are physically capable of performing their jobs.

> Since physical ability generally declines with age, mandatory retirement at 50 serves to remove from police service those whose fitness for uniformed work presumptively has diminished with age. . . . There is no indication that [the challenged statute] has the effect of excluding from service so few officers who are in fact unqualified as to render age 50 a criterion wholly unrelated to the objective of the statute.

Although the state could advance its objective more precisely by individualized testing of police officers after the age of fifty, the equal protection clause, when rationality is the test, does not command that it do so.

Hortonville Joint School District No. 1 v. Hortonville Education Association, 426 U.S. 482 (1976)

Facts: A teachers' union went on strike in violation of Wisconsin law after failing to conclude a collective-bargaining agreement with a local school board. After the striking teachers were provided notice and a hearing to explain their actions, the school board voted to terminate their employment. The union brought suit in state court alleging, *inter alia*, that the board's lack of neutrality in the collective-bargaining dispute disqualified it from evaluating and determining the appropriate sanctions for the striking teachers under the due process clause of the Fourteenth Amendment. The Wisconsin Supreme Court sustained the union's claim.

Question: Did the due process clause disqualify the school board from making the decision to terminate the employment of the striking teachers?

Decision: No. Opinion by Chief Justice Burger. Vote: 6–3, Stewart, Brennan, and Marshall dissenting.

Reasons: Although the school board was involved in the collective-bargaining negotiations which led to the teachers' strike, there was nothing in the record to indicate that its members harbored any personal animosity or had a personal or financial conflict of interest that would cast doubt on their impartiality. Thus, the narrow issue in this case was whether the involvement of the board in the negotiations constitutionally barred its decision to fire the striking teachers.

Due process is a flexible concept shaped in part by the "individual's stake in the decision at issue as well as the State's interest in a particular procedure for making it." Here, the interests of the teachers were to avoid termination of employment. But since their unlawful striking activity was conceded, there was no danger of a factual error on this critical issue. On the other hand, the interest of the state in vesting the school board with authority to terminate the employment of striking teachers is substantial. The decision of the board whether or not to exercise that authority implicates the interests of the school system, parents and children, and taxpayers. The decision had significant governmental policy-making aspects that state law vests exclusively in elected local school boards. Moreover,

> the state legislature has given to the Board the power to employ and dismiss teachers, as a part of the balance it has struck in the area of municipal labor relations; altering those statutory powers as a matter of federal due process clearly changes that balance. Permitting the Board to make the decision at issue here preserves its control over school district affairs, leaves the balance of power in labor relations where the state legislature struck it, and assures that the decision whether to dismiss the teachers will be made by the body responsible for that decision under state law.

Accordingly, constitutional due process did not disqualify the board from making the decision to terminate the employment of the striking teachers.

Fitzpatrick v. Bitzer, 427 U.S. 445 (1976)

Facts: The 1972 amendments to Title VII of the Civil Rights Act of 1964 authorize federal courts to award money damages and attorneys' fees in suits brought by private individuals against a state to redress employment discrimination on the basis of "race, color, religion, sex, or national origin." Present and retired male state employees of Connecticut brought suit claiming that the state's retirement benefit plan discriminated against them on the basis of sex in violation of Title VII. The federal district court upheld the claim and granted injunctive relief. It concluded, however, that the Eleventh Amendment precluded an award of damages or attorneys' fees against the state.

Question: Does the Eleventh Amendment prohibit an award of damages or attorneys' fees against a state in private suits brought under Title VII of the Civil Rights Act?

Decision: No. Opinion by Justice Rehnquist. Vote: 9–0.

Reasons: Generally speaking, the Eleventh Amendment prohibits federal courts from entertaining a private suit against a state without its consent. For this purpose, a suit against a state is one that seeks monetary damages that will be paid out of the state treasury.

To a limited extent, however, the Fourteenth Amendment eroded the immunity of a state under the Eleventh Amendment. Section 5 of the Fourteenth Amendment expressly authorizes Congress to enact "appropriate legislation" to enforce its substantive provisions. Section 1 of the Fourteenth Amendment prohibits a state, *inter alia,* from denying "any person . . . the equal protection of the laws." The 1972 amendments of Title VII constitute appropriate legislation to enforce section 1.

> When Congress acts pursuant to section 5, . . . it is exercising . . . authority under one section of a constitutional Amendment whose other sections by their own terms embody limitations on state authority. We think that Congress may, in determining what is "appropriate legislation" for the purpose of enforcing the provisions of the Fourteenth Amendment, provide for private suits against States or state officials which are constitutionally impermissible in other contexts.

Church and State

In 1971, the Supreme Court established a three-pronged test to determine whether statutes providing state aid to church-related schools violate the establishment clause of the First Amendment.[56] To satisfy that clause, the statute must have a secular legislative purpose; its primary effect must neither advance nor inhibit religion; and it must avoid fostering an excessive government entanglement with religion. The Court has failed, however, to apply its three-pronged test in accord with clear and consistent principles.[57] This has resulted in considerable confusion over what types and quantity of state aid to church-related schools will pass constitutional scrutiny.

This term, the Court approved a state subsidy program benefiting church-related colleges that required annual legislative funding (*Roemer v. Board of Public Works of Maryland*, 426 U.S. 736 [1976]). Only last term, in contrast, the Court indicated that state aid requiring continuing appropriations would be unconstitutional because it would increase the likelihood of political divisions along religious lines, a principal evil that the establishment clause was designed to prevent (*Meek v. Pittenger*, 421 U.S. 349 [1975]). Ironically, the inability of the Court to construct a clear dividing line between constitutionally permissible and impermissible state aid to church-related schools has probably promoted political debate and divisiveness on this issue in legislative bodies.

Roemer v. *Board of Public Works of Maryland*, 426 U.S. 736 (1976)

Facts: A Maryland statute authorizes the payment of state funds to private colleges or universities within the state that satisfy certain minimum criteria and which refrain from awarding "only seminarian or theological degrees." The state subsidy is provided annually, and its amount is based upon the number of full-time pupils, excluding those in seminary or theological academic programs, attending the qualifying institution. No part of the state subsidy may be used for sectarian purposes. The administration of the subsidy program is entrusted to the Board of Public Works and the Council for Higher Education. The council determines which institutions qualify for a subsidy and which are ineligible because they award primarily theological or seminary degrees. The council also requires qualifying

---

[56] Lemon v. Kurtzman, 403 U.S. 602 (1971).

[57] Compare Tilton v. Richardson, 403 U.S. 672 (1971), Hunt v. McNair, 413 U.S. 743 (1973), and Lemon v. Kurtzman, 411 U.S. 193 (1973) (Lemon II), with Committee for Public Education and Religious Liberty v. Nyquist, 413 U.S. 756 (1973), Levitt v. Committee for Public Education and Religious Liberty, 413 U.S. 472 (1973), and Meek v. Pittenger, 421 U.S. 349 (1975).

institutions to provide affidavits describing the specific nonsectarian uses that are planned for the subsidy. Sufficient documentation of the expenditure of state funds must be maintained to permit an audit confirming that no expenditures have been made for sectarian purposes.

In 1972, eighteen institutions qualified to receive $1.8 million in state funds. Five of the eighteen institutions were church-related and were to receive $603,000. Before disbursement, however, suit was brought challenging the constitutionality of the state subsidies as a violation of the establishment clause of the First Amendment. The district court rejected the claim.

Question: Does the Maryland program of state subsidies to private colleges and universities violate the establishment clause of the First Amendment?

Decision: No. Plurality opinion by Justice Blackmun. Vote: 5–4, White and Rehnquist concurring, Stevens, Brennan, Stewart, and Marshall dissenting.

Reasons: The First Amendment, as applicable to the states through the Fourteenth Amendment, prohibits any law "respecting an establishment of religion." That command, however, has never been interpreted to require a "hermetic separation" between the state and religious activity. "Neutrality is what is required. The State must confine itself to secular objectives, and neither advance nor impede religious activity."

The Court has developed a three-pronged test to determine whether statutes affording state aid to church-related schools satisfy the establishment clause. First, the statute must have a secular legislative purpose. Second, the primary effect must neither advance nor inhibit religious practices. Third, it must not foster an excessive government entanglement with religion. It was conceded that the purpose of Maryland's subsidy program is "the secular one of supporting private higher education generally, as an economic alternative to a wholly public system."

With regard to the primary-effect test, *Hunt* v. *McNair*, 413 U.S. 734 (1973), established two propositions: "(1) that no state aid at all [may] go to institutions that are so 'pervasively sectarian' that secular activities cannot be separated from sectarian ones, and (2) that if secular activities *can* be separated out, they alone may be funded." (Emphasis in original.)

The district court concluded that the recipient church-related colleges are not pervasively sectarian. It found that only one of them reported to the Catholic Church. Attendance at religious exercises

131

was not required. Mandatory courses in religion or theology were taught in an atmosphere of intellectual freedom. Although some classes commenced with prayer, that fact alone did not inject religion into the academic program. Recruitment of faculty and selection of students were made without regard to religion. The findings of the district court were not "clearly erroneous" and therefore justified the conclusion that the church-related colleges were not pervasively sectarian.

The district court also found that the state subsidies assisted only "the secular side" of the recipient institutions. By statute, none of the funds can be used for sectarian purposes. "We must assume that the colleges, and the Council [for Higher Education], will exercise their delegated control over use of the funds in compliance with the statutory, and therefore the constitutional, mandate." Accordingly, Maryland's subsidy program satisfies the primary-effect test under the *Hunt* standards.

The excessive-entanglement test in this case focuses on the degree of government supervision needed to distribute the subsidies and assure their expenditure for proper purposes. Because the church-related institutions perform essentially secular educational functions, there is little danger that nominally secular activities will be infused with religious significance. Consequently, state officials will not have to monitor secular classes to ensure their avoidance of religious indoctrination. Although the funding is provided annually and is subject to legislative review, this fact alone does not constitute excessive entanglement. The potential for political divisiveness on religious grounds is reduced in this case because the aided institutions serve a widely dispersed constituency as opposed to one of local students. Moreover, more than two-thirds of the aided institutions lack any religious affiliation. Finally, any audit of the state funds will be "quick and non-judgmental." All these factors cumulatively considered supported the conclusion that any entanglement with religion involved in Maryland's subsidy program would not be constitutionally excessive.

Serbian Eastern Orthodox Diocese for the United States of America and Canada v. Dionisije Milivojevich, 426 U.S. 696 (1976)

Facts: In 1963, the Holy Assembly of Bishops and the Holy Synod of the Serbian Orthodox Church (Mother Church) suspended and ultimately removed Dionisije Milivojevich (Dionisije) as bishop of the American-Canadian Diocese of that church. The Mother Church also reorganized the American-Canadian Diocese into three dioceses. In 1964 the Holy Assembly and Holy Synod defrocked Dionisije as a bishop and cleric of the Mother Church. As a consequence of these actions, Dionisije lost control over the assets of the American-Canadian Diocese held in a not-for-profit corporation. He brought suit in Illinois state court seeking to enjoin the Mother Church from interference with diocesan assets and a declaration that he was the true diocesan bishop. The Illinois Supreme Court invalidated Dionisije's removal and defrockment on the ground that the Mother Church proceedings resulting in those actions were "arbitrary" in failing to conform to the church's own constitution and penal code. The court also ruled that the diocesan reorganization was invalid because it exceeded the authority of the Mother Church to effectuate such changes without diocesan approval. Review of the decision of the court was sought on the theory that its inquiry and interpretation of the rules and laws of the Mother Church violated the establishment clause of the First Amendment.

Question: Did the judgment of the Illinois Supreme Court contravene the establishment clause in rejecting the decisions of the highest ecclesiastical tribunals of the Mother Church and substituting its own inquiry into church polity and resolutions?

Decision: Yes. Opinion by Justice Brennan. Vote: 7–2, Rehnquist and Stevens dissenting.

Reasons: At the outset, the Court noted that

> where resolution of the disputes cannot be made without extensive inquiry by civil courts into religious law and polity, the First and Fourteenth Amendments mandate that civil courts shall not disturb the decisions of the highest ecclesiastical tribunal within a church of hierarchial polity, but must accept such decisions as binding on them, in their application to the religious issues of doctrine or polity before them.

The main religious dispute in this case concerns the validity of the removal and defrockment of Dionisije. Its resolution requires an inquiry into ecclesiastical matters not fit for civil tribunals. Although the determination of the removal and defrockment issues would also decide the control of church property, that fact does not justify intervention by civil courts. As the Court observed in *Presbyterian Church* v. *Hull Church,* 393 U.S. 440 (1969):

> First Amendment values are plainly jeopardized when church property litigation is made to turn on the resolution by civil

courts of controversies over religious doctrine and practice. If civil courts undertake to resolve such controversies in order to adjudicate the property dispute, the hazards are ever present in inhibiting the free development of religious doctrine and of implicating secular interests in matters of purely ecclesiastical concern. . . . [T]he [First] Amendment therefore commands civil courts to decide church property disputes without resolving underlying controversies over religious doctrine.

The Illinois Supreme Court concluded that the decisions of the Mother Church were arbitrary because made in violation of its own laws and procedures. Whether or not narrowly limited civil court review of decisions of church tribunals might be available if "fraud" or "collusion" is alleged, it is clear that review is unavailable to test for arbitrariness

in the sense of an inquiry whether the decisions of the highest ecclesiastical tribunal of a hierarchical church complied with church laws and regulations. . . . For civil courts to analyze whether the ecclesiastical actions of a church judicatory are in that sense "arbitrary" must inherently entail inquiry into the procedures that canon or ecclesiastical law supposedly require the church adjudicatory to follow, or else into the substantive criteria by which they are supposedly to decide the ecclesiastical question. But this is exactly the inquiry that the First Amendment prohibits.

Accordingly, the Illinois Supreme Court violated the First Amendment in overturning the removal and defrockment of Dionisije by the Mother Church on the ground of arbitrariness.

Similarly, the state court erred in holding that the reorganization of the American-Canadian Diocese into three dioceses exceeded the Mother Church's jurisdiction. In reaching that decision, "the Supreme Court of Illinois substituted its interpretation of the Diocesan and Mother Church constitutions for that of the highest ecclesiastical tribunals in which church law vests authority to make that interpretation. This the First and Fourteenth Amendments forbid."

Aliens

Over the past decade, approximately 375,000 aliens have been admitted annually for permanent residence in the United States.[58] Rough estimates place the number of illegal aliens in the United States

[58] See Department of Justice, *1975 Annual Report of the Attorney General*, p. 166.

in the millions,[59] many of whom enter the country in search of employment. The decisions of the Court concerning aliens thus have considerable impact.

This term the Court continued to afford special protection to lawfully admitted aliens[60] in holding unconstitutional a U.S. Civil Service Commission regulation excluding them from employment by the federal government and a Puerto Rican statute excluding them from employment as civil engineers (*Hampton v. Wong*, 426 U.S. 88 [1976]; *Examining Board of Engineers, Architects, and Surveyors v. Flores de Otero*, 426 U.S. 572 [1976]). However, the Court upheld restrictions on the rights of aliens to receive Medicare benefits (*Mathews v. Diaz*, 426 U.S. 67 [1976]).

With regard to illegal aliens, the decisions of the Court bolstered the authority of the state and federal governments in detecting and deterring illegal entry. In *DeCanas v. Bica*, 424 U.S. 351 (1976), the Court upheld a California statute prohibiting the knowing employment of illegal aliens that injures lawful resident workers.[61] In *United States v. Martinez-Fuerte*, 428 U.S. 543 (1976), the Court upheld the use of fixed traffic checkpoints by border patrol officers for the purpose of discovering illegal aliens (see section entitled "Powers of the Police and Prosecutors").

Hampton v. Wong, 426 U.S. 88 (1976)

Facts: A United States Civil Service Commission regulation prohibited resident aliens from employment in the federal competitive civil service. Resident aliens brought suit challenging the constitutionality of the regulation on the ground that it arbitrarily discriminated between citizens and noncitizens in violation of the due process clause of the Fifth Amendment.

---

[59] See statement of Leonard F. Chapman, commissioner of the Immigration and Naturalization Service, before the Senate Subcommittee on Immigration and Naturalization, 94th Congress, 2nd session, March 17, 1976.

[60] In Graham v. Richardson, 403 U.S. 365 (1971), the Court concluded that state laws classifying persons on the basis of their being aliens are inherently suspect and can be constitutionally justified only by a compelling state interest. *Graham* struck down an Arizona statute requiring aliens but not citizens to satisfy a durational residency requirement to qualify for welfare benefits. The Court invalidated a state statute excluding aliens from the practice of law in In re Griffiths, 413 U.S. 717 (1973). In Sugarman v. Dougall, 413 U.S. 634 (1973), the Court held that a New York civil service statute excluding aliens from appointment to any position in the competitive class violated the equal protection clause of the Fourteenth Amendment.

[61] Pending legislation in Congress would make it unlawful under federal law to employ illegal aliens knowingly. See H.R. 1663, 95th Congress, 1st session (1977).

Question: Is the challenged Civil Service Commission regulation constitutional?

Decision: No. Opinion by Justice Stevens. Vote: 5–4, Rehnquist, Burger, White, and Blackmun dissenting.

Reasons: The due process clause of the Fifth Amendment and the equal protection clause of the Fourteenth Amendment limit the authority of the federal and state governments to classify persons subject to their respective jurisdictions. The constitutional mandates of due process and equal protection require that both the federal and state governments "govern impartially." The guarantees of due process and equal protection are not coextensive, however. Equal protection provides greater safeguards against arbitrary discrimination by the states. In addition,

> there may be overriding national interests which justify selective federal legislation that would be unacceptable for an individual State. On the other hand, when a federal rule is applicable to only a limited territory, such as the District of Columbia, or an insular possession, and when there is no special national interest involved, the Due Process Clause has been construed as having the same significance as the Equal Protection Clause.

At issue here is a federal regulation with nationwide application. The federal government possesses paramount power over immigration and naturalization. "Overriding national interests may provide a justification for a citizenship requirement in the federal service even though an identical requirement may not be enforced by a State."[62] On the other hand, aliens are a disadvantaged class lacking the franchise and familiarity with our language and customs. The challenged regulation deprives this group of a significant economic interest by making them ineligible for employment in a major sector of the economy. Accordingly, some judicial scrutiny of the discriminatory features of the regulation is constitutionally mandated.

> When the Federal Government asserts an overriding national interest as justification for a discriminatory rule which would violate the Equal Protection Clause if adopted by a

---

[62] In *Sugarman v. Dougall*, 413 U.S. 634 (1973), the Court struck down a New York civil service statute excluding aliens from appointment to any position in the competitive class on the ground that it violated the equal protection clause. The *Sugarman* decision, however, did not preclude states from making individual determinations that particular persons could be denied employment for non-citizenship or requiring that a class of sensitive employment positions be reserved for citizens.

State, due process requires that there be a legitimate basis for presuming that the rule was actually intended to serve that interest. If the agency which promulgates the rule has direct responsibility for fostering or protecting that interest, it may reasonably be presumed that the asserted interest was the actual predicate for the rule. That presumption would, of course, be fortified by an appropriate statement of reasons identifying the relevant interest. Alternatively, if the rule were expressly mandated by the Congress or the President, we might presume that any interest which might rationally be served by the rule did in fact give rise to its adoption.

In this case . . . several interests [have been identified] which the Congress or the President might deem sufficient to justify the exclusion of noncitizens from the federal service. . . . [F]or example, . . . the broad exclusion may facilitate the President's negotiation of treaties with foreign powers by enabling him to offer employment opportunities to citizens of a given foreign country in exchange for reciprocal concessions—an offer he could not make if those aliens were already eligible for federal jobs. Alternatively, . . . reserving the federal service for citizens [may provide] an appropriate incentive to aliens to qualify for naturalization and thereby to participate more effectively in our society. [In addition], the citizenship requirement has been imposed in the United States with substantial consistency for over 100 years and accords with international law and the practice of most foreign countries. Finally, . . . the need for undivided loyalty in certain sensitive positions clearly justifies a citizenship requirement in at least some parts of the federal service, and . . . the broad exclusion serves the valid administrative purpose of avoiding the trouble and expense of classifying those positions which properly belong in executive or sensitive categories.

The last interest, however, is the only one which could reasonably be presumed to have influenced the Civil Service Commission in adopting the challenged regulation. This point is critical because neither the President nor the Congress has ever required the commission to adopt the regulation. It may be assumed that both these institutions, with responsibilities over naturalization and foreign affairs, could constitutionally have mandated the regulation for the legitimate purposes of either encouraging aliens to become naturalized or assisting the President in treaty negotiations. The Civil Service Commission, however, lacks any authority to act in these areas of concern. Its "business . . . [is] to adopt and enforce regulations which will best promote the efficiency of the federal civil service." In fulfilling its duties in this regard, the commission's regulation might be justified by the "administrative desirability of having one simple rule excluding all noncitizens when it is manifest that citizenship is an appropriate and legitimate requirement for some important and sensitive positions," but

> for several reasons that justification is unacceptable in this case. The Civil Service Commission . . . has an obligation to perform its responsibilities with some degree of expertise, and to make known the reasons for its important decisions. There is nothing in the record before us, nor in matter of which we may properly take judicial notice, to indicate that the Commission actually made any considered evaluation of the relative desirability of a simple exclusionary rule on the one hand, or the value to the service of enlarging the pool of eligible employees on the other. Nor can we reasonably infer that the administrative burden of establishing the job classifications for which citizenship is an appropriate requirement would be a particularly onerous task for an expert in personnel matters. . . . Of greater significance, however, is the quality of the interest at stake. Any fair balancing of the public interest in avoiding the wholesale deprivation of employment opportunities caused by the Commission's indiscriminate policy, as opposed to what may be nothing more than a hypothetical justification, requires rejection of the argument of administrative convenience in this case.

Postscript: After *Wong* was decided, President Ford issued an executive order barring aliens from the civil service (Executive Order No. 11,935, *Federal Register*, vol. 41 [1976], p. 37301).

Examining Board of Engineers, Architects and Surveyors v. *Flores de Otero*, 426 U.S. 572 (1976)

Facts: A Puerto Rican statute permitted only U.S. citizens to practice privately as civil engineers. Otherwise qualified aliens brought suit under 42 U.S. Code 1983 challenging the constitutionality of that statute in the federal district court in Puerto Rico. The jurisdiction of the district court was invoked under 28 U.S. Code 1343(3). That section gives district courts jurisdiction over suits alleging deprivation of federal constitutional rights under color of any "State law." Section 1983 authorizes "every person" to sue to redress the deprivation of constitutional rights under color of law "of any State or Territory." The defendants claimed that jurisdiction was lacking under section 1343(3) because Puerto Rico was a territory, not a state, and the section 1983 actions challenged a territorial, not a state law.

The district court rejected the challenge to its jurisdiction and upheld constitutional attack by the plaintiffs on the Puerto Rican statute.

Question: Were the decisions of the district court on the jurisdictional and constitutional issues correct?

Decision: Yes. Opinion by Justice Blackmun. Vote: 7–1, Rehnquist dissenting. Stevens did not participate.

Reasons: Although section 1343(3) omits mention of constitutional deprivations under color of territorial law as opposed to state law, its legislative history clearly shows a design to encompass all suits authorized by 42 U.S. Code 1983. Accordingly, since section 1983 authorizes constitutional attacks on territorial statutes, jurisdiction was properly invoked under section 1343(3).

The constitutional issue turns largely on the question of the extent to which federal constitutional protections extend to residents of Puerto Rico. Although past decisions on that issue lack a consistent theory, it is clear that under *Downes* v. *Bidwell*, 182 U.S. 244 (1901), and *Balzac* v. *Puerto Rico*, 258 U.S. 298 (1922), such residents are protected by the due process clause of the Fifth Amendment and the equal protection clause of the Fourteenth Amendment. Under either of these guarantees, "the statutory restrictions on the ability of aliens to engage in the otherwise lawful private practice of civil engineering is plainly unconstitutional." Recent decisions in *Graham* v. *Richardson*, 403 U.S. 365 (1971), *Sugarman* v. *Dougall*, 413 U.S. 634 (1973), and *In re Griffiths*, 413 U.S. 717 (1973), establish that state or territorial statutory classifications based upon alienage will be upheld only if necessary to accomplish a substantial and constitutionally permissible objective.

Puerto Rico offered three justifications for its virtual ban of aliens from private civil engineering. First, it was alleged that the statute was designed to prevent the influx of Spanish-speaking aliens into the field of civil engineering. That discriminatory purpose violates both the equal protection and due process clauses, however, and conflicts with the federal government's plenary authority over the regulation of immigration.

The second asserted justification was to raise the low standard of living of American citizens in Puerto Rico. That type of purpose, however, was held constitutionally impermissible more than fifty years ago in *Truax* v. *Raich*, 293 U.S. 33 (1915).

Third, the discrimination against aliens was claimed to advance the legitimate interest of providing civil engineering clients an assurance of financial accountability if a building for which the engineer is responsible collapses within 10 years of construction. . . . [But] United States citizenship is not a guarantee that a civil engineer will continue to reside in Puerto Rico or even in the United States, and it bears no particular or rational relationship to skill, competence, or financial responsibility. . . . Puerto Rico has available to it other ample tools to achieve the goal of an engineer's financial responsibility without indiscriminately prohibiting the private practice of civil engineering by a class of otherwise qualified professionals.

Mathews v. *Diaz*, 426 U.S. 67 (1976)

Facts: Under the Social Security Act, 42 U.S. Code 1395o(2), resident citizens who are sixty-five or older are eligible to participate in the Medicare supplemental insurance program. An alien, however, is denied eligibility unless, in addition to satisfying the age requirement, he has been admitted for permanent residence and has resided in the United States for at least five years. Aliens who were excluded from the Medicare supplemental insurance program for failing to meet either the permanent or durational residency requirements brought suit challenging their constitutionality. A three-judge federal district court held that the challenged eligibility requirements unjustifiably discriminated against aliens in violation of the due process clause of the Fifth Amendment.

Question: May Congress constitutionally limit the eligibility of aliens for the Medicare supplemental insurance program to those who have been admitted for permanent residence and have resided within the United States for five years?

Decision: Yes. Opinion by Justice Stevens. Vote: 9–0.

Reasons: Although the due process clause protects aliens and citizens alike, Congress, in the exercise of its broad power over naturalization and immigration, may establish rules for aliens that would be unacceptable if applied to citizens.

In particular, the fact that Congress has provided some welfare benefits for citizens does not require it to provide like benefits for *all* aliens. Neither the overnight visitor, the unfriendly agent of a hostile foreign power, the resident diplomat, nor the illegal entrant, can advance even a colorable constitutional claim to a share in the bounty that a conscientious sovereign makes available to its own citizens and *some* of its guests. The decision to share that bounty with our guests may take into account the character of the relationship between the alien and this country: Congress may decide that as the alien's tie grows stronger, so does the strength of his claim to an equal share of that munificence. [Emphasis in original.]

Matters concerning aliens involve foreign policy issues over which the legislative branch or the executive branch exercises primary responsibility. Those branches need broad latitude in dealing with aliens because of the rapidly changing world environment. Accordingly, the judiciary should exercise a "narrow standard of review of decisions made by the Congress or the President" in this area.

Congress clearly has no constitutional duty to provide welfare benefits to all aliens. Providing such benefits only to aliens that satisfy both a permanent and a durational residency requirement is not wholly irrational. Its general aim is to provide benefits to aliens that presumably most resemble citizens. Although the line separating eligible and ineligible aliens might have been drawn elsewhere, that is the type of policy choice the Constitution commits to congressional judgment.

DeCanas v. *Bica*, 424 U.S. 351 (1976)

Facts: A California statute prohibits the knowing employment of illegal aliens if such employment would adversely affect lawful resident workers. In defending a suit for violating the statute, farm labor contractors claimed it was unconstitutional on two theories: first, that the Constitution bars states from attempting to regulate immigration, and second, that the comprehensive federal scheme for regulating immigration and naturalization in the Immigration and Nationality Act (INA) preempted the state statute under the supremacy clause of the Constitution.

Question: Is the California statute unconstitutional?

Decision: No. Opinion by Justice Brennan. Vote: 8–0. Stevens did not participate.

Reasons: The federal government unquestionably has exclusive constitutional power to regulate immigration. A state statute is not barred by this rule, however, simply because it concerns aliens. The regulation of immigration generally concerns a determination of who should be admitted or excluded from the country and the conditions under which a legal entrant may remain. The challenged California statute, in contrast, concerns employment of aliens lacking any rights to remain in the country. Designed to strengthen California's economy, the statute cannot be characterized as a constitutionally proscribed regulation of immigration merely because of some speculative and indirect impact on the flow of aliens.

Neither is the statute preempted by the INA. The standards for determining preemption were stated in *Florida Lime & Avocado Growers* v. *Paul*, 373 U.S. 132 (1963): "federal regulation . . . should not be deemed pre-emptive of state regulatory power in the absence of persuasive reasons—either that the nature of the regulated subject matter permits no other conclusion, or that Congress has unmistakably so ordained."

Here, the challenged statute is designed to protect California workers from the adverse effects of illegal aliens on employment, wages and working conditions, and labor unions. It is akin to child labor laws, minimum and other wage laws, and workmen's compensation laws, all within the mainstream of the state police power. In light of California's acute problem with illegal aliens because of its border with Mexico, the challenged statute is a reasonable attempt to protect its economy.

In addition, there is no indication that the INA was intended to preclude states from regulating the employment of illegal aliens. At most, that act evidences only a peripheral concern with that subject by exempting employment of illegal aliens from the federal crime of "harbor[ing] illegal entrants." Furthermore, the federal Farm Labor Contractor Regulation Act authorizes supplementary state laws regulating employment of illegal aliens by farm labor contractors. Thus, Congress has not "unmistakably . . . ordained" the preemption of the California statute.

The Court remanded the case to the California state courts, however, to determine whether the statute, as properly construed, would bar the knowing employment of aliens authorized to work under federal law, although not entitled to lawful residence. The Court indicated that such a construction would be in direct conflict with federal laws.

Prisons and the Rights of Prisoners

At present, there are approximately 250,000 prisoners in state and federal penal institutions. In fiscal year 1976, 15.2 percent of all civil actions filed in federal district courts were petitions by prisoners.[63] A

---

[63] See *1976 Annual Report of the Administrative Office of the U.S. Courts* (Washington: U.S. Government Printing Office, 1976), p. 93.

state prisoner seeking habeas corpus relief and a federal prisoner seeking section 2255 relief are generally authorized to attack their convictions on the ground that they were obtained in violation of the Constitution. In a series of cases beginning at least in 1938,[64] the Supreme Court has enormously expanded the opportunities and grounds for obtaining habeas corpus or section 2255 relief.[65] These decisions have been accompanied by a corresponding increase in the number of such suits filed.[66]

In two significant cases this term, the Court abruptly reduced the ability of prisoners to attack their convictions collaterally. In virtually overruling *Kaufman v. United States*, 394 U.S. 217 (1969), the Court held that a state prisoner could not obtain federal habeas corpus relief on the ground that evidence obtained in violation of the Fourth Amendment was used in his trial if that claim was fully and fairly litigated in state courts (*Stone v. Powell*, 428 U.S. 465 [1976]). The landmark decision by the Court in *Fay v. Noia*, 372 U.S. 391 (1963), concerning waiver of constitutional rights [67] was also disavowed in *Estelle v. Williams*, 425 U.S. 501 (1976). There the Court held that a prisoner, unconstitutionally tried in prison garb, was precluded from obtaining habeas corpus relief because his lawyer failed to object to the prisoner's attire at trial. The *Stone* and *Estelle* decisions come at a time of growing disenchantment with the existing provisions concerning habeas corpus and section 2255 on at least two grounds. First, they authorize reversal of convictions for reasons unrelated to the guilt or innocence of the prisoner. Second, they permit challenges to convictions years or even decades after trial when evidence relevant to the prisoner's claim is at best stale and often difficult, if not impossible, to obtain.

---

[64] Johnson v. Zerbst, 304 U.S. 458.

[65] See note 44 of "Overview."

[66] Between fiscal 1966 and 1975, habeas corpus and section 2255 suits increased 47 percent and 68 percent, respectively. See *1975 Annual Report of the Administrative Office of the U.S. Courts*, pp. xi-49.

[67] *Noia* concluded that a state prisoner waives his right to raise particular federal claims in habeas corpus only through an intentional relinquishment or abandonment of the claims. The Court elaborated on this standard for determining waiver: "If a habeas applicant, after consultation with competent counsel or otherwise, understandingly and knowingly forewent the privilege of seeking to vindicate his federal claims in the state courts, whether for strategy, tactical, or any other reasons, that can fairly be described as the deliberate by-passing of state procedures, then it is open to the federal court on habeas to deny him all relief if the state courts refused to entertain his federal claims on the merits. . . . We wish it clearly understood that the standard here put forth depends on the considered choice of the petitioner. . . . A choice made by counsel not participated in by the petitioner does not automatically bar relief."

Prison inmates were unsuccessful in seeking to expand their constitutional rights in relation to disciplinary proceedings initially recognized in *Wolff* v. *McDonnell*, 418 U.S. 539 (1974).[68] The Court ruled that an inmate lacks a constitutional right to a hearing before transfer to a penal institution with less favorable living conditions, whether or not the transfer was for disciplinary reasons (*Meachum* v. *Fano*, 427 U.S. 215 [1976]; *Montanye* v. *Haymes*, 427 U.S. 236 [1976]. With regard to disciplinary proceedings, the Court held that an inmate:

- is not entitled to a written explanation for denying him rights of cross-examination;
- is not entitled to counsel simply because the disciplinary charges might also constitute a crime; and
- lacks a Fifth Amendment right to prevent the drawing of adverse inferences from his silence (*Baxter* v. *Palmigiano*, 425 U.S. 308 [1976]).

The *Baxter* and *Meachum* decisions reflected in part the unmistakable inclination of the Court this term to disfavor constitutional claims that would involve the federal judiciary in the day-to-day administration of government.

Stone v. *Powell*, 428 U.S. 465 (1976)

Facts: A state prisoner sought federal habeas corpus relief on the ground that evidence obtained in violation of the Fourth Amendment was unconstitutionally admitted at his criminal trial.[69] The state argued that if such an issue was raised and fairly considered by state courts, federal courts should not redetermine the question in habeas corpus proceedings.

Question: Should a federal court consider, in ruling on a petition for habeas corpus relief filed by a state prisoner, a claim that evidence obtained by an unconstitutional search or seizure was introduced at

---

[68] There the Court held that an inmate facing loss of good-time credits in a disciplinary hearing was entitled to written notice of the charges against him, an opportunity to prepare a defense, and a written statement as to the evidence relied upon and reasons for any adverse action taken. In addition, he has a right to call witnesses and present documentary evidence in his behalf if his doing so would not be unduly hazardous to institutional safety or correctional goals.

[69] In Mapp v. Ohio, 367 U.S. 643 (1961), the Court held that a state is constitutionally prohibited from using evidence obtained in violation of the Fourth Amendment rights of the accused in his criminal trial.

his trial, when he has previously been afforded an opportunity for full and fair litigation of his claim in the state courts?

Decision: No. Opinion by Justice Powell. Vote: 6–3, Brennan, White, and Marshall dissenting.

Reasons: Past decisions in *Fay* v. *Noia*, 372 U.S. 391 (1963), and *Kaufman* v. *United States*, 394 U.S. 217 (1969), have generally been interpreted to authorize both state and federal prisoners to claim any constitutional violation infecting their trials as a basis for collateral relief. The Court has never specifically held, however, that a state prisoner could obtain habeas corpus relief on the basis of a violation of the Fourth Amendment exclusionary rule.

The primary purpose of the exclusionary rule is to deter Fourth Amendment violations. In determining the exact scope of the rule, however, the Court has also considered the needs of effective law enforcement and the harm caused by the exclusion of relevant and reliable evidence in judicial proceedings. For example, the Court has declined to extend the rule to grand jury proceedings or to exclude the use of unconstitutionally obtained evidence for impeachment purposes. Thus, in deciding whether state prisoners, who have had a full and fair review of their exclusionary rule claims in state courts, should be permitted to raise the claim again on federal habeas corpus review, two factors must be balanced: the incremental deterrence of Fourth Amendment violations and the costs of impairing the judicial truth-finding process.

The costs of the exclusionary rule are great. In mandating the exclusion of reliable evidence at trial, the rule may operate to free the guilty. In contrast, the deterrence value of the rule will be reduced only marginally, at best, if federal courts are precluded from hearing such claims *de novo* on habeas corpus review. Accordingly, "where the State has provided an opportunity for full and fair litigation of a Fourth Amendment claim, a state prisoner may not be granted federal habeas corpus relief on the ground that evidence obtained in an unconstitutional search or seizure was introduced at his trial."

The Court specifically rejected the argument that state courts could not be trusted to apply the exclusionary rule fairly. It stated that

despite differences in institutional environment and the unsympathetic attitude to federal constitutional claims of some state judges in years past, we are unwilling to assume that there now exists a general lack of appropriate sensitivity to constitutional rights in the trial and appellate courts of the several States.

Estelle v. *Williams*, 425 U.S. 501 (1976)

Facts: A state prisoner sought federal habeas corpus relief on the ground that his trial was constitutionally tainted because he was tried in prison clothing. Although represented by counsel, the prisoner failed to request of the trial judge that he be tried in civilian clothes. A federal court of appeals upheld the prisoner's claim.

Questions: (1) Does compelling an accused to wear identifiable prison clothing at his trial by jury violate constitutional due process or equal protection? (2) Was the element of compulsion lacking in this case because of the prisoner's failure to raise any objection at trial?

Decision: Yes to both questions. Opinion by Chief Justice Burger. Vote: 8–0 on the first question and 6–2 on the second, Brennan and Marshall dissenting. Stevens did not participate.

Reasons: The right to a fair trial safeguarded by the Fourteenth Amendment entitles a defendant to a presumption of innocence. That presumption is impaired when the attire of an accused marks him as a prison inmate. Common sense and experience indicate that a juror's judgment will be affected by such clothing. In addition, the vast majority of defendants tried in prison garb are those too poor to post bail prior to trial. Compelling only that group to stand trial in prison clothing would thus violate equal protection. The state lacks any legitimate interest in compelling an accused to wear prison clothes.

The failure of the defendant to raise any objection at trial in this case, however, tends to indicate that his wearing of prison garb was not compelled by the state. Defense counsel was aware of the defendant's constitutional right to be tried in civilian clothes. An accused in some cases might desire to be tried in prison garments in the hope of eliciting the sympathy of the jury. The trial judge thus had no reason or duty to inquire whether the defendant lacked knowledge of his constitutional right to trial in civilian clothes.

> Nothing in this record, therefore, warrants a conclusion that [the defendant] was compelled to stand trial in jail garb or that there was sufficient reason to excuse the failure to raise the issue before trial. . . . Under our adversary system, once a defendant has the assistance of counsel, the vast array of trial decisions, strategic and tactical, which must be made before and during trial, rests with the accused and his attorney. Any other approach would rewrite the duties of trial judges and counsel in our legal system.

Meachum v. *Fano*, 427 U.S. 215 (1976)

Facts: Massachusetts state correctional officials received confidential information that several inmates at Norfolk, a medium-security institution, were guilty of serious misconduct. After a hearing in which each was entitled to present evidence, the inmates were transferred to maximum-security facilities having less favorable living conditions than those at Norfolk. The inmates brought suit attacking the constitutionality of their transfers on the ground that due process required a more extensive fact-finding hearing before subjecting them to less favorable living conditions. Their transfers, it was claimed, deprived the inmates of a "liberty" interest protected by the Fourteenth Amendment.

Question: Were the inmates entitled to a hearing under the due process clause of the Fourteenth Amendment before transfer to maximum-security facilities?

Decision: No. Opinion by Justice White. Vote: 6–3, Stevens, Brennan, and Marshall dissenting.

Reasons: Protected liberty interests under the Fourteenth Amendment derive from either state law or the Constitution.

[T]he Due Process Clause [does not] in and of itself protect a duly convicted prisoner against transfer from one institution to another within the state prison system. Confinement in any of the State's institutions is within the normal limits or range of custody which the conviction has authorized the State to impose. That life in one prison is much more disagreeable than in another does not in itself signify that a Fourteenth Amendment liberty interest is implicated when a prisoner is transferred to the institution with the more severe rules.

Similarly, Massachusetts law created no protectable liberty interest in avoiding transfer from one institution to another. Massachusetts correction officials have the authority to order transfer of inmates with virtually unlimited discretion. Their transfer authority is not conditioned upon proof of specified events or serious misconduct.

Whatever expectation the prisoner may have in remaining at a particular prison so long as he behaves himself, it is too ephemeral and insubstantial to trigger procedural due process protections as long as prison officials have discretion to transfer him for whatever reason or for no reason at all.

147

Holding that arrangements like this are within reach of the procedural protections of the Due Process Clause would place the Clause astride the day-to-day functioning of state prisons and involve the judiciary in issues and discretionary decisions that are not the business of federal judges. We decline to so interpret and apply the Due Process Clause. The federal courts do not sit to supervise state prisons, the administration of which is of acute interest to the States.

In a companion case, *Montanye* v. *Haymes*, 427 U.S. 236 (1976), the Court relied upon *Meachum* in holding that a state may constitutionally transfer prisoners among its various penal institutions for disciplinary purposes without providing a hearing.

Baxter v. *Palmigiano*, 425 U.S. 308 (1976)

Facts: Inmates of both California and Rhode Island penal institutions brought separate suits challenging the constitutionality of certain disciplinary procedures used in those institutions. In the California case, a federal appeals court held that in light of *Wolff* v. *McDonnell*, 418 U.S. 539 (1974), inmates were constitutionally entitled to the following protections: notice and a right to respond if temporary suspension of privileges is contemplated; a written explanation for denying cross-examination rights in a disciplinary hearing, or the denial would be presumptive evidence of abuse of discretion; and a right to counsel if the disciplinary charges might also constitute a crime. In the Rhode Island case, a federal court of appeals held that an inmate's exercise of his right to remain silent under the Fifth Amendment in a disciplinary proceeding could not be used to draw adverse inferences against him in that or future proceedings.

Question: Were the constitutional rules enunciated by the federal appeals courts for prison disciplinary hearings erroneous?

Decision: Yes. Opinion by Justice White. Vote: 6–2, Brennan and Marshall dissenting. Stevens did not participate.

Reasons: In *Wolff* v. *McDonnell*, the Court held that except in narrow circumstances, an inmate has no constitutional right to either retained or appointed counsel in disciplinary proceedings. The appeals courts concluded, nevertheless, that counsel was required when disciplinary charges might involve criminal conduct in order to render statements made by inmates in the prison hearing admissible under *Miranda* v. *Arizona*, 384 U.S. 436 (1966), and *Mathis* v. *United States*, 391 U.S. 1 (1968), in subsequent state court criminal prosecutions for the same conduct. *Miranda* and *Mathis*, however, require counsel during custodial interrogation of a person suspected of criminal conduct only if statements of the accused are to be used in a criminal prosecution. "The Court has never held, and we decline to do so now, that the requirements of those cases must be met to render pretrial statements admissible in other than criminal cases."

It was also error to hold that the Fifth Amendment prohibits the drawing of adverse inferences against an inmate for his failure to testify in disciplinary hearings. In a series of cases from *Garrity v. New Jersey*, 385 U.S. 493 (1967), to *Lefkowitz v. Turley*, 414 U.S. 70 (1973), the Court has held that a state may not terminate employment or eligibility to contract with the state solely because an employee or contractor refuses to waive his Fifth Amendment privilege in disciplinary investigations or proceedings. That constitutional rule is inapplicable, however, when the invocation of the privilege is not treated as a final admission but only as partial evidence of guilt. "This does not smack of an invalid attempt by the State to compel testimony without granting immunity or to penalize the exercise of the privilege."

The rule requiring a written statement of reasons for denying an inmate a right to cross-examine a witness in disciplinary proceedings is contrary to *Wolff*. There the Court held that no constitutional right of cross-examination attached in such hearings. "Mandating confrontation and cross-examination, except where prison officials can justify their denial on one or more grounds that appeal to judges, effectively preempts the area that *Wolff* left to the sound discretion of prison officials."

Finally, it was improper for the court of appeals in the California case to reach the question of whether minimum due process procedures applied when only temporary loss of privileges is at stake because all of the inmate plaintiffs faced more severe penalties for their alleged misconduct. *Wolff* expressly left open the issue of whether the degree of "liberty" at stake in loss of privileges, as opposed to deprivation of good time, was sufficient to qualify for due process protection.

Francis v. *Henderson*, 425 U.S. 536 (1976)

Facts: A state prisoner sought federal habeas corpus relief on the ground that blacks had been unconstitutionally excluded from the grand jury that indicted him. The prisoner had failed without good cause to make a pretrial challenge to the composition of the grand jury as state law required. A federal court of appeals held that the failure to challenge the constitutionality of the grand jury in a timely fashion precluded its assertion as a ground for federal habeas corpus relief.

Question: Was the decision of the court of appeals correct?

Decision: Yes. Opinion by Justice Stewart. Vote: 6–1, Brennan dissenting. Marshall and Stevens did not participate.

Reasons: In *Davis* v. *United States,* 411 U.S. 233 (1973), the Court held that a federal prisoner who failed to make a pretrial challenge to the composition of the grand jury that indicted him as required by the Federal Rules of Criminal Procedure could not belatedly raise such a challenge in seeking collateral relief under 28 U.S. Code 2255. The purpose of rules requiring that claims of defects in the institution of criminal proceedings be made before trial is to permit the defects to be cured before the court, the witnesses, and the parties have gone to the burden and expense of a trial. In addition, such rules prevent a defendant from withholding objections with a view toward raising them to upset an otherwise valid conviction at a time when reprosecution would be difficult. These legitimate concerns underlie the state law at issue in this case.

> If, as *Davis* held, the federal courts must give effect to these important . . . concerns in section 2255 proceedings, then surely considerations of comity and federalism require that they give no less effect to the same clear interests when asked to overturn state criminal convictions. . . . [T]here-fore, . . . the rule of *Davis* v. *United States* applies with equal force when a federal court is asked in a habeas corpus proceeding to overturn a state court conviction because of an allegedly unconstitutional grand jury indictment. . . . [T]hat rule requires . . . not only a showing of "cause" for the defendant's failure to challenge the composition of the grand jury before trial, but also a showing of actual prejudice [before relief should be granted].

United States v. MacCollom, 426 U.S. 317 (1976)

Facts: Under 28 U.S. Code 753(f), an indigent federal prisoner seeking to void his conviction collaterally under 28 U.S. Code 2255 [70] may obtain a free trial transcript to assist in preparing his petition only

---

[70] Section 2255 authorizes a federal prisoner to attack his conviction on the ground that it was obtained in violation of the Constitution or federal statutes. It authorizes relief identical to that available to a state prisoner seeking habeas corpus relief under 28 U.S. Code 2241 (Hill v. United States, 368 U.S. 424 [1962]).

"if the trial judge certifies that the suit . . . is not frivolous and that the transcript is needed to decide the issue presented." An indigent is entitled to a free transcript without restriction, however, if he appeals his conviction directly. An indigent federal prisoner, who failed to appeal his conviction, sought section 2255 relief two years later on the grounds of incompetency of counsel and insufficiency of the evidence to convict. He asserted that, without a transcript of his trial, adequate presentation of his claims would be impossible.

The district court rejected the claims and declined to authorize the provision of a transcript of the trial. The prisoner appealed, contending that the failure to provide free trial transcripts to all indigents seeking section 2255 relief constituted impermissible discrimination contrary to due process because wealthier prisoners could purchase the transcripts.

Question: Does the due process clause of the Fifth Amendment entitle all indigent federal prisoners seeking section 2255 relief to a free trial transcript?

Decision: No. Plurality opinion by Justice Rehnquist. Vote: 5–4, Blackmun concurring, Brennan, Marshall, Stevens, and White dissenting.

Reasons: The due process clause prohibits the government from arbitrarily discriminating among particular classes, but it does not guarantee absolute equality or equal advantages. In criminal proceedings, *Ross v. Moffitt*, 417 U.S. 600 (1974), established that due process requires only "an adequate opportunity to present [one's] claim fairly." In this case, the prisoner could have obtained a free transcript if he had challenged his conviction on direct appeal. The prisoner having forgone that opportunity, due process

> does not require the Government to furnish to the indigent a delayed duplicate of a right of appeal with attendant free transcript which it offered in the first instance, even though a criminal defendant of means might well decide to purchase such a transcript in pursuit of relief under section 2255. The basic question is one of adequacy of [the prisoner's] access to procedures for review of his conviction, . . . and it must be decided in the light of avenues which [he] chose not to follow as well as those he now seeks to widen. We think it enough at the collateral relief stage that Congress has provided that the transcript be paid for by public funds if one demonstrates to a district judge that his section 2255 claim is not frivolous, and that the transcript is needed to decide the issue presented.

151

Government Regulation of Business and Commerce

At present, at least some type of federal regulation touches nearly all businesses of consequence.[71] Extensive federal regulation of the environment is of relatively recent vintage. The landmark National Environmental Policy Act (NEPA) was passed in 1969.[72] Both Earth Day and the Clean Air Act amendments came in 1970.[73] The amendments to the Federal Water Pollution Control Act were passed in 1972.[74] These complex environmental laws pose many difficult problems of interpretation that have generated an increasing number of lawsuits.[75] This term the Court decided three significant environmental cases. It held that NEPA does not require federal agencies to prepare an environmental impact statement with regard to "contemplated" as opposed to concrete programs that would significantly affect the quality of the human environment (*Kleppe v. Sierra Club*, 427 U.S. 390 [1976]). It also concluded that an environmental impact statement was not required before the Department of Housing and Urban Development approved land sales under the Interstate Land Sales Full Disclosure Act (*Flint Ridge Development Co. v. Scenic Rivers Association of Oklahoma*, 426 U.S. 776 [1976]). In a decision that may threaten the economic viability of many businesses, the Court held that the 1970 amendments to the Clean Air Act preclude federal rejection of a state's air pollution standards on the ground that they are economically or technologically infeasible (*Union Electric Co. v. Environmental Protection Agency*, 427 U.S. 246 [1976]).

In contrast to environmental controls on business, federal antitrust laws have a long history dating from the enactment of the Sherman Act in 1890.[76] This term the Court reversed the probusiness trend of antitrust decisions begun in recent years[77] by narrowly con-

---

[71] See Thomas D. Morgan, *Economic Regulation of Business* (St. Paul, Minn.: West Publishing Co., 1975), pp. 2-4.

[72] P.L. 91-190.

[73] P.L. 91-604.

[74] P.L. 92-500.

[75] In fiscal 1973, 270 environmental cases were filed in federal district courts. That number rose to 343 in fiscal 1974, to 406 in fiscal 1975, and to 499 in fiscal 1976; *1975 Annual Report of the Administrative Office of the U.S. Courts*, pp. ix-60; also, *1976 Annual Report of the Administrative Office of the U.S. Courts*, pp. i-14.

[76] 26 Stat. 209.

[77] See United States v. National Association of Securities Dealers, 422 U.S. 694 (1975); United States v. Citizens and Southern National Bank, 422 U.S. 86 (1975); United States v. American Building Maintenance Industries, 422 U.S. 271 (1975); United States v. General Dynamics Corp., 415 U.S. 486 (1974); United States v. Marine Bancorporation, 418 U.S. 602 (1974).

struing the so-called state action immunity doctrine recognized in *Parker* v. *Brown*, 317 U.S. 341 (1943).[78] A plurality opinion by Justice Stevens concluded that *Parker* immunized only state officials from private treble damage antitrust suits. The Court stated, however, that private conduct might justifiably be exempt from antitrust attack in two situations: first, where the conduct was compelled under state law and was not privately inspired; and second, where the conduct was permitted under a state regulatory scheme and was necessary to make the scheme work. Without deciding whether such exemptions from the federal antitrust laws should be implied, the plurality concluded that a private electrical utility company's privately initiated practice of distributing free light bulbs to its residential customers could not validly claim whatever protection such exemptions might offer (*Cantor* v. *Detroit Edison Co.*, 428 U.S. 579 [1976]).

Numerous state and local laws restrict advertising and solicitation by members of certain professions such as lawyers, doctors, architects, and engineers. The plurality reasoning in *Cantor* may render the private conduct of these professionals in conformity with anticompetitive laws restricting or prohibiting the use of advertising and competitive bidding suspect under the antitrust laws.

Securities law, like antitrust law, receives the recurrent attention of the Court. As with antitrust decisions, the Court has in recent securities cases generally ruled in favor of business, departing from the spirit of earlier decisions that liberally construed the securities laws in seeking to provide maximum protection for outside investors.[79] In contrast to antitrust, however, this term the Court continued to rule in favor of corporate insiders and business interests in the three important securities cases it decided. Most significant, the Court held that Rule 10b-5 promulgated under the Securities Exchange Act of 1934 does not authorize a purchaser or seller of securities to sue for damages on the basis of negligent as opposed to fraudulent conduct (*Ernst & Ernst* v. *Hochfelder*, 425 U.S. 185 [1976]). The Court also ruled that a stockholder does not become a "corporate insider" and thus required to disgorge any profits made on a purchase and sale of the corporate stock within six months until *after* he acquires more than 10 percent of the stock of the corporation (*Foremost-*

---

[78] There the Court held that state officials acting pursuant to an express statutory scheme for restricting the production and distribution of raisins were immune from suit under the Sherman Act.

[79] Compare New York State Superintendent of Insurance v. Bankers Life and Casualty Co., 404 U.S. 6 (1971), and J. I. Case v. Borak, 377 U.S. 426 (1964), with Kern County Land Co. v. Occidental Petroleum Corp., 411 U.S. 582 (1973), and United Housing Foundation v. Forman, 421 U.S. 837 (1975).

McKesson v. *Provident Securities Co.*, 423 U.S. 232 [1976]). With regard to solicitation of corporate proxies, the Court ruled that the federal prohibition against the omission of any "material fact" applies only to facts that a reasonable shareholder would probably consider important in deciding how to vote (*TSC Industries, Inc.* v. *Northway, Inc.*, 426 U.S. 438 [1976]).

In recent years, many developers, builders, and others have expressed concern over the increasing use of zoning ordinances or laws designed to limit population growth. A recent decision by a federal court of appeals rejected a constitutional challenge to the controlled-growth plan of Petaluma, California, limiting new housing with five or more units to 500 units annually.[80] A related problem for developers and persons with low incomes is so-called referendum zoning. One type requires the approval of any change in zoning by referendums. It is used only in a few cities and towns throughout the country.[81] Various planning authorities have stated that the use of referendums for determining changes in zoning might deter real estate development, obstruct rational planning, and result in favoring industrial projects over low-income housing projects.[82] This term the Court rejected a constitutional attack on the required use of a referendum to obtain a zoning change (*City of Eastlake* v. *Forest City Enterprises*, 426 U.S. 668 [1976]).

At present, U.S. companies do a large volume of business with foreign governments or government-controlled corporations. This volume will undoubtedly grow as trade with Eastern European countries and others with government-controlled economies increases.[83] The decision of the Court this term in *Alfred Dunhill of London, Inc.* v. *Republic of Cuba*, 425 U.S. 682 (1976), will encourage American businesses to conclude commercial dealings with foreign states. The Court ruled that neither sovereign immunity nor the act-of-state doctrine prevents U.S. courts from ordering a foreign government-controlled corporation to repay funds mistakenly paid by a company located in America. More significant, the plurality opinion by Justice White concluded that neither sovereign immunity nor the act-of-state

---

[80] Construction Industry Association of Sonoma County v. City of Petaluma, 522 F.2d 897 (9th Cir. 1975), certiorari denied, 424 U.S. 934 (1976).

[81] See *Washington Post*, August 7, 1976.

[82] Ibid.

[83] During the first five months of 1976, aggregate U.S. exports to "socialist" countries were approximately $1.8 billion, an 81 percent increase over the same period in 1975. The United States imported approximately $420 million from the socialist countries for the first five months of 1976, a 12 percent increase over comparable 1975 import figures. See U.S. Department of Commerce, Bureau of East West Trade, *U.S. Trade Status with Socialist Countries*, June 13, 1976.

doctrine could ever protect "the repudiation of a purely commercial obligation owed by a foreign sovereign or by one of its commercial instrumentalities." Congress subsequently passed legislation generally denying a foreign state immunity from suit in courts of the United States or of the states in any case premised upon a commercial activity of the foreign state that causes a direct effect in the United States.[84]

Kleppe v. *Sierra Club*, 427 U.S. 390 (1976)

Facts: Section 102(2)(c) of the National Environmental Policy Act (NEPA) requires all federal agencies to prepare an environmental impact statement (EIS) in connection with "every recommendation or report on proposals for legislation or other major Federal actions significantly affecting the quality of the human environment." The Department of the Interior and other federal agencies are responsible for issuing coal leases, approving mining grants, and taking other action necessary for the development of coal reserves on land owned or controlled by the federal government. Alleging a widespread government interest in the development of federal coal reserves in the so-called Northern Great Plains region (encompassing parts of Wyoming, Montana, North Dakota, and South Dakota), the Sierra Club and other environmental organizations brought suit against several federal agencies to prevent any further development unless an EIS was prepared on the entire region. The district court dismissed the suit, finding that the federal government lacked any plan for developing the region. The court of appeals reversed and remanded. It found that federal agencies were "contemplating" a program for developing the Northern Great Plains region and that necessary information would be available to prepare an EIS for the contemplated program. Accordingly, the court of appeals remanded, with instructions to federal officials to inform the district court, after completion of an interim report on the issue, of their intent to control coal development in the Northern Great Plains. It ruled that an EIS would be required if such control was contemplated.

Question: Did the court of appeals err in ruling that in some circumstances NEPA requires preparation of an EIS in connection with contemplated, as opposed to concrete, proposals for major federal action significantly affecting the quality of the human environment?

Decision: Yes. Opinion by Justice Powell. Vote: 7–2, Marshall and Brennan dissenting.

---

[84] P.L. 94-583.

Reasons: NEPA clearly states that an EIS is required only when a proposed recommendation or report is made. Neither its language nor legislative history supports the conclusion that in some circumstances contemplated action triggers the application of NEPA.

> A court has no authority to depart from the statutory language and, by a balancing of court-devised factors, determine a point during the germination process of a potential proposal at which an impact statement *should be prepared.* Such an assertion of judicial authority would leave the agencies uncertain as to their procedural duties under NEPA, would invite judicial involvement in the day-to-day decision-making process of the agencies, and would invite litigation. As the contemplation of a project and the accompanying study thereof do not necessarily result in a proposal for major federal action, it may be assumed that the balancing process devised by the Court of Appeals also would result in the preparation of a good many unnecessary impact statements. [Emphasis in original.]

It was also argued that because all coal-related projects in the Northern Great Plains region would have an intimate environmental relationship to one another, NEPA required a regional EIS before permitting a single proposed project to proceed. The Court agreed that NEPA "may require a comprehensive impact statement in certain situations where several proposed actions are pending at the same time." It is the primary responsibility of the federal agencies involved, however, to determine whether proposed actions are environmentally interrelated. Their judgments on such matters should be overturned only if they are shown to be "arbitrary." The federal agencies concerned with coal development did not act arbitrarily in concluding that the interrelationship of environmental impacts caused by particular proposed coal-related projects within the Northern Great Plains region would not be regionwide.

Flint Ridge Development Co. v. *Scenic Rivers Association of Oklahoma,* 426 U.S. 776 (1976)

Facts: The Interstate Land Sales Full Disclosure Act (Disclosure Act) generally prohibits a developer of unimproved land, subdivided into fifty or more lots, from selling or leasing any lot unless certain disclosures are made both to the secretary of the Department of Housing and Urban Development (HUD) and to the purchaser. The developer must file a "statement of record" with the secretary containing information concerning the title of the land, the terms and conditions for disposing of lots, the conditions of the subdivision, including access, noise, safety, sewage, utilities, and proximity to municipalities, and the nature of the developer's proposed improvements and various other specified data. The statement becomes effective and triggers the developer's right to sell thirty days after filing, unless the secretary determines that it is incomplete or inaccurate in some material respect.

A developer of land adjacent to the Illinois River filed a statement of record with the secretary relating to approximately 1,000 residential lots. After amendment, the statement became effective and sales of lots commenced. An environmental organization brought suit to enjoin the sales on the ground that HUD was required to file an environmental impact statement (EIS) under the National Environmental Policy Act (NEPA) before permitting the statement of record to become effective. NEPA requires all U.S. agencies, "to the fullest extent possible," to prepare environmental impact statements before undertaking "major Federal actions significantly affecting the quality of the human environment." The district court ruled in favor of the environmentalists and the court of appeals affirmed.

Question: Must HUD prepare an EIS before allowing a statement of record under the Disclosure Act to become effective?

Decision: No. Opinion by Justice Marshall. Vote: 8–0. Powell did not participate.

Reasons: NEPA requires the preparation of environmental impact statements "to the fullest extent possible." With that phrase NEPA recognizes that when preparation of an EIS would "unavoidabl[y] conflict" with other statutory requirements, the statement is not required. It is clear that the secretary could not prepare an EIS without creating an "irreconcilable and fundamental conflict with her duties under the Disclosure Act."

That act requires automatic approval of a truthful and complete statement of record thirty days after filing. It would be impossible to prepare an adequate EIS during that period. The secretary lacks any discretion to extend the thirty-day period for the purpose of preparing an EIS.

> In sum, even if the Secretary's action in this case constituted major federal action significantly affecting the quality of the human environment so that an environmental impact statement would ordinarily be required, there would be a clear and fundamental conflict of statutory duty. The Secretary cannot comply with her duty to allow statements of record to

go into effect within 30 days of filing, absent inaccurate or incomplete disclosure, and simultaneously prepare impact statements on proposed developments. In these circumstances, we find that NEPA's impact statement requirement is inapplicable.

Union Electric Co. v. *Environmental Protection Agency*, 427 U.S. 246 (1976)

Facts: Under section 110(a)(1) of the 1970 amendments to the Clean Air Act, each state must develop a plan designed to achieve national primary ambient air quality standards—those necessary to protect public health—"as expeditiously as practicable but . . . in no case later than three years from the date of [Environmental Protection Agency (EPA)] approval of such plan." A state plan must also provide for the attainment of national secondary ambient air quality standards—those necessary to protect public welfare—within a "reasonable time." Section 110(a)(2) provides that the administrator of the EPA "shall approve" a proposed plan if it meets eight specified criteria and has been adopted after public notice and hearing. Under section 307(b)(1), the administrator's approval of a state plan may be challenged in a court of appeals within thirty days, or after thirty days if newly discovered evidence justifies a belated challenge.

An electric utility company sought belated judicial review of an approved Missouri plan to attain national primary standards for sulfur dioxide, claiming that new evidence showed the plan to be economically and technologically infeasible. In holding that the challenge was untimely, the court of appeals reasoned that review of an approved plan after the initial thirty-day period is authorized only if the new evidence would have required the administrator to have disapproved the state plan from the outset. It concluded that economic and technological infeasibility provide no basis for the administrator to disapprove a proposed state plan.

Question: Was the decision of the court of appeals correct?

Decision: Yes. Opinion by Justice Marshall for a unanimous Court.

Reasons: It is clear that section 307(b)(1) authorizes judicial review only of the action of the administrator in approving a proposed state plan. Thus, any new evidence claimed to justify judicial review must be such that it would have required the administrator to disapprove the proposed plan if the evidence had been known when the plan was first presented.

None of the eight criteria that a state plan must satisfy require that economic or technological infeasibility be considered in its design. The language of the act, its legislative history, and the three-year deadline for achieving primary air quality standards justify this conclusion. Congress intended to permit states to force businesses to develop new air pollution technology or close down.

> [If] a State makes the legislative determination that it desires a particular air quality by a certain date and that it is willing to force technology to attain it—or lose a certain industry if attainment is not possible—such a determination is fully consistent with the structure and purpose of the Amendments, and section 110(a)(2)(B) provides no basis for the EPA Administrator to object to the determination on the ground of infeasibility. . . . Technology forcing is a concept somewhat new to our national experience and it necessarily entails certain risks. But Congress considered those risks in passing the 1970 Amendments and decided that the dangers posed by uncontrolled air pollution made them worth taking.

Cantor v. *Detroit Edison Co.*, 428 U.S. 579 (1976)

Facts: A private electrical utility company in Michigan supplies light bulbs to its residential customers without any additional charge. Its electricity rates, including the omission of any separate charge for light bulbs, were subject to approval by the state public service commission and could not be altered without its approval. A retailer of light bulbs brought suit against the utility under the Sherman Act claiming that its practice of distributing "free" light bulbs to electricity customers constituted an unlawful tying arrangement and an abuse of its monopoly power in the distribution of electricity. The district court dismissed the suit on the theory that the challenged practice was exempt from antitrust attack under *Parker* v. *Brown*, 317 U.S. 341 (1943), because it had been approved by the public service commission.

Question: Is the challenged practice of distributing light bulbs to electricity customers without additional charge exempt from Sherman Act scrutiny under the authority of *Parker* v. *Brown*?

Decision: No. Plurality opinion by Justice Stevens. Vote: 6–3, Burger and Blackmun concurring, Stewart, Powell, and Rehnquist dissenting.

Reasons: The exemption from the antitrust laws clearly authorized by *Parker* v. *Brown* is very narrow. There the Court held that state officials were immune from private treble damage antitrust suits challenging the legality of actions taken pursuant to express legislative command. Because the defendant in this case is a private utility rather than a state official, *Parker* does not control its disposition.

It is argued, nevertheless, that private conduct required by state law should be exempt from antitrust attack. Two reasons might support such a rule. First, it seems unjust to penalize a private party under federal law for doing nothing more than obeying the commands of his state sovereign. Second, Congress may not have intended to apply its antitrust laws to areas of the economy already pervasively regulated by the states, such as the retail sale of electricity. The first justification is absent here because the public service commission did not require the private utility to distribute free light bulbs. The second reason lacks force because there is no necessary inconsistency between state regulation and federal antitrust mandates. Additionally, if inconsistency appears, there is no reason to believe that Congress intended to subordinate the federal interest to that of the state in every case. Finally, the antitrust suit in this case challenged a practice in the essentially unregulated electric light bulb market.

The Court has implied antitrust exemptions for activity taken under federal regulatory legislation only to the minimum extent necessary to make the regulatory scheme work. "[A]ssuming that there are situations in which the existence of state regulation should give rise to an implied exemption, the standards for ascertaining the existence and scope of such an exemption surely must be at least as severe as those applied to federal regulatory legislation." Granting antitrust immunity to the utility in its distribution of free light bulbs is not necessary to effectuate state regulation of the retail distribution and sale of electricity.

Ernst & Ernst v. *Hochfelder*, 425 U.S. 185 (1976)

Facts: An accounting firm was sued for damages under Securities and Exchange Commission (SEC) Rule 10b-5 and section 10(b) of the Securities Exchange Act for alleged negligence in failing to discover certain fraudulent acts committed by the president and principal stockholder of a brokerage firm. (Rule 10b-5 generally prohibits the use of manipulative or deceptive practices in connection with the purchase or sale of any security.) The accounting firm moved to dismiss the suit on the theory that a private suit for damages under

Rule 10b-5 must allege an intent to deceive, manipulate, or defraud rather than mere negligence.

Question: Does Rule 10b-5 authorize a private suit for damages based upon negligence?

Decision: No. Opinion by Justice Powell. Vote: 6–2, Brennan and Blackmun dissenting. Stevens did not participate.

Reasons: Rule 10b-5 was promulgated pursuant to section 10(b) of the Securities Exchange Act of 1934. That section makes unlawful the use of "any manipulative or deceptive device or contrivance" in violation of SEC rules. The words *manipulative, deceptive, device,* and *contrivance* unmistakably indicate a "congressional intent to proscribe conduct quite different from negligence." That conclusion is also supported by the legislative history of the 1934 act.

The SEC, nevertheless, contends that Rule 10b-5 encompassed both intentional and negligent behavior. But that rule was promulgated pursuant to section 10(b) and thus cannot substantively expand its scope.

When a statute speaks so specifically in terms of manipulation and deception, and of implementing devices and contrivances—the commonly understood terminology of intentional wrongdoing—and when its history reflects no more expansive intent, we are quite unwilling to extend the scope of the statute to negligent conduct.

Foremost-McKesson, Inc. v. *Provident Securities Co.,* 423 U.S. 232 (1976)

Facts: In exchange for the sale of its assets, Provident Securities Co. received more than 10 percent of Foremost-McKesson's equity securities. A few days later, Provident sold the equity securities for a profit. Foremost-McKesson sued Provident under section 16(b) of the Securities Exchange Act of 1934 to recover the profit. That section provides that a corporation may recover for itself the profits realized on a purchase and sale of its securities within six months by a director, officer, or beneficial owner of more than 10 percent of that corporation's securities. With regard to a beneficial owner, however, the section applies only if the owner exceeded the 10 percent figure both at the time of purchase and at the time of sale. Provident contended that section 16(b) was inapplicable to the challenged sale of Foremost-McKesson securities because it was not a 10 percent owner of Foremost-McKesson at the time of their purchase.

Question: For purposes of section 16(b) of the Securities Exchange Act, is a person who purchases securities that place his holdings above the 10 percent level a 10 percent owner at the time of that purchase so that profits realized on the sale of those securities within six months may be recovered?

Decision: No. Opinion by Justice Powell. Vote: 8–0. Stevens did not participate.

Reasons: Congress enacted section 16(b) to prevent certain persons with inside information about their corporations to profit in a class of stock transactions in which the possibility of misusing that information was great. "It accomplished this by defining directors, officers, and beneficial owners as those presumed to have access to inside information and enacting a flat rule that a corporation could recover the profits these insiders made on a pair of security transactions within six months."

The legislative history of section 16(b), however, indicates that Congress intended to limit its application to those 10 percent beneficial owners who possessed that status at the time of both the purchase and the sale in question. That interpretation is consistent with the statute's general purpose of imposing liability without fault, but only within narrowly drawn limits.

Congress recognized that trading by mere stockholders, moreover, in contrast to that by directors or officers, was "subject to abuse only when the size of their holdings afforded the potential for access to corporate information. . . . It would not be consistent with this perceived distinction to impose liability on the basis of a purchase made when the percentage of stock ownership requisite to insider status had not been acquired."

Congress has enacted other statutes, unrestricted by the limitations in section 16(b), to provide sanctions against actual as opposed to presumed abuse of inside information in securities trading.

TSC Industries, Inc. v. *Northway, Inc.,* 426 U.S. 438 (1976)

Facts: Rule 14a-9, promulgated by the Securities and Exchange Commission under section 14a of the Securities Exchange Act of 1934, prohibits proxy solicitations that are "false or misleading with respect to any material fact." TSC Industries and National Industries prepared a joint proxy statement in successfully seeking the approval of shareholders of National's proposed acquisition of TSC. A disappointed TSC shareholder brought suit against both companies alleging, *inter alia,* that the proxy statement violated Rule 14a-9 by omitting material facts relating to the degree of National's control over TSC and the benefits of the acquisition to TSC shareholders. The district court denied the shareholder's motion for summary judgment. The court of appeals reversed. It held that a fact is material for purposes of Rule 14a-9 if a reasonable shareholder "might" consider it important in deciding how to vote. Under this standard of materiality, the court of appeals held that summary judgment was warranted.

Question: Did the court of appeals err in construing the term *material fact* in Rule 14a-9?

Decision: Yes. Opinion by Justice Marshall. Vote: 8–0. Stevens did not participate.

Reasons: The purpose of Rule 14a-9 is to promote intelligent voting decisions by stockholders by ensuring that proxies will explain the questions at issue fairly and thoroughly. To this end, false or misleading statements or omissions of material facts in proxy statements are prohibited. If the term *material fact* is construed too broadly, however,

> not only may the corporation and its management be subjected to liability for insignificant omissions or misstatements, but also management's fear of exposing itself to substantial liability may cause it simply to bury the shareholder in an avalanche of trivial information—a result that is hardly conducive to informed decisionmaking. Precisely these dangers are presented, we think, by the definition of a material fact adopted by the Court of Appeals in this case— a fact which a reasonable shareholder *might* consider important. . . . The general standard of materiality that we think best comports with the policies of Rule 14a-9 is as follows: an omitted fact is material if there is a substantial likelihood that a reasonable shareholder would consider it important in deciding how to vote. . . . It does not require proof of a substantial likelihood that disclosure of the omitted fact would have caused the reasonable investor to change his vote. What the standard does contemplate is a showing of a substantial likelihood that, under all the circumstances, the omitted fact would have assumed actual significance in the deliberations of the reasonable shareholder. [Emphasis in original.]

The Court concluded that under this standard of materiality, summary judgment for the shareholder was unwarranted.

City of Eastlake v. Forest City Enterprises, Inc., 426 U.S. 668 (1976)

Facts: The city charter of Eastlake, Ohio, requires that any zoning changes approved by the city council also be ratified by a 55 percent vote in a referendum. The city council approved a real estate developer's request to change the zoning on an eight-acre parcel from light industrial to zoning that would permit construction of a multifamily, high-rise apartment building. The zoning change failed, however, to obtain the requisite 55 percent support in a referendum. The developer brought suit in Ohio state court alleging that the referendum requirement in the city charter constituted an unconstitutional delegation of legislative power to the people in violation of the due process clause of the Fourteenth Amendment. That claim was upheld by the Ohio Supreme Court.

Question: Does the challenged municipal referendum requirement for proposed zoning changes violate the due process clause?

Decision: No. Opinion by Chief Justice Burger. Vote: 6–3, Powell, Stevens, and Brennan dissenting.

Reasons: It would be erroneous to characterize the zoning referendum requirement as a delegation of legislative power.

> Under our constitutional assumptions, all power derives from the people, who can delegate it to representative instruments which they create.... In establishing legislative bodies, the people can reserve to themselves power to deal directly with matters which might otherwise be assigned to the legislature.

The Ohio Constitution specifically reserves the power of referendum to the people of each municipality on all legislative action that municipalities are authorized to undertake. Accordingly, the challenged referendum provision did not involve a delegation of legislative power.

The Ohio Supreme Court erred in holding that the lack of any standards to guide voters in making decisions in the referendum violated due process because zoning changes "[would] be made dependent upon the potentially arbitrary and unreasonable whims of the voting public." Although the U.S. Supreme Court has held that a congressional delegation of power to a regulatory authority must be accompanied by "discernible standards" to guide its actions, "this doctrine is inapplicable where ... we deal with a power reserved by the people to themselves."

If a zoning restriction on particular land is arbitrary or unreasonable, then *Euclid v. Amber Realty Co.*, 272 U.S. 365 (1926), authorizes a constitutional remedy under the due process clause. Here, however, no claim is made that the existing light industrial zoning on the developer's eight-acre parcel is unreasonable.

Finally, *Eubank v. City of Richmond*, 226 U.S. 137 (1912), and *Washington ex rel Seattle Title Trust Co. v. Roberge*, 278 U.S. 116 (1928), provide no basis for invalidating the referendum requirement. In *Eubank*, the Court struck down a city ordinance which conferred the power to establish building setback lines upon the owners of two-thirds of the property abutting any street. In *Roberge*, the Court held unconstitutional an ordinance which authorized the owners of two-thirds of the property within 400 feet of any proposed residential homes for the aged to reject the proposal. In contrast to the referendum provision in this case, however, both *Eubank* and *Roberge* involved the delegation of legislative power "to a *narrow segment* of the community, not to the people at large. . . . As a basic instrument of democratic government, the referendum process does not, in itself, violate the Due Process Clause of the Fourteenth Amendment when applied to a rezoning ordinance." (Emphasis in original.)

Alfred Dunhill of London, Inc. v. Republic of Cuba, 425 U.S. 682 (1976)

Facts: Alfred Dunhill of London (Dunhill) imported Havana cigars from Cuba. In 1960, the Cuban government confiscated the business and assets of the five leading manufacturers of such cigars who had previously sold to Dunhill. After the confiscation, Dunhill paid the government-controlled manufacturers $148,000 for shipments of cigars made before the confiscation. The former owners of the Cuban companies brought suit against Dunhill and others seeking, *inter alia*, payment for their preconfiscation shipments. The district court ruled that the former owners were entitled to payment on the alternative grounds that the 1960 confiscation did not reach existing accounts receivable and that the U.S. courts will not recognize confiscations of property located in the United States, including accounts receivable, by foreign governments. Dunhill then claimed that its payment to the Cuban-controlled companies for preconfiscation debts had been made in error and that it was entitled to recover that sum from the Republic of Cuba, which was already a party to this complex suit. Cuba denied the claim and asserted that in any event its refusal to honor the alleged obligation constituted an "act of state" that could not be questioned in U.S. courts. The district court upheld Dunhill's claim to repayment and rejected Cuba's assertion that its mere refusal to honor the claim constituted an "act of state."

Question: Was the decision of the district court correct?

Decision: Yes. Plurality opinion by Justice White. Vote: 5–4, Marshall, Brennan, Stewart, and Blackmun dissenting.

Reasons: The act-of-state doctrine precludes U.S. courts from inquiring into the validity of public acts which a recognized foreign country takes within its own territory. The doctrine applies to government action taken within the boundaries of the foreign sovereign.

The burden of proving an act of state in this case was on the Cuban-controlled companies. The only evidence adduced on this issue was a stated declination to pay over the funds legally due Dunhill. There was no evidence that these companies had authority, in addition to operating commercial businesses, to repudiate under the cloak of sovereignty any debts incurred by these businesses. Because of this failure of proof, the refusal to pay Dunhill cannot be deemed an act of state. In addition, "no statute, decree, order or resolution of the Cuban government itself was offered in evidence indicating that Cuba had repudiated her obligations in general or any class thereof or that she had as a sovereign matter determined to confiscate the amounts due [Dunhill]." Accordingly, the district court properly rejected the act-of-state defense.

Even if the Cuban government in its sovereign capacity had repudiated its debt to Dunhill, moreover, "we are . . . persuaded . . . that the concept of an act of state should not be extended to include the repudiation of a purely commercial obligation owed by a foreign sovereign or by one of its commercial instrumentalities." That was also the view of the solicitor general and the Department of State.

> The major underpinning of the act of state doctrine is the policy of foreclosing court adjudications involving the legality of acts of foreign states on their own soil that might embarrass the Executive Branch of our Government in the conduct of our foreign relations. . . . But based on the presently expressed views of those who conduct our relations with foreign countries, we are in no sense compelled to recognize as an act of state the purely commercial conduct of foreign governments in order to avoid embarrassing conflicts with the Executive Branch.

The Department of State holds the view at present that the defense of sovereign immunity should preclude from review in U.S.

courts only "causes of action arising out of . . . public or governmental actions and not with respect to those arising out of its commercial or proprietary actions." The purpose of this restrictive view of immunity is the promotion of international commercial intercourse by assuring those doing business with foreign governments "that their rights will be determined in the courts whenever possible." This assurance has gained importance in recent times because of the sharply increased participation of foreign sovereigns in the international commercial market. For that reason, many other countries have adopted the restrictive approach to immunity.

> Of equal importance is the fact that subjecting foreign governments to the rule of law in their commercial dealings presents a much smaller risk of affronting their sovereignty than would an attempt to pass on the legality of their governmental acts. For all the reasons which led the Executive Branch to adopt the restrictive theory of sovereign immunity, we hold that the mere assertion of sovereignty as a defense to a claim arising out of purely commercial acts by a foreign sovereign is no more effective if given the label "Act of State" than if it is given the label "sovereign immunity."

New Orleans v. *Dukes*, 427 U.S. 297 (1976)

Facts: To preserve the distinctive charm, character, and economic vitality of the French Quarter of the city, New Orleans enacted an ordinance in 1972 generally prohibiting the sale of foodstuffs from pushcarts there. A "grandfather clause" exemption was provided for two vendors, however, who had, for at least eight years before 1972, continuously sold foodstuffs in the French Quarter. A vendor who failed to qualify for the exemption brought suit challenging the constitutionality of the ordinance on the ground that the grandfather clause lacked sufficient rationality to survive the command of the equal protection clause of the Fourteenth Amendment. Relying on *Morey* v. *Doud*, 354 U.S. 457 (1957),[85] a federal court of appeals upheld the challenge. It reasoned that the ordinance created a protected monopoly for a favored class of vendors without regard to whether they were more likely than others to preserve the charm, character, and economic vitality of the French Quarter.

---

[85] There the Court struck down under the equal protection clause a state statute exempting only money orders issued by the American Express Company from the general prohibition against issuance of money orders absent a state license and submission to state regulation.

Question: Does the New Orleans ordinance violate the equal protection clause?

Decision: No. Per curiam opinion. Vote: 8–0. Stevens did not participate.

Reasons: Laws aimed at economic regulation survive equal protection attack if rationally related to a legitimate state interest. The challenged ordinance sought to further the legitimate objective of preserving the appearance and custom of the French Quarter valued by its residents and attractive to tourists. It was rational for New Orleans to conclude that the presence of vendors of foodstuffs in the Quarter would obstruct that objective. Its choice to forbid most, but not all, such vendors was constitutionally permissible. In the area of economic regulation, problems may be addressed incrementally. In addition,

> the city could reasonably decide that newer businesses were less likely to have built up substantial reliance interests in continued operation in the Vieux Carre and that the two vendors which qualified under the "grandfather clause"— both of which had operated in the area for over 20 years rather than only eight—had themselves become part of the distinctive character and charm that distinguishes the [French Quarter]. We cannot say that these judgments so lack rationality that they constitute a constitutionally impermissible denial of equal protection.

The reliance by the court of appeals on *Morey* v. *Doud* was misplaced. "*Morey* was the only case in the last half century to invalidate a wholly economic regulation solely on equal protection grounds, and we are now satisfied that the decision was erroneous . . . [and] that it should be, and it is, overruled."

NAACP v. *Federal Power Commission*, 425 U.S. 662 (1976)

Facts: The National Association for the Advancement of Colored People (NAACP) and several other organizations petitioned the Federal Power Commission to issue a rule that would have required the companies it regulated to adopt affirmative action programs to combat employment discrimination and would have authorized victims of such discrimination to file complaints with the commission. The commission refused to adopt the proposed rule on the ground that it lacked jurisdiction to regulate the employment practices of the companies subject to its economic regulatory purview. The court of appeals reversed and remanded. It held that the commission possessed authority to consider, in performing its economic regulatory functions, including licensing and rate review, evidence that a company discriminates in its employment practices. However, the court rejected the NAACP claim that the commission had authority to adopt its proposed rule.

Question: Was the decision of the court of appeals correct?

Decision: Yes. Opinion by Justice Stewart. Vote: 8–0. Marshall did not participate.

Reasons: Under the Natural Gas Act and Federal Power Act, the commission is directed to establish "just and reasonable" rates for the transmission and sale of electric energy and for the transportation and sale of natural gas. Pursuant to this authority, the commission "clearly has the duty to prevent its regulatees from charging rates based upon illegal, duplicative, or unnecessary labor costs. To the extent that such costs are demonstrably the product of a regulatee's discriminatory employment practices, the Commission should disallow them."

The NAACP contends that because the commission is statutorily directed to act in the "public interest," it has authority to issue the proposed rule calling for affirmative action and other measures to eliminate employment discrimination. However, "the use of the words 'public interest' in the Gas and Power Acts is not a directive to the Commission to seek to eradicate discrimination, but rather is a charge to promote the orderly production of plentiful supplies of electric energy and natural gas at just and reasonable rates."

The Great Atlantic & Pacific Tea Company v. Cottrell, 424 U.S. 366 (1976)

Facts: A Mississippi regulation prohibits the sale of milk and milk products in Mississippi from another state unless that state permits the sale of Mississippi milk and milk products on a reciprocal basis. (Mississippi also required that the out-of-state milk satisfy certain standards of sanitation to qualify for sale there.) A Louisiana milk producer was denied the right to sell in Mississippi solely because Louisiana failed to satisfy the reciprocity requirement. The producer challenged the constitutionality of the Mississippi requirement on the ground that it burdened interstate commerce unduly.

Question: Does the Mississippi milk reciprocity regulation constitute an undue burden on interstate commerce in violation of the commerce clause, Article I, section 8, clause 3 of the Constitution?

Decision: Yes. Opinion by Justice Brennan. Vote: 8–0. Stevens did not participate.

Reasons: The purpose of the commerce clause is to create an area of free trade among the several states. Nevertheless, the clause permits state statutes that burden interstate commerce if certain conditions are satisfied. Where the statute is nondiscriminatory, advances a legitimate local public interest, and only incidentally affects interstate commerce, it will be upheld "unless the burden imposed on such commerce is clearly excessive in relation to the putative local benefits."

In this case, the challenged reciprocity regulation failed to advance any legitimate Mississippi interest. The Mississippi regulation barred wholesome milk that satisfied its standards of sanitation from sale to its residents. Mississippi argues, nevertheless, that its reciprocity requirement advances the interests of the commerce clause by encouraging states to eliminate hypertechnical milk-inspection standards. However, "Mississippi may not use the threat of economic isolation as a weapon to force sister States to enter into even a desirable reciprocity agreement."

Labor Law

Labor unions were successful in the two significant decisions of the Court under the National Labor Relations Act. It ruled that the states lacked authority to impose sanctions on unions for encouraging their members to refuse overtime work (*International Association of Machinists & Aerospace Workers* v. *Wisconsin Employment Relations Commission*, 427 U.S. 132 [1976]). In *Buffalo Forge Co.* v. *United Steelworkers of America*, 428 U.S. 397 (1976), the Court held that federal courts lacked jurisdiction to enjoin so-called sympathy strikes by unions that might violate their collective-bargaining agreements. Shortly after *Buffalo Forge* was decided, a series of wildcat sympathy strikes in the coal industry occurred involving at times more than 100,000 miners and lasting approximately four weeks. The strikes were apparently in support of a complaint by a local union about the actions of federal courts concerning the operation of grievance machinery. They resulted in the loss of millions of tons of coal production. *Buffalo Forge* apparently precluded the issuance of back-to-work injunctions.[86]

International Association of Machinists & Aerospace Workers v. Wisconsin Employment Relations Commission, 427 U.S. 132 (1976)

Facts: The National Labor Relations Board (NLRB) ruled that the refusal of union members to work overtime during collective-bargaining negotiations with their employer was not an unfair labor practice under the National Labor Relations Act (NLRA). The employer obtained a ruling from the Wisconsin Employment Relations Commission, however, ordering the union to cease encouraging concerted refusals to accept overtime work on the ground that such activity was an unfair labor practice under state law. The commission rejected the argument that its jurisdiction over the concerted refusals to accept overtime was preempted by the National Labor Relations Act.

Question: Was the authority of the commission to issue its unfair labor-practice ruling preempted by federal labor policy?

Decision: Yes. Opinion by Justice Brennan. Vote: 6–3, Stevens, Stewart, and Rehnquist dissenting.

Reasons: The Court has interpreted the NLRA to preempt state regulation of legitimate economic sanctions used to support collective-bargaining positions. In *NLRB* v. *Insurance Agents International Union*, 361 U.S. 477 (1960), the Court concluded that the NLRA did not prohibit a union from urging its members to commit harassing acts designed to interfere with the conduct of the employer's business in order to exert economic pressure in furtherance of the union's bargaining demands. *Insurance Agents* held that the challenged union activity was a legitimate economic weapon under the NLRA. Similarly, in this case the concerted refusal of union members to accept overtime work in support of their bargaining demands was a legitimate means under federal law of pressuring the employer. The employer can counter that pressure by use of his own economic strength and sanctions, but he cannot seek the aid of state law or state authorities for this purpose. Otherwise, a legitimate union bargaining weapon under federal law could be frustrated by the application of state law.

---

[86] See *Business Week*, August 30, 1976, p. 30; U.S. Steel Corp. v. United Mine Workers of America, 45 U.S.L.W. 2318 (3rd Cir. 1976).

Buffalo Forge Co. v. United Steelworkers of America, 428 U.S. 397 (1976)

Facts: A collective-bargaining agreement between a union representing production-and-maintenance (P&M) employees and an employer provided for arbitration of any dispute concerning its meaning or application. The agreement also prohibited strikes by P&M employees. When P&M employees honored the picket lines of a sister union against the employer, the employer brought suit under section 301(a) of the Labor Management Relations Act (LMRA) claiming a violation of the no-strike provision, or, in the alternative, that the question whether the work stoppage violated the no-strike provision was arbitrable. The employer sought damages, an injunction against the strike, and an order compelling arbitration of the no-strike question. The district court held that section 4 of the Norris-LaGuardia Act precluded the issuance of an injunction against the strike, even if it stemmed from an arbitrable dispute over the interpretation of the collective-bargaining agreement.

Question: Does the Norris-LaGuardia Act prohibit a federal court from enjoining a sympathy strike pending decision by an arbitrator as to whether the strike is forbidden by an express no-strike clause in a collective-bargaining contract to which the striking union is a party?

Decision: Yes. Opinion by Justice White. Vote: 5–4, Stevens, Brennan, Marshall, and Powell dissenting.

Reasons: Section 4 of the Norris-LaGuardia Act generally prohibits federal courts from enjoining strikes. In *Boys Markets, Inc. v. Retail Clerks Union,* 398 U.S. 235 (1970), however, the Court carved out a limited exception to that general prohibition in order to advance the strong congressional preference in favor of settling disputes by arbitration when it is provided for in collective-bargaining agreements. *Boys Markets* held that a federal court could enjoin a union from striking over a dispute which it was contractually bound to arbitrate at the behest of the employer.

Boys Markets, however, clearly fails to cover this case. The strike was not over any dispute between the P&M union and the employer that was subject to arbitration. Rather, it was a sympathy strike in favor of sister unions.

> [N]either its causes nor the issue underlying it were subject to the settlement procedures provided by the contract be-

tween the employer and respondents. The strike had neither the purpose nor the effect of denying or evading an obligation to arbitrate or of depriving the employer of his bargain.

An injunction was not authorized simply because the strike was alleged to have violated the no-strike provision. Although section 301 of the LMRA generally authorizes federal courts to enforce collective-bargaining agreements, it was not intended to override the anti-injunction policy of the Norris-LaGuardia Act except as specified in *Boys Markets*.

> If an injunction could issue against the strike in this case, so in proper circumstances could a court enjoin any other alleged breach of contract pending the exhaustion of the applicable grievance and arbitration provisions. . . . The court in such cases would be permitted, if the dispute was arbitrable, to hold hearings, make findings of fact, interpret the applicable provisions of the contract and issue injunctions so as to restore the status quo or to otherwise regulate the relationship of the parties pending exhaustion of the arbitration process. This would cut deeply into the policy of the Norris-LaGuardia Act and make the courts potential participants in a wide range of arbitrable disputes . . . for the purpose of preliminarily dealing with the merits of the factual and legal issues that are subjects for the arbitrator and of issuing injunctions that would otherwise be forbidden by the Norris-LaGuardia Act.

Usery v. *Turner Elkhorn Mining Co.*, 428 U.S. 1 (1976)

Facts: Title IV of the Federal Coal Mine Health and Safety Act of 1969 requires coal mine employers to pay benefits to certain former and current employees suffering from black-lung disease (pneumoconiosis). The survivors of these miners are also entitled to benefits if death was either caused by pneumoconiosis or occurred while the miner was totally disabled by that disease.

Title IV prescribes several presumptions for use in determining whether a miner is totally disabled because of black-lung disease and thus entitled to benefits. A miner shown by X-ray or other clinical evidence to be afflicted with complicated pneumoconiosis is "irrebuttably presumed" to be totally disabled on account of pneumoconiosis; if he has died, it is irrebuttably presumed that he was totally disabled by pneumoconiosis at the time of his death and that his death was attributable to pneumoconiosis.

The act also provides three presumptions that a coal operator may rebut to avoid liability. First, if a miner with ten or more years' employment in the mines contracts pneumoconiosis, it is rebuttably presumed that the disease arose out of such employment. Second, if a miner with ten or more years' employment in the mines died from a respiratory disease, it is rebuttably presumed that his death was attributable to pneumoconiosis. Finally, if a miner, or the survivor of a miner, with fifteen or more years' employment in underground coal mines is able, despite the absence of clinical evidence of complicated pneumoconiosis, to demonstrate a totally disabling respiratory or pulmonary impairment, the act rebuttably presumes that the total disability is attributable to pneumoconiosis, that the miner was totally disabled by pneumoconiosis when he died, and that the miner's death was caused by pneumoconiosis. In addition, the act provides that a chest X-ray is insufficient evidence by itself to rebut any of these presumptions.

Several coal mine operators brought suit claiming that Title IV violates the due process clause of the Fifth Amendment insofar as it requires payments to miners who left employment in the industry before the effective date of the act. The presumptions in Title IV were also alleged to limit the ability of the operators to defend against claims in violation of due process.

Question: Do the challenged provisions of Title IV violate the due process clause of the Fifth Amendment?

Decision: No. Opinion by Justice Marshall. Vote: 5–3, Powell, Stewart, and Rehnquist dissenting in part. Stevens did not participate.

Reasons: Legislation regulating the burdens and benefits of economic life violate due process only if without any rational basis. Title IV has some retrospective effect insofar as it requires compensation for disabilities caused by employment that terminated prior to its enactment. Because retrospective application of statutes may upset legitimate expectations, greater justification is required to satisfy due process than if the legislation operated only prospectively. In this case, coal mine operators might have sought to minimize the danger of black-lung disease before enactment of Title IV if they knew they would be liable to miners suffering from that disease.

We find, however, that the imposition of liability for the effects of disabilities bred in the past is justified as a rational measure to spread the costs of the employees' disabilities to those who have profited from the fruits of their labor—the operators and the coal consumers. . . . [The coal mine operators] claim, however, that the Act spreads costs in an arbitrary and irrational manner by basing liability upon past employment relationships, rather than taxing all coal mine operators presently in business. . . . [T]hey argue that the liability scheme gives an unfair competitive advantage to new entrants into the industry, who are not saddled with the burden of compensation for inactive miners' disabilities. . . . But . . . it is for Congress to choose between imposing the burden of inactive miners' disabilities on all operators, including new entrants and farsighted early operators who might have taken steps to minimize black lung dangers, or to impose that liability solely on those early operators whose profits may have been increased at the expense of their employees' health. . . . It is enough to say that the Act approaches the problem of cost-spreading rationally; whether a broader cost-spreading scheme would have been wiser or more practical under the circumstances is not a question of constitutional dimension.

The challenges to the statutory presumptions also lack merit. Title IV irrefutably presumes that a miner is totally disabled and entitled to compensation if he demonstrates clinically an affliction with complicated pneumoconiosis arising out of his employment. Because Congress could rationally have required the payment of benefits to employees solely because of impairment of health, due process is not violated simply because Congress chose to accomplish that result through the use of an irrebuttable presumption of total disability.

Title IV, by virtue of a second irrebuttable presumption, in effect grants benefits to the survivors of any miner who during his lifetime had contracted pneumoconiosis arising out of employment in the mines, regardless of whether the miner's death was caused by pneumoconiosis. These benefits are designed in part to compensate for injury suffered by a miner or his dependents prior to his death because of the physical and emotional stress engendered by black-lung disease. "[W]e cannot say that the scheme is wholly unreasonable in providing benefits for those who were most likely to have shared the miner's suffering."

The three challenged rebuttable presumptions pass constitutional scrutiny if there is a rational connection between the proven and the presumed fact. The coal operators argue that the selection of ten years' employment to trigger two of the presumptions is irrational.

But it is agreed here that pneumoconiosis is caused by breathing coal dust, and that the likelihood of a miner's developing the disease rests upon both the concentration of dust to which he was exposed and the duration of his exposure. Against this scientific background, it was not beyond Congress' authority to refer to exposure factors in establishing a presumption that throws the burden of going forward on the operators. And in view of the medical evidence before Congress indicating the noticeable incidence of pneumoconiosis in cases of miners with 10 years' employment in the mines, we cannot say that [the choice of 10 years to trigger the presumption was arbitrary].

The choice of fifteen years' employment in underground mines, coupled with a totally disabling respiratory or pulmonary disease, to trigger a presumption that black-lung disease caused the disability was also attacked. Congress chose fifteen years, however, in light of expert testimony that it marks "the beginning of linear increase in the prevalence of the disease with years spent underground." Accordingly, that number has a firm rational basis.

Finally, the operators attacked the provision prohibiting a denial of benefits solely on the basis of chest X-rays.

Congress was presented with significant evidence demonstrating that X-ray testing that fails to disclose pneumoconiosis cannot be depended upon as a trustworthy indicator of the absence of the disease. . . . [It] was [thus] faced with the problem of determining which side should bear the burden of [this] unreliability. . . . That Congress ultimately determined "to resolve doubts in favor of the disabled miner" [was not irrational].

Social Security

At present, approximately 32 million persons receive social security benefits at a cost of $67 billion annually.[87] The number of social security cases filed in federal district courts has risen from 537 in fiscal 1961 to 10,355 in fiscal 1976.[88] Two significant social security cases reached the Supreme Court this term.

The Court departed from a line of recent decisions according special judicial protection to illegitimate children[89] in *Mathews* v.

---

[87] See *1976 Economic Report of the President* (Washington: United States Government Printing Office, 1976), p. 111.

[88] See *1976 Annual Report of the Administrative Office of the U.S. Courts*, pp. 1-15.

[89] See Jimenez v. Weinberger, 417 U.S. 628 (1974); New Jersey Welfare Rights Organization v. Cahill, 411 U.S. 619 (1973); Gomez v. Perez, 409 U.S. 535 (1973); Weber v. Aetna Casualty and Surety Co., 406 U.S. 164 (1972); Levy v. Louisiana, 391 U.S. 68 (1968); but see Labine v. Vincent, 401 U.S. 532 (1971).

Lucas, 427 U.S. 495 (1976). There the Court upheld social security provisions that discriminated against a certain class of illegitimate children for purposes of qualifying for survivors' benefits. In rejecting a constitutional challenge to the discrimination, the Court gave considerable weight to the "administrative convenience" served by inflexible rules. This contrasted with past decisions finding administrative convenience an insufficient government interest to justify an otherwise unconstitutional discrimination.[90] In *Mathews* v. *Eldridge*, 424 U.S. 319 (1976), the Court again attached considerable weight to administrative convenience, in addition to fiscal burdens, in declining to require a trial type of hearing before the termination of social security disability benefits.

Mathews v. *Lucas*, 427 U.S. 495 (1976)

Facts: For purposes of qualifying for survivors' benefits, the Social Security Act divides children into two categories. Children automatically qualify for such benefits if they are legitimate or entitled to inherit personal property from their parents' estate. An illegitimate child also automatically qualifies if the deceased parent was not validly married to the other parent only because of a nonobvious legal defect, in writing had acknowledged the child to be his, had been judicially determined to be the child's father, or had been judicially ordered to support the child. Other illegitimate children qualify for survivors' benefits only if the father was living with the child or contributing to his support at the time of death. Illegitimate children in the latter category filed suit claiming that the provisions of the Social Security Act making it more difficult for them to qualify for survivors' benefits than for legitimate and certain illegitimate children violated due process. They had to prove economic dependency upon or presence of the father whereas the others did not.

Question: Do the challenged provisions of the Social Security Act violate due process?

Decision: No. Opinion by Justice Blackmun. Vote: 6–3, Stevens, Brennan, and Marshall dissenting.

Reasons: The discrimination against a certain class of illegitimate children under the surviving-children provisions of the act must be sustained if it has a rational basis. Stricter judicial scrutiny would be inappropriate.

---

[90] See Shapiro v. Thompson, 394 U.S. 618, 636-37 (1969); Memorial Hospital v. Maricopa County, 415 U.S. 250, 267-69 (1974).

> [W]hile the law has long placed the illegitimate child in an inferior position relative to the legitimate in certain circumstances, particularly in regard to obligations of support or other aspects of family law, . . . perhaps in part because the roots of the discrimination rest in the conduct of the parents rather than the child, and perhaps in part because illegitimacy does not carry an obvious badge, as race or sex do, this discrimination against illegitimates has never approached the severity or pervasiveness of the historic legal and political discrimination against women and Negroes.

Because illegitimates do not need special protection from the majoritarian political process, exacting standards of judicial review in this case are not warranted.

The congressional purpose in providing for surviving children's benefits was to replace the economic support that was previously provided by the deceased parent. To serve "administrative convenience," Congress chose to presume that children in some categories would always have been dependent on their deceased parents for support and thus should qualify without special proof of dependency.

> Such presumptions in aid of administrative functions, though they may approximate, rather than precisely mirror, the results that case-by-case adjudication would show, are permissible under the Fifth Amendment, so long as that lack of precise equivalence does not exceed the bounds of substantiality tolerated by the applicable level of scrutiny.

It was rational for Congress to presume that legitimate children and those entitled to inherit from the decedent's estate would be dependent on their deceased parents for support. Children of an invalid marriage also are typically dependent on the parents' income. A paternity decree or judicial support order usually results in the parents' support for the child, and one who in writing acknowledges his responsibility for a child can be expected to support him. Congress was not required to presume dependency in these circumstances.

> But the constitutional question is not whether such a presumption is required, but whether it is permitted. . . . Drawing upon its own practical experience, Congress has tailored statutory classifications in accord with its calculations of the likelihood of actual support suggested by a narrow set of objective and apparently reasonable indicators. Our role is simply to determine whether Congress' assumptions are so inconsistent or insubstantial as not to be reasonably supportive of its conclusions that individualized factual inquiry

in order to isolate each nondependent child in a given class of cases is unwarranted as an administrative exercise. In the end, the precise accuracy of Congress' calculations is not a matter of specialized judicial competence; and we have no basis to question their detail beyond the evident consistency and substantiality.

In conclusion, Congress acted rationally and thus within the boundaries of due process in presuming the economic dependency of legitimate children and certain classes of illegitimate children for the purpose of obtaining survivors' benefits. Those presumptions substantially aid the legitimate goal of administrative convenience in the award of such benefits.

Mathews v. *Eldridge*, 424 U.S. 319 (1976)

Facts: The procedures for terminating social security disability benefits were challenged as unconstitutional in violation of due process. To establish initial and continuing entitlement to disability benefits, a worker must show that he is unable to perform "substantial gainful activity by reason of any medically determinable physical or mental impairment" of certain severity. The physical or mental impairment must be proven by means of "medically acceptable clinical and laboratory diagnostic techniques." The questioned procedures for determining whether disability benefits should be terminated were as follows:

The state monitoring agency obtained information concerning the recipient's health through his answers to a questionnaire and from his sources of medical treatment. This information caused the agency to conclude that benefits should be terminated, and the recipient was so informed, provided with a summary of the evidence against him, and afforded an opportunity to review the medical reports and other evidence in his case file. The recipient was also permitted to respond to the agency in writing and to submit additional evidence. At that point, the agency, for stated reasons, tentatively decided to terminate his disability benefits on an effective date two months after the medical recovery was found to have occurred. The recipient then had the right to obtain *de novo* review of the adverse decision in an evidentiary hearing before an administrative law judge. If the decision there was adverse, the recipient could seek discretionary review by the federal social security administration appeals council, and ultimately could obtain judicial review as of right. If the termination decision was reversed, the recipient would receive retroactive benefits.

It was claimed that the termination procedures were unconstitutional because an "evidentiary" hearing was not provided prior to termination. (Under *Goldberg v. Kelly*, 397 U.S. 254 [1970], such a hearing must include the following elements: [1] timely and adequate notice detailing the reasons for the proposed termination, [2] an effective opportunity for the recipient to defend by confronting any adverse witnesses and by presenting his own arguments and evidence orally, [3] use of retained counsel, if desired, [4] an impartial decision maker, [5] a decision based upon the evidence adduced at the hearing, and [6] a statement of reasons for the decision and the evidence relied on. The challenged termination procedures lacked element [2].)

Question: Do the procedures for terminating social security disability benefits violate due process?

Decision: No. Opinion by Justice Powell. Vote: 6–2, Brennan and Marshall dissenting. Stevens did not participate.

Reasons: Constitutional due process is a flexible concept, and the procedural protections which it requires before the government may deprive an individual of property or liberty depend upon three distinct factors:

> first, the private interest that will be affected by the official action; second, the risk of an erroneous deprivation of such interest through the procedures used, and the probable value, if any, of additional or substitute procedural safeguards; and finally, the government's interest, including the function involved and the fiscal and administrative burdens that the additional or substitute procedural requirement would entail.

In this case, the disabled recipient's sole interest was in the uninterrupted receipt of benefits pending a final administrative decision of his claim, since retroactive relief is afforded if he ultimately prevails. That interest could be significant if the worker is relatively poor. He may have access to other private resources, however, and welfare will be available if the termination of his disability benefits places him or his family below the subsistence level. The potential for economic hardship is thus less than that in *Goldberg v. Kelly*, where the Court held that due process required an evidentiary hearing before the termination of welfare benefits.

In addition, the risk of an erroneous termination decision is relatively small. The decision will generally turn upon routine, standard, and unbiased medical reports by physician specialists who have treated the recipient. The value of requiring that the recipient be provided an opportunity to confront the physicians and make an oral presentation is thus small. Moreover, the challenged procedures provide safeguards against mistakes by obtaining medical information from the recipient through questionnaires and providing him with access to all information relied upon in making the termination decision.

Lastly, the fiscal interest of the government in avoiding an evidentiary hearing prior to termination in every case is considerable. The costs of the additional procedures, moreover, may operate to reduce the funds available for deserving recipients, since social welfare budgets are limited.

Accordingly, the balance of relevant interests justifies the conclusion that the challenged administrative procedures fully comport with due process. The ultimate question raised by these types of cases is when judicial procedures must be constitutionally imposed upon administrative action to assure fairness. Due process requires only that "the procedures be tailored, in light of the decision to be made, to the capacities and circumstances of those who are to be heard, '. . . to insure that they are given a meaningful opportunity to present their case.' " (Quoting *Goldberg*, pp. 268–69.)

Taxation and Import Fees

In recent years, both the federal government and many state and municipal governments have suffered large budget deficits caused in part by the recession and expanding social welfare expenditures.[91] The federal budget deficit was $65.6 billion in fiscal 1976. The aggregate deficits of state and local governments were approximately $1.3 billion in 1975.[92] These deficits exert pressure on the various governments to seek additional sources of revenue.

This term the Court eliminated a barrier to additional local revenue in upholding the imposition of a nondiscriminatory personal property tax on imported tires maintained as inventory in a distribution warehouse (*Michelin Tire Corp.* v. *Wages*, 423 U.S. 276 [1976]). In rejecting the argument that such a tax was prohibited by the export-import clause of the Constitution, the Court overruled its 1871 decision in *Low* v. *Austin*, 13 Wall. 29 (1871). The states of Pennsylvania, Maine, Massachusetts, and Vermont, however, were

---

[91] Total public welfare spending, federal, state, and local, rose from $77 billion in 1965 to $287 billion in 1975, including an increase of $47 billion from 1974 to 1975. "The Welfare State v. the Public Welfare," *Fortune*, June 1976, p. 132.

[92] This figure excludes social insurance funds that state and local governments cannot use for their own purposes. In 1972, the comparable figure was a surplus of $5.6 billion.

unsuccessful in seeking to recover lost revenues from states that had unconstitutionally levied an income tax against their residents (*Pennsylvania* v. *New Jersey*, 426 U.S. 660 [1976]).

The national energy crisis also generated an important Court decision. For the purpose of reducing oil imports and stimulating Congress to pass needed energy legislation, on January 23, 1975, President Ford increased license fees on the importation of crude oil and petroleum products. He purported to act under the authority of the Trade Expansion Act. Several states and other plaintiffs brought suit claiming that the act failed to authorize the license fees. The Court rejected that claim in *Federal Energy Administration* v. *Algonquin SNG, Inc.*, 426 U.S. 548 (1976). Before that decision, Congress passed the Energy Policy and Conservation Act (EPCA) [93] which seeks to increase the country's energy independence. President Ford eliminated the increase in oil-import license fees shortly after enactment of EPCA.

Michelin Tire Corp. v. *Wages*, 423 U.S. 276 (1976)

Facts: A county assessed ad valorem property taxes against imported tires maintained as inventory in a distribution warehouse. Except for sorting by size and style, the tires were stored in the same form in which they were delivered. The importer unsuccessfully claimed in state court that the taxes were prohibited by Article I, section 10, clause 2 of the Constitution (import-export clause) which provides that "[n]o State shall, without the consent of Congress, lay any Imposts or Duties on Imports or Exports, except what may be absolutely necessary for executing its Inspection Laws." The importer argued that the clause, as interpreted in *Low* v. *Austin*, 13 Wall. 29 (1871), prohibits a state from imposing a nondiscriminatory ad valorem property tax on imported goods until they lose their character as imports and become incorporated into the mass of property in the state.

Question: Does the challenged tax violate the import-export clause?

Decision: No. Opinion by Justice Brennan. Vote: 8–0. Stevens did not participate.

---

[93] P.L. 94-163. The act seeks to increase energy independence by, *inter alia*, gradually deregulating the price of domestically produced crude oil, creating a strategic petroleum reserve, and requiring improved automotive fuel economy.

Reasons: Three main concerns prompted the adoption of the import-export clause that confers on the federal government the exclusive authority to lay imposts and duties on imports: the need for the nation to speak with one voice when regulating commercial relations with foreign governments; the need to provide a major source of revenue for the federal government; and the desire to promote harmony among the states, which might be frustrated if coastal states were permitted in effect to tax citizens of inland states by taxing imported goods merely flowing through their ports.

Nothing in the history of the Import-Export Clause even remotely suggests that a nondiscriminatory ad valorem property tax which is also imposed on imported goods that are no longer in import transit was the type of exaction that was regarded as objectionable by the Framers of the Constitution. For such an exaction, unlike discriminatory state taxation against imported goods as imports, was not regarded as an impediment that severely hampered commerce or constituted a form of tribute by seaboard States to the disadvantage of the interior States.

It is obvious that such nondiscriminatory property taxation can have no impact whatsoever on the Federal Government's exclusive regulation of foreign commerce, probably the most important purpose of the clause's prohibition. By definition, such a tax does not fall on imports as such because of their place of origin. It cannot be used to create special protective tariffs or particular preferences for certain domestic goods, and it cannot be applied selectively to encourage or discourage any importation in a manner inconsistent with federal regulation.

In addition, the tax is not in substance an impost or duty. It is levied in return for the cost of such services as police and fire protection, not for the privilege of importing.

Finally, the challenged tax is not predicated upon a favorable geographical location which would permit coastal states to profit at the expense of interior states. Thus, "prohibition of nondiscriminatory ad valorem property taxation would not further the objectives of the Import-Export Clause, . . . [and] we decline to presume it was intended to embrace taxation that does not create the evils the clause was specifically intended to eliminate."

Low v. Austin was based upon a misreading of *Brown v. Maryland,* 12 Wheat. 419 (1827), and the *License Cases,* 5 How. 504 (1847), and is thus overruled.

Pennsylvania v. *New Jersey*, 426 U.S. 660 (1976)

Facts: In *Austin* v. *New Hampshire*, 420 U.S. 656 (1975), the Court held that a New Hampshire income tax levied solely on non-residents violated the privileges and immunities clause of the Constitution. Thereafter, Pennsylvania sought to file a complaint against New Jersey (which, like New Hampshire, levies an income tax only on nonresidents), and Maine, Massachusetts, and Vermont sought to file suit against New Hampshire under the original jurisdiction of the Supreme Court. The complaints sought monetary recovery on two distinct theories. First, the plaintiff states contended that because they provided income tax credits to their residents in the amount of the unconstitutionally imposed income taxes paid to New Jersey and New Hampshire, they were entitled to recover the amount of tax revenues thereby diverted. Second, Pennsylvania sought to sue as *parens patriae* on behalf of its citizens to recover the amount of unconstitutionally levied income taxes paid to New Jersey.

Question: Should the plaintiff states be permitted to file their bills of complaint?

Decision: No. Per curiam opinion. Vote: 5–2, Brennan and White dissenting. Powell and Stevens did not participate.

Reasons: The original jurisdiction of the Supreme Court can only be invoked by a plaintiff state to remedy an injury "directly caused by the actions of another State." Neither of the defendant states in this case caused injury in the form of diverted taxes and revenues to the plaintiff states; rather those injuries flowed from the legislative decisions of the plaintiffs to offer income tax credits to their residents for taxes paid to the defendant states. The alleged injuries to the plaintiff's were thus "self-inflicted." In addition, the plaintiff states have no independent rights to assert under the privileges and immunities or equal protection clause because these constitutional guarantees protect only persons, not states.

Pennsylvania's attempt to sue as *parens patriae* is equally unavailing.

> It has . . . become settled doctrine that a State has standing to sue [in that capacity] only when its sovereign or quasi-sovereign interests are implicated and it is not merely litigating as a volunteer the personal claims of its citizens. . . . This rule is a salutary one. For if, by the simple expedient of bringing an action in the name of a State, this Court's original jurisdiction could be invoked to resolve what are,

after all, suits to redress private grievances, our docket would be inundated. And, more important, the critical distinction, articulated in Art. III, section 2, of the Constitution, between suits brought by "Citizens" and those brought by "States" would evaporate.

Pennsylvania's *parens patriae* claim "represents nothing more than a collectivity of private suits" to recover taxes unlawfully withheld by New Jersey. The claim implicates none of the sovereign or quasi-sovereign interests of Pennsylvania and thus cannot serve to invoke the original jurisdiction of the Supreme Court.

Federal Energy Administration v. *Algonquin SNG, Inc.*, 426 U.S. 548 (1976)

Facts: Section 232(b) of the Trade Expansion Act of 1962, 19 U.S. Code 1862(b), provides that if the secretary of the Treasury finds that an "article is being imported into the United States in such quantities or under such circumstances as to threaten to impair the national security," the President is authorized to "take such action, and for such time, as he deems necessary to adjust the imports of [the] article and its derivatives so that . . . imports [of the article] will not threaten to impair the national security." Pursuant to this authority, President Ford imposed license fees on the importation of crude oil and petroleum products. Eight states, utility companies, and other plaintiffs brought suit challenging the legality of the President's action under section 232(b). They claimed that section 232(b) authorized the imposition of import quotas, but not license fees or other monetary charges, in order to reduce imports. That claim was rejected by the district court, but sustained by the court of appeals.

Question: Were the license fees imposed on importation of crude oil and petroleum products authorized by section 232(b)?

Decision: Yes. Opinion by Justice Marshall for a unanimous Court.

Reasons: The argument that section 232(b) must be narrowly construed to avoid a serious question of unconstitutional delegation of legislative power lacks merit. In *Hampton & Co.* v. *United States*, 276 U.S. 394 (1928), the Court established the general rule that Congress may delegate authority to the President if it provides an "intelligible principle" to guide his actions.

Section 232(b) easily fulfills that test. It establishes clear preconditions to Presidential action—*inter alia*, a finding by the Secretary of the Treasury that an "article is being imported into the United States in such quantities or under such circumstances as to threaten to impair the national security." Moreover, . . . [t]he President can act only to the extent "he deems necessary to adjust the imports of such article and its derivatives so that such imports will not threaten to impair the national security." . . . In light of these factors . . . we see no looming problem of improper delegation that should affect our reading of section 232(b).

On its face, section 232(b) "seems clearly to grant [the President] a measure of discretion in determining the method to be used to adjust imports." Neither the language of the statute nor its lengthy legislative history supports the argument that the authority of the President to "adjust" imports was limited to the use of quotas as opposed to monetary exactions, such as license fees. "To the contrary, [the] original enactment [of section 232(b)], and its subsequent re-enactment in 1958, 1962, and 1974 in the face of repeated expressions from Members of Congress and the Executive Branch as to their broad understanding of its language, all lead to the conclusion that section 232(b) does in fact authorize the actions of the President challenged here."

Freedom of Information

In 1974, Congress considerably increased the ability of persons to obtain government records under the Freedom of Information Act.[94] The 1974 amendments have contributed to a large rise in the number of freedom of information (FOI) requests and lawsuits.[95] The Supreme Court has decided several important FOI cases in recent years

---

[94] See P.L. 93-502. The 1974 amendments eased the burden of obtaining agency records in at least four important respects. First, the grounds for withholding records concerning classified information or investigatory files were narrowed. Second, the nonexempt portion of any record containing exempt information must be disclosed if it is reasonably segregable. Third, an agency is permitted to charge a fee to a requester equal only to the direct costs of search for and duplication of the document. Fourth, an agency must generally make a final response to a request for information within thirty days.

[95] The Food and Drug Administration, for example, received 13,140 FOI requests in 1975 compared with only 2,644 in 1974. See *Washington Post*, July 27, 1976. The Justice Department estimates that approximately 450 FOI suits are now pending. See *Washington Post*, July 26, 1976.

as its use has grown.[96] This term the Court narrowly construed two exemptions from the general disclosure requirements of the act in ordering the disclosure of individual case summaries concerning military honor or ethics code violations if they are edited sufficiently to protect the identity of the accused (*Department of the Air Force* v. *Rose*, 425 U.S. 352 [1976]).

Department of the Air Force v. Rose, 425 U.S. 352 (1976)

Facts: Under the Freedom of Information Act, the United States Air Force Academy was requested to provide the case summaries of individuals charged with violations of the honor code or the ethics code, with personal references or other identifying information deleted. (The act requires agencies of the federal government to disclose all reasonably well described records requested by any person except those falling within any of nine exempt categories.) Copies of the summaries were routinely posted on forty squadron bulletin boards throughout the academy and distributed to faculty and administrative officials. The request was denied on the grounds that the summaries fell within both exemptions 2 and 6, 5 U.S. Code 552(b)(2), (6). Exemption 2 protects "matters . . . related solely to the internal personnel rules and practices of an agency." Exemption 6 protects "personnel and medical files and similar files the disclosure of which would constitute a clearly unwarranted invasion of personal privacy." A federal court of appeals rejected the exemption 2 claim, but ruled that the rights of privacy of the cadets concerned, protected by exemption 6, might be jeopardized if the case summaries were released in the form requested. Accordingly, it directed the district court to work with the academy in editing the summaries with the purpose of minimizing the likelihood that any cadet involved would be identified by public disclosure. The court of appeals concluded that a case summary was protected by exemption 6 if the editing process could not safeguard the privacy of the cadet, but not otherwise.

Question: Was the decision of the court of appeals correct?

Decision: Yes. Opinion by Justice Brennan. Vote: 5–3, Burger, Blackmun, and Rehnquist dissenting. Stevens did not participate.

---

96 See Environmental Protection Agency v. Mink, 410 U.S. 73 (1973); Renegotiation Board v. Bannercraft Clothing Co., 415 U.S. 1 (1974); National Labor Relations Board v. Sears, Roebuck & Co., 421 U.S. 132 (1975); Renegotiation Board v. Grumman Aircraft Engineering Corp., 421 U.S. 168 (1975); Administrator, Federal Aviation Administration v. Robertson, 422 U.S. 255 (1975).

Reasons: Exemption 2 has a muddied legislative history. The relevant House report indicated that operating rules and manuals of agencies would be covered, but not such items as employee relations and working conditions. The corresponding Senate report indicated that the latter items were of the only type intended to fall within exemption 2. The Senate report is the more reliable indicator of congressional intent because it was the only one considered by both houses of Congress. "[A]t least where the situation is not one where disclosure may risk circumvention of agency regulation, Exemption 2 is not applicable to matters subject to . . . genuine and significant public interest" as opposed to matters "in which the public could not reasonably be expected to have an interest."

The case summaries at issue did not relate solely to the internal workings of the academy. The public has an enormous stake in knowing how the codes of honor and ethics of the military are administered. The effectiveness of those codes is directly related to the reliability and strength of the armed forces. Thus, exemption 2 did not cover the case summaries involving violations of the codes of honor and ethics.

Exemption 6 protects certain files whose disclosure would invade individual privacy. Its interpretation requires a balancing between the rights of individuals to privacy and public rights to government information. Disclosing the case summaries creates a risk to the involved cadet that he may be publicly identified and stigmatized. The summaries may have been forgotten by those with earlier access within the academy. Thus, disclosure would implicate substantial privacy interests of the concerned cadet. The court of appeals was thus correct in ordering that all identifying information be edited before disclosure of a case summary. In this connection, deletions should be made not only with reference to what the public might know about a subject cadet, "but also from the vantage of those who would have been familiar, as fellow cadets or Academy staff, with other aspects of his career at the Academy."

INDEX OF CASES

SUBJECT INDEX